Cincinnati Silversmiths
Jewelers, Watch and Clockmakers

Cincinnati Silversmiths
Jewelers, Watch and Clockmakers

Through 1850
Also Listing the More Prominent Men in These Trades
from 1851 until 1900

*With A New Appendix Featuring Ohio
Silversmiths Working Outside of Cincinnati
Compiled from Ms. Beckman's notes by Maurice Meslans
with notes by Wm. Erik Voss*

Elizabeth D. Beckman

Commonwealth Book Company
St. Martin, Ohio
2014

Copyright 1975
Elizabeth D. Beckman
Cincinnati, OH

New Material Copyright 2014
Maurice Meslans
Wm. Erik Voss
Betsey Beckman

ISBN: 099053510X

Cover photograph: punch bowl by Loring Andrews Company of Cincinnati, Ohio. Sold at auction in 2006 for $9200. Courtesy of Cowan's Auctions, Cincinnati, Ohio.

Table of Contents

About the Author	iv
Foreward by Robert Alan Green	v
Foreward by Carol Macht, Ph. D	vii
Acknowledgments	viii
Illustrations	ix
Introduction	xi
Cincinnati Silversmiths, Jewelers, Watch and Clockmakers Through 1850	1
Cincinnati Silversmiths, Jewelers, Watch and Clockmakers Listed Only Once in the Directories (1819-1850)	153
A List of Prominent Cincinnati Silversmiths, Jewelers, Watch and Clockmakers (1850-1900)	155
Bibliography	156
Index	161
Appendix: Ohio Silversmiths and Related Trades Working Outside Cincinnati	169

*This book is dedicated to my husband
Vincent and my daughters
Betsey and Julie*

ABOUT THE AUTHOR

Elizabeth Desloge Beckman, known to her friends as Betty Beckman, was born on January 20, 1921 in St. Louis, Missouri. She attended St. Mary's College in South Bend, Indiana, where she earned a BA in Art in 1942, and soon thereafter worked as a draftsman in the war effort. On the shores of Lake Michigan, Betty met Vincent H. Beckman, whom she married in 1943. After the war, they made their home in Cincinnati, where Vince established a respected law practice and the couple raised their six children.

Betty Beckman, November 6, 1975, being recognized in the Cincinnati Post for the newly published *Cincinnati Silversmiths*. Photo courtesy of E. W. Scripps.

Betty's creativity was the hallmark of her life. As a young mother, she designed campaign material and dynamically supported her husband in his long career in Cincinnati politics. In the early 1960's, she bought a summer house in Michigan and oversaw its renovation, furnishing the house with objets trouvés and treasures she refinished by hand. A few years later, Betty designed and built a residence in the Clifton area of Cincinnati and decorated it with many of her prized antiques. She later opened an Interior Design business, "The id Shop," where she combined her passion for collectibles with art and décor.

In the early 1970's, while researching several pieces of Cincinnati silver, Betty found that there were no published resources identifying Cincinnati's silver makers, marks, or design elements. She combed newspapers, museum files, directories, and cemeteries to create a thorough catalogue of Cincinnati silversmiths from the earliest days of the Queen City to the dawn of the 20th century. Cincinnati Art Museum curator Amy Miller Dehan has recently written a spectacular new book, *Cincinnati Silver: 1788-1940*, in which she acknowledges that Betty's original publication "has been, and will continue to be, a 'bible' for many of us, and it is from her superlative study" that this new study "dares to grow." (Dehan, 8)

On July 23, 1981, a handful of years after the publication of her book, Betty lost her battle with cancer. *Cincinnati Silversmiths, Jewelers, Watch and Clockmakers* remains to this day a treasure for her family, a useful research guide for the antiques community, and a seminal piece of Cincinnati's estimable arts heritage.

Betsey Beckman
May, 2014

FOREWORD

The late Dr. George Barton Cutten, former President of Colgate University, and his wife Minnie W. Cutten, were an outstanding research team whose writings set forth much new data on Early American Silver, its makers and their marks. They were among the first to illustrate hallmarks in the tradition of Hollis French, Stephen G.C. Ensko, and Ernest M. Currier, but they went even further in publishing detailed biographical material, announcements, and extracts from old records. Another early writer in this field was Rhea Mansfield Knittle of Ashland, Ohio, who wrote a pamphlet on Ohio Silversmiths and Pewterers in 1943. Dr. Cutten maintained a friendship and correspondence with Mrs. Knittle as evidenced by a presentation copy of her book from his library, now bequeathed to Colgate. After a long search, and through the intervention of a sympathetic librarian in Ashland, Ohio, I was able to purchase another presentation copy for my own collection, and a careful reading of it whetted my appetite for further study of silver from the Ohio area.

For many years I amassed notes on the silversmiths, watchmakers and jewelers of Ohio, welcomed each public reference to makers, each appearance of examples of their work in periodicals or the market place, and carried out an extensive correspondence with others sharing this common interest with me. While I was preparing an article on the subject last year for the *Magazine Silver,* (Issue for Jan-Feb., 1975), Mrs. Elizabeth D. Beckman wrote to me of her work. We met in Cincinnati and after carefully reviewing for voluminous material, I came to the inescapable conclusion that her manuscript warranted immediate publication.

While the title of this book would appear to limit its scope to Cincinnati, it is in reality much more than a small area study. By including a wealth of source material in the form of full advertisements, announcements, and similiar records we have a well documented and fully illustrated reference work for all who are concerned with the origins and development of American silver and related trades in the "Western Country".

Only Mr. E. Milby Burton, in his definitive regional study, *"South Carolina Silversmiths"* achieved similiar extensive documentation in one volume. The research required to write so detailed and accurate an account as this, is both painstaking and time consuming; yet it is only thus that important facts can be assembled for the enlightenment of readers with so wide a spectrum of interests. Authoritative information on silversmiths, watchmakers, clockmakers and jewelers requires the perusal of countless periodicals, journals, directories, census reports, books, trade cards, account books and ledgers, town, city, county and church records, as well as visits to grave sites. Mrs. Beckman has done all this with understanding and humor, so that for the first time in almost two hundred years, we have a factual account of unsurpassed usefulness to genealogists, horologists, collectors of militaria, antique instrument specialists, optometrists, as well as those interested in engraving, local history, jewelry manufacture, silversmithing, early trade practices and advertising.

The style of Cincinnati silver during the first half of the 19th Century requires a special comment. Many of the craftsmen came from European countries or the British Isles via the Eastern Seaboard States to settle in this burgeoning metropolis on the Ohio River. Some remained only a part of their working lives and moved on. The handsome neo-classic water pitchers and tea services of Edward Kinsey and his brother David and their fine beakers, or julep cups, compare favorably in quality of workmanship and style to any produced in Philadelphia or Kentucky. But the most distinctive style of Cincinnati fiddle handled spoons developed in the late 1840's. The bowls of these spoons seem small, and the handles very large by comparison. These handles are of a very exaggerated hour glass shape terminating in a wide rounded end. All of the Cincinnati smiths of the time made variations of this shape and "Cincinnati" spoons of this period are very easy to recognize.

Another form worthy of note is the flatware of Herman Duhme of Duhme & Co. This twist-stem silver is quite imaginative and was widely copied. The twist appears first on the shanks of sucket forks of the 17th Century, and the wire handles of the earliest dram cups, but it does not appear as a favored embellishment until this firm revived this simple decorative technique. Combined with bright-out engraving, Duhme created new patterns whose influences survive to this day.

The inclusion in this book of extensive excerpts from the diary of Jacob Deterly is also of much interest, in that, only through this account by an actual silversmith, watchmaker, and instrument repairman, are we able to garner information about his contemporaries during the years he spent in Cincinnati: 1819 to 1833. There are a few surviving ledgers, account books and letter books of the early workers such as those of Paul Revere, Joseph Richardson, Edward Lang of Salem, the shop records of Daniel Burnap, clockmaker, and the Design Book of William Faris, silversmith and clockmaker, the last mentioned republished in my edition of Pleasants & Sill's, *Maryland Silversmiths,* 1972. Even holographic material, in the form of receipts for goods, services and letters, is quite rare bearing the hand of those busy artisans. In so far as a diary is concerned, it would appear that of Jacob Deterly falls into this class, for no other early 19th Century diary of this category of artisan, and of this quality, has come to my notice.

The wealth of additional data from the Deterly chronicle, including the relationships among the fraternity of workers in Cincinnati in those early years, has fleshed out these characters and given to them heightened personalities and new dimensions.

One final thought. A number of the workers whose names appear in this book are mentioned but briefly, for the recorded facts about them in Ohio are, in reality, scant. Yet this small amount of information may prove of substantial value to future researchers and afford answers to a variety of unresolved problems. In reviewing the manuscript we have already encountered this pleasant experience, and we are confident that countless others will do, as they place this volume among their most valued regional silver classics.

ROBERT ALAN GREEN

FOREWORD

It is not difficult to write a foreword for this book on Cincinnati silversmiths which has been long overdue. The subject has been covered only spottily and in most cases most inaccurately. The author has labored for three years using directories, newspaper advertisements, courthouse records, wills and diaries. No stone has been left unturned in order to identify the personalities and the corpus of works of the local silversmiths.

It is interesting to note the amount of movement amongst these artisans which bespeaks the breakdown of the old guild system of Great Britain and the Continental countries. For example, Samuel Best emigrated from Ilminster, England to Philadelphia, Pennsylvania, thence to Limestone, Kentucky, became prominent in Cincinnati, Ohio and finally worked and died in Rising Sun, Indiana.

This book which draws examples from both museums and private collections should prove to be an indispensable tool to both curators and collectors.

Carol Macht Ph.D.
Senior Curator
Curator, Decorative Arts
Cincinnati Art Museum

ACKNOWLEDGMENTS

No book requiring research can be written without help, and I want to thank all who gave of their time and knowledge to make this book a reality.

First, my friends at the Cincinnati Historical Society, Stephen Starr, the Director, and all the staff who make the long hours of research more pleasant, and my special thanks to Frances Forman, Laura Chace, and Peter Hawkins.

Secondly, Dr. Carol Macht and Debbie Long at the Cincinnati Art Museum, who made my job so much easier with their wonderful cooperation.

Third, a special in memoriam to Mrs. Grace Dallow whose knowledge of genealogy was so helpful, and whose friendship meant so much to me.

Fourth, to Paul and Alma Brunner for the tremendous help they gave me in sharing their knowledge of Cincinnati silver and for their many kindnesses to me.

Fifth, to all the other persons who helped me, including the staffs at the Ohio Historical Society, Lebanon Historical Society, Glendower Museum, University of Cincinnati Archives, Winterthur Museum, Hamilton County Court House, Spring Grove Cemetery, and Jane Sikes, John and Jane Diehl, Maurice Meslans, Betty and Jim Sutherland, Red Bostain, Emmy Todd, Max Harter, Joe Teel, Chuck Wilcox, Ann Rottinghaus, Sam West, Lucille Heizer, Teel Hilton, H. Collis Reid, Tom Janszen, Dick Olberding, Robert A. Green, Peggy Pennington, Larry Melvin, Russell Lutes, Pat Mertz, Ruth H. Roach, Lucy Hiatt, Rucker Rich, Foster Stearns, Roger Newstedt, Alfred Mahan, Marilyn White, and my friends Jay, Phyllis, Gilbert, E.K., and Ralph.

And last but not least a special thanks to Susanne de Risi for her patience in typing my manuscript.

                                          Elizabeth D. Beckman
                                          1 North Cliff Terrace
                                          Cincinnati, Ohio 45220

ILLUSTRATIONS

1.	Cincinnati fiddle handled flat ware from the late 1840's and early 1850's by various makers	xii
2.	Twist handled and engraved flat ware by Cincinnati makers	xiii
3.	Engraved Victorian ewer, goblets and tray by Duhme & Co.	xiv
4.	Silver mounted French paste jewelry	xv
5.	English watch made for E. & D. Kinsey	xv
6.	Cincinnati salt spoons and a reproduction tablespoon	3
7.	Four piece tea set bearing the mark Beggs & Smith	10
8.	Enlargement of the mark appearing on illustration 9	10
9.	Detail of the tea pot appearing in illustration 7	10
10.	Examples of early Cincinnati table and teaspoons	15
11.	Cup by S. Best and spectacles by Scovil & Kinsey	18
12.	Enlargement of mark appearing on Scovil & Kinsey spectacles	18
13.	Cincinnati spoons from the 1830's	29
14.	Punch ladles by Clayton and Scovil & Co.	32
15.	Punch ladle and cup marked W & D (Woodruff & Deterly) cup by N.L. Hazen and miniature spoon by McGrew & Beggs	42
16.	Condiment set by Duhme & Co.	52
17.	Soup tureen by Herman Duhme	53
18.	N.L. Hazen handled cup	66
19.	E.H. Hill mustard spoon	67
20.	J.G. Joseph sauce ladle	75
21.	Mark which appears on illustration 20	75
22.	Sugar tongs by N.L. Hazen and J. Draper, sauce ladle by Luke Kent Sr.	78
23.	D. Kinsey three piece tea set	82
24.	Photograph of David Kinsey	83
25.	Cups by E. & D. Kinsey	85
26.	Water pitcher by Edward Kinsey	86
27.	Mark which appears on E. Kinsey water pitcher	87
28.	Pair of A. McGrew spoons	93
29.	W.W. McGrew water pitcher	95
30.	Detail of handle of illustration 29	95
31.	A. Palmer sugar bowl	105
32.	Sugar tongs by Rhodes, Anthony & Co. and W. McGrew, gravy ladle by Allen & Rhodes	117
33.	Cups by Scovil & Co. and Scovil & Kinsey	122
34.	Mark which appears on cup in illustration 33	122
35.	Verdin town clock mechanism	141
36.	Luman Watson clock	143
37.	Cups by Willey & Co., Scovil, Willey & Co. and Willey & Blaksley	147
38.	Enlargement of mark appearing on Willey & Blaksley cup	147
39.	E. Woodruff spoon	150

INTRODUCTION

Cincinnati was founed in 1788 but it was the signing of the Treaty of Greenville in 1795, resolving the troubles with the Indians, which opened the Ohio territory for permanent settlement. Cincinnati, partly because of its location on the Ohio River, grew in leaps and bounds and as early as 1832 was called "The Queen City of the West".

The aim of this book is to tell of the contribution made by Cincinnati craftsmen, mainly in hand-made silver, and to establish their rightful place in the history of American craftsmen in this field.

From the research done, covering the years from the founding of Cincinnati through 1850, it would seem that there were more silversmiths, jewelers, watch and clockmakers working in Cincinnati during this time than in any other city in the midwest. This is not surprising when we consider that Cincinnati was founded before Chicago and Cleveland, and was in 1850 the 6th largest city in the United States. The city abounded in craftsmen in many fields and products made in Cincinnati were being shipped all over the midwest.

The book also covers some of the prominent companies in existence after the Civil War, as many Cincinnati products in gold, silver and jewelry were well known at that time. For example, silver and jewelry made in the great houses of Duhme and C. Oskamp were being sold all over the midwest, the John Holland Pen Co. was shipping all over the United States, and the Dueber Watch Case Co. was producing coin silver watch cases which were being sold from Maine to California.

But to go back to the beginnings, the story is partly told by the silver which has survived, and illustrations of some existing examples appear throughout the book. The book covers each man whose name appeared in a Cincinnati directory as a silversmith, jeweler, watch or clockmaker, and each man who advertised at one of the above trades through 1850. In some cases only one ad was found, in others life histories were found, in others information from newspapers, census records, Court House records of wills and marriages, and cemetery records were put together to tell something of the lives of these men. A new dimension was added in 1972, when the diary of an early Cincinnati silversmith, Jacob Deterly, was printed. With this new material, much additional information was gained. Actual quotes are used throughout the book, including some of Deterly's amusing comments on incidents of the time. But the most unique feature of the book is the reproduction of the ads as they originally appeared. Approximately 175 ads are reproduced and give information about the silver and jewelry brought back from the east, the variety of articles carried in the shops, and the items of silver made in the shops. Some ads included commentaries on the times, and one ad even included a dissertation on the evils of credit buying.

The men who came to Cincinnati to work as silversmiths, jewelers, watch and clockmakers came from many places, cities of the east, England, France, Germany, etc. All must have had some spirit of adventure to leave their homes for this new city in the midwest. Their coming brought refinements such as silver spoons and jewelry to the frontier town of Cincinnati.

The early Cincinnati silver which has survived is for the most part well made and generally of simple graceful design, which would be fitting for life at the time. Many of the silversmiths made only silver spoons and ladles, and were also watchmakers, repairing watches and jewelry; others were spectacle makers, also advertising that they made silver spoons; others advertised that they made holloware, although not a large amount of holloware has survived. Possibly the publishing of this book and a revival of interest in these Cincinnati craftsmen will bring more of their work to light.

The early Cincinnati spoon styles followed those of the east. A few coffin end silver pieces have survived, and illustrated on page 42 is a Cincinnati coffin end soup ladle. The next style to appear was the fiddle handle and illustrated on page 15 is a grouping of spoons in this style by early Cincinnati makers. Cincinnati spoons from the 1830's have a rather broad handle and spoons of this type appear in the illustration on page 29. In the 1840's and early 1850's a very exaggerated fiddle handled shape evolved in Cincinnati. The illustration below includes spoons by many Cincinnati silversmiths and shows the evolution of this shape. Although spoons with a somewhat similar shape from other parts of the country have been seen, none have the exaggerated shape of the spoons appearing on the right in the illustration. This shape disappeared in the 1850's and was replaced by the late fiddle shape which continued to be made in the 1860's and 1870's.

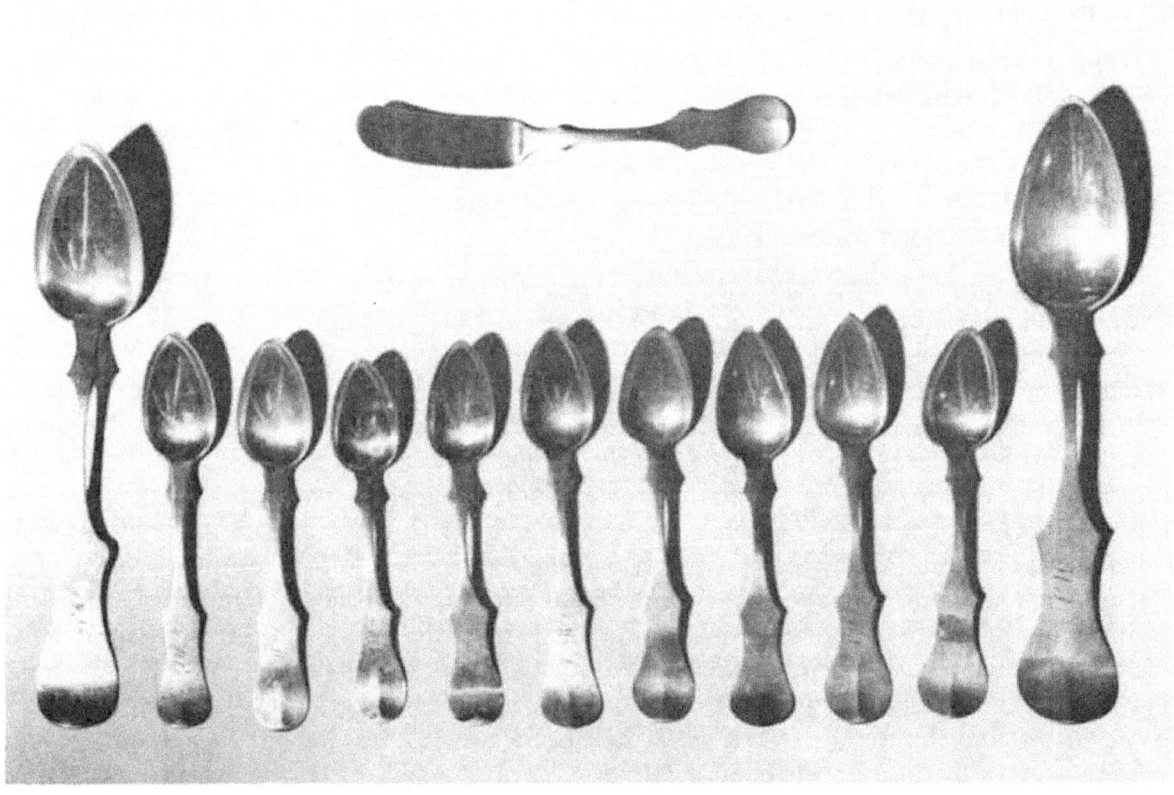

Fiddle handled spoons of the 1840's and early 1850's by Cincinnati makers. Left to right, T. Oskamp, Owen & Read, N. L. Hazen, Owen & Carley, T. Oskamp, J. Owen, W. McGrew, J. Draper, Owen & Carley, McGrew & Beggs, and Owen & Carley, butterknife above by McGrew & Beggs. The marks on the above spoons all appear in a cartouche.

Private collections.

It is not surprising to find in the late 1850's that the Kinseys began to make twist handled flatware. This style was to become very popular and continued to be made for many years. Illustrated on the following page are examples of twist handled flatware made by Duhme & Co., the Kinseys, C. Oskamp and C. Hellebush. Complete sets of twist handled flatware were made by Duhme & Co., the earlier sets in coin silver and the later sets in sterling silver.

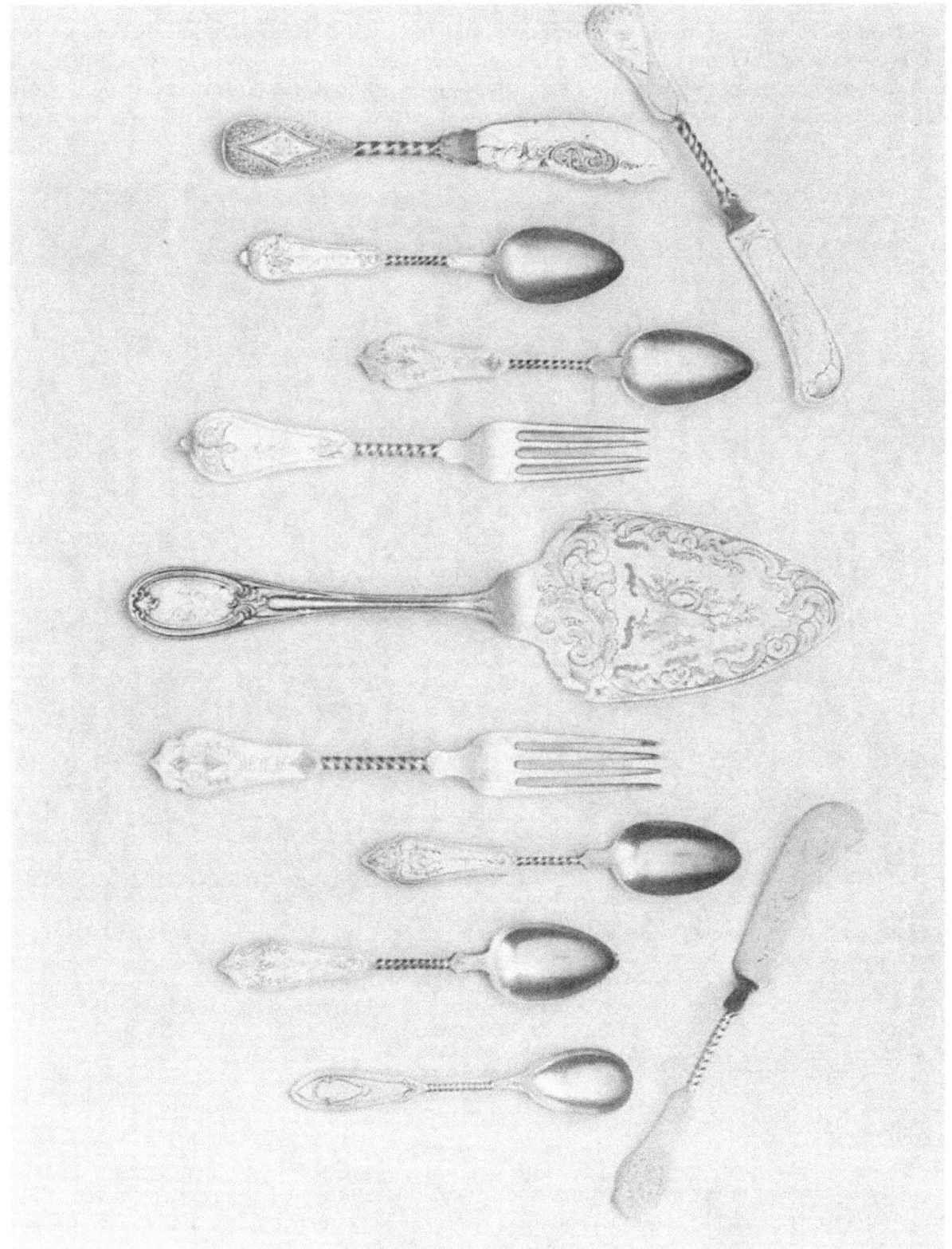

Twist handled and engraved flatware by Cincinnati makers. From left to right the following marks are found, butter knife, Duhme, spoon, Duhme and Co., spoon, C. Hellebush, fork, Duhme, large engraved serving piece, Palmer & Owen, fork, C. Hellebush, spoon, C. Oskamp, spoon, Duhme & Co., spoon Duhme, butterknife above left, E. & D. Kinsey, butterknife above right, David Kinsey. All of the above pieces are in private collections.

Holloware was also made in Cincinnati after the Civil War and Duhme & Co. was the largest producer. Duhme silver can be found today all over the United States. Illustrated below, and on pages 52 and 53, are examples of some of the fine holloware made by Duhme & Co. Also illustrated on page 95 is a Victorian silver water pitcher marked W.W. McGrew.

An elegant Victorian engraved presentation set, consisting of ewer, goblets and tray, bearing the following inscription:

Presented to his honor the Mayor,
Charles Jacob Jr.
by his friends.
Cincinnati, Nov. 22nd, 1880

The set is marked Duhme & Co., and also is marked with the Duhme hallmark.

Private collection.

As can be seen in the above photo, and other illustrations of Duhme silver included in the book, silver made by Duhme and Co. was of a very high quality and can compare favorably with any silver produced at the time.

A large amount of jewelry, too, was made in Cincinnati over the years, if we are to judge by the number of men who were listed as jewelry manufacturers. Jewelry was also brought in from the east and sold in the shops. But since there were no laws governing the marking of jewelry, very little is marked and consequently it is very difficult to trace. The included picture shows an early piece of silver mounted French paste jewelry bearing an early French hallmark and maker's mark. If the American craftsmen had marked their jewelry in a similar manner the identification of antique jewelry would be simple. In some cases jewelry had been found in the original box marked with the jeweler's name, but such examples are fairly rare.

In the watchmaking business we find that most of the early watchmakers were selling watches imported from England and the Continent. Illustrated below is an English watch bearing the mark of E. & D. Kinsey on the case. It is not unlikely that watches made by Cincinnati craftsmen will be discovered and our knowledge of this subject will be increased.

A piece of early French paste jewelry bearing an early French hallmark and maker's mark.

A gold hunters case watch, marked on the face M.I. Tobias & Co., Liverpool, the case marked E. & D. Kinsey, Cincinnati O., this mark incised and in a half circle.

Private collection.

Many of the early Cincinnati silversmiths were also watch and clockmakers, but a few men do not fit in this category and were only clockmakers. Very little research has been done in this field except for Luman Watson, about whom much has been written. The inclusion of clockmakers in this book adds much new information for those interested in horology.

Hopefully, this book will be a beginning. Its publication should make us more aware of the contribution of Cincinnati craftsmen and with this knowledge more examples of their work may be discovered for future generations to enjoy.

Biographies of Cincinnati Silversmiths Jewelers Watch and Clockmakers working prior to 1851 listed alphabetically

Abbreviations Used

b. born

d. died

w. working in Cincinnati

For the convenience of readers, partnerships are listed alphabetically by the surname of the first partner. They are listed following the biographical account of the last man with that surname. Partnerships are listed only when a definite date is known.

ALLEN, CALEB, JR. *(b. 1808, d. 1873)* .... *(w. 1833-1873)*

Caleb Allen had a long career as a silversmith and jeweler in Cincinnati. He was born in Providence, Rhode Island in 1808, the son of Caleb and Hannah Allen. Exactly when Allen arrived in Cincinnati is unknown, but C. Allen & Co. existed prior to June of 1833, when the firm of Allen & Rhodes was formed. (See ad under P. Scovil.) The included newspaper notice announced the formation of Allen & Rhodes.

NOTICE.—The subscribers having formed a connection in business under the firm of ALLEN & RHODES, would inform the public that they will manufacture and keep for sale, an extensive assortment of JEWELRY. They have just received from New York and Philadelphia, Gold and silver Lever English and French Watches, gold chains; coral, Jett and fillagree Ear Rings and Pins, fine Cutlery, with a general assortment of Fancy Goods, &c; all of which they offer at wholesale at a small advance, at No. 36, Lower Market street, up stairs.

C. ALLEN,
THOS. F. RHODES,

june 17   47tf

Cincinnati Daily Gazette, June 17, 1833

The 1834 Cincinnati Directory listed Caleb Allen as a jeweler with Thomas Rhodes. Business must have been good, as the notice for apprentices which appears below was carried by the newspaper in 1834.

WANTED,
BY the subscribers, two boys as apprentices to the Jewelry business; also, two to the manufacturing of silver ware. Those between the age of sixteen and eighteen would be preferred; those that can come well recommended only need apply.
ALLEN & RHODES.

ap 18   4tf

Cincinnati Daily Gazette, April 18, 1834

In August of the same year Allen & Rhodes took John G. Anthony into the firm and the name became Allen, Rhodes & Co. (See Thomas F. Rhodes.)

Like so many shops of the period, Allen, Rhodes & Co. carried a variety of articles, and the February 18, 1835 *Cincinnati Daily Gazette* carried their ad for accordions. Then in December of the same year they advertized that they carried dental supplies!

The 1836 Cincinnati Directory, listed Allen

Rhodes & Co. as silver plate manufacturers, and this same directory carried the following ad:

ALLEN, RHODES & CO.
MANUFACTURE SILVER PLATE AND JEWELRY,
AND KEEP FOR SALE,
At wholesale only,
Watches, Cutlery, and Fancy Goods:
Also
A LARGE ASSORTMENT OF WATCH-MAKER'S TOOLS,
And watch materials.

By 1837 Allen & Rhodes were no longer partners and an ad for C. Allen & Co. appeared in the Western Address Directory of that year.

In 1840 the following ad appeared in the Cincinnati Directory, listing Caleb and his brother William H. Allen as partners in C. Allen and Co.

C. ALLEN & CO.,
MANUFACTURERS OF JEWELRY,
DEALERS IN
Clocks, Watches, Watch-Tools and Materials,
and
FANCY GOODS GENERALLY;
N. E. corner of Main and Columbia streets,
CINCINNATI:
C. ALLEN,   WM. H. ALLEN.

For some unknown reason the 1842 through 1844 Directories listed Caleb Allen with no occupation and indicated that brother William had formed his own company. In 1846, however, William and Caleb formed another partnership (C. & W.H. Allen) which was to last until Caleb's death in 1873.

The 1851-1852 Cincinnati Directory carried the following ad for the Allen brothers:

Court House records of 1835 listed the marriage of Caleb Allen to Caroline Hastings, from Massachusetts. From the 1850 Census we learned that Caleb and Caroline had three sons and four daughters; Caleb was listed as a jeweler with $11,500 in property.

Flat silver exists bearing the following marks:

C. Allen & Co.   Allen & Rhodes

ALLEN, RHODES & Co

(This mark also appears in a cartouche with a serrated edge.)

A salt spoon bearing the first mark illustrated above appears below, a tablespoon by Allen, Rhodes & Co. is shown below, and a gravy ladle by Allen & Rhodes on page 117.

Cincinnati spoons, the salt spoon on the left marked Clayton in a cartouche, the second salt spoon marked J. Draper in a cartouche, the third salt spoon marked C. Allen & Co. in a banner. The tablespoon on the right is a pewter spoon, recently made from the C. Symmes spoon mold belonging to the Cincinnati Historical Society.

Private collections.

ALLEN, WILLIAM H. *(b. 1813, d. 1889)* .... **(w. 1839-1873)**

William H. Allen was the son of Caleb and Hannah Allen and the younger brother of Caleb Allen, Jr. He was born in Providence, Rhode Island in 1813.

The first recorded evidence of his arrival in Cincinnati is the directory listing of 1839, at which time he was with C. Allen & Co. The 1842 Cincinnati Directory listed him as a silversmith and carried the included ad.

> 230   FOURTH WARD.
> Allen William H. silversmith, corner Main and 2d—boards A. Mann
>
> ---
> **WILLIAM H. ALLEN,**
> *North East corner of Main and Columbia Streets,*
> CINCINNATI,
> *MANUFACTURER OF JEWELRY,*
> AND
> Dealer in Clocks, Watches,
> WATCH MATERIALS AND TOOLS,
> Fine Cutlery and Fancy Goods, Musical Boxes, &c. &c. &c.
> ---

The 1843 and 1844 Directories listed Allen as a silversmith on Main between Third and Fourth.

From 1846 until 1873 William worked with his brother Caleb (C. & W.H. Allen). Following the death of Caleb, the business seems to have terminated, as William was listed in the directory at 402 W. Fourth, with no occupation given.

William Allen died in 1889 and is buried in Spring Grove Cemetery.

Possibly silver marked W.H. Allen exists, and if so, this book may help to bring it to light.

ALLEN & RHODES .... *(1833-1834)*

ALLEN, RHODES & CO. .... *(1834-1837)*

C. ALLEN & CO. .... *(1833) (1837-1840)*

C. & W.H. ALLEN .... *(1846-1873)*

ANDREWS, DAVID B. *(b. 1822, d. ?)* .... (w. 1849-1863)

The first Cincinnati Directory listing of David Andrews occurred in 1849, when he was listed as a watchmaker. Andrews may have come to Cincinnati from Elyria, Ohio, as a D. B. Andrews advertised his dry goods store in Elyria in Kimball's Business Directory of 1846.

Cincinnati Commercial, November 6, 1849

Several ads were found for D. B. Andrews in Cincinnati newspapers of 1849. The included ad appeared in November of that year.

The 1850 census listed David Andrews as 28, male, a silversmith from Ireland.

Gray & Co.'s *Business Mirror of 1851-1852* carried the following ad, and Andrews continued to be listed in the directories as a jeweler until 1863.

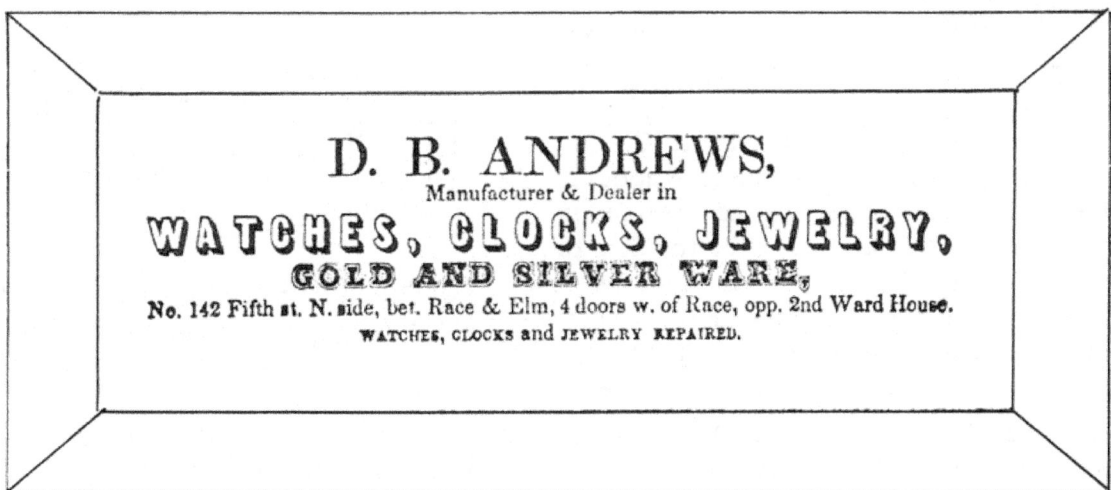

ANGE, SOLOMON *(b. 1788, d. 1861)* .... (w. 1834-1861)

Solomon Ange was born in Switzerland on December 15, 1788. Currier lists him as working in New York in 1827 and 1828.

The first notice found of Ange's appearance in Cincinnati was a record of his marriage in 1834 to Maria B. Damiael. In 1836 the Cincinnati Directory listed Ange as a silversmith, and the 1839 Directory listed him as a jeweler and goldsmith.

Succeeding directories listed Ange as working as a watchmaker and jeweler at various addresses on Second Street, Walnut Street and Central Avenue, until his death in 1861.

Ange's wife Maria must have died, since cemetery records show his wife as Evaline Mennet, born in Kentucky. Three children of Evaline and Solomon, Theodore, Eliza and William Henry, are buried with their parents in Spring Grove Cemetery.

Ange's shop was listed in business directories, but no ads were found in the newspapers, and no examples of silver marked with his name have been seen.

ANTHONY, John G. *(b. 1810, d. ?)* .... (w. 1834-1837)

John G. Anthony worked for several years as a silversmith in Cincinnati. In 1834 he became a partner of C. Allen and T. F. Rhodes in the firm of Allen, Rhodes & Co. (See notice under Thomas F. Rhodes.)

Anthony was possibly the brother-in-law of Rhodes, as his wife was Ann Rhodes, and one son was named Thomas Rhodes Anthony. In 1836 T. F. Rhodes and Anthony were advertising the firm of Rhodes & Anthony, and the included ad appeared in the newspaper, stating that they carried an assortment of silverware of their own manufacture. This firm was also called Rhodes, Anthony & Co.; silver with these marks has been seen.

Anthony's name appeared in the 1836 Directory working for Allen, Rhodes & Co., although this is the same year in which Rhodes & Anthony advertised. In 1837 an ad appeared in the Western Address Directory for the firm of Rhodes, Anthony & Carley, manufacturers of jewelry and silverware. By the time of the publishing of the next directory in 1839 Anthony was listed with no occupation given and Rhodes' name did not appear at all. In later directories, Anthony was listed as a clerk, accountant, bookseller, and as an insurance agent.

> **NOTICE.**
> THE Subscribers have just received their Fall Supply of Goods, which they offer at Wholesale on the most accommodating terms. Their Stock consists of—
> Jewelry, a very extensive and well selected assortment.
> Silver Spoons, Pencil Cases, Thimbles, Spectacles, &c.
> Watches, Clocks, Watch Chains and Keys, Watch Materials, and Tools of every description usually called for by Watchmakers.
> ALSO,
> A Complete Assortment of Toys and Fancy Goods, generally.
> Gold Foil, Plate, Wire, and Tools for Dentists' use.
> They also make to order, Silver Spoons, Tumblers, &c. and keep constantly on hand an assortment of Silver Ware of their own manufacture. RHODES & ANTHONY.
> No. 50, Main st. Cincinnati.
> oct 8   68tf
> ☞ The Dayton Journal, Richmond Palladium, Indianapolis Journal, Republican Banner, Madison, Ia., Louisville Journal, Lexington Intelligencer, Maysville Eagle, and Missouri Republican, St. Louis, will give the above 3 insertions, and charge this office.

Cincinnati Daily Gazette, October 8, 1836

The 1850 Cincinnati Census listed Anthony as forty years old, from Rhode Island, with no occupation given. It also included his wife Ann, three sons and two daughters.

The following are reproductions of the marks used:

Rhodes & Anthony   *Rhodes, Anthony & Co*

Illustrated on page 117 is a sugar tongs marked Rhodes, Anthony & Co.

ASPINWALL, CHAUNCEY B. *(b. 1801, d. 1882)* .... (w. 1846-1855; w. 1865-1882)

Cutten notes in his book on silversmiths, watchmakers and jewelers of the state of New York, that C.B. Aspinwall advertised as a jeweler in Oswego, N.Y. in 1831 and 1832. At that time he was a partner of Griffing (Aspinwall & Griffing).

The first listing of Aspinwall in Cincinnati appeared in the 1846 Cincinnati Directory, where he was listed as a watchmaker. From 1848 until 1852 he was listed as a watchmaker and jeweler at 5 Clinton Buildings. In 1853 he became a partner of Eyster (Aspinwall & Eyster). By 1855 he was working alone again as a jeweler.

From 1856 until 1865 Aspinwall was listed with a variety of occupations including agent, patent right agent, and real estate agent.

By 1865 he was back in the jewelry business, and he continued as a jeweler until his death in 1882. During these years the directory listing was C.B. Aspinwall & Co., at 183 West 8th.

Born in New York State in 1801, Chauncey B. Aspinwall died in Cincinnati in 1882. His wife Sara was born in Lebanon, Connecticut in 1805 and died in Cincinnati in 1864. Children of this marriage listed in the 1850 Census were William Henry, Edward, Theodore and Mary.

ATKINSON, JOHN V. *(b. 1812, d. 1883)* .... (w. 1843-1852; w. 1866-1879)

John V. Atkinson was born in England in 1812. We can assume that he lived for a time in Kentucky before coming to Cincinnati, as cemetery records include a George Atkinson, son of John V. Atkinson, born in Kentucky in 1838.

In 1843 the Cincinnati Directory listed Atkinson as a watchmaker on 5th between John and Smith. Succeeding directories up to 1853 listed him as a watchmaker, for most of these years on Western Row. From 1853 to 1863 Atkinson had a Queensware and Crockery store at 92 West 5th. By 1866 Atkinson had returned to his old business and he was listed as a watchmaker or jeweler until 1879.

Atkinson died in 1883 and is buried in Spring Grove Cemetery, as are his wife Jeanette and his children George, Emma, Edward, John and Clarence.

BAILEY, GAMALIEL .... (w. 1834-1846)

Gamaliel Bailey must have come directly from Philadelphia to Cincinnati. Brix lists him as a watchmaker in Philadelphia from 1828 to 1833 and his name appeared in the Cincinnati Directory as a watchmaker in 1834.

Earlier information about Bailey was found in Williams' book on the silversmiths of New Jersey. Mr. Williams states, "Bailey was a pioneer American follower of John Wesley, and before he settled in Mt. Holly, New Jersey in 1807, he was a travelling Methodist preacher. He organized a class which became the foundation of the Methodist Episcopal Church in Mt. Holly." (p. 72) Williams also states that Bailey worked as a silversmith in Mt. Holly, where he had a shop on Main St. He was succeeded in the shop by Peter Hill in 1821.

Information is scarce about Bailey in Cincinnati. We know that he worked as a watchmaker on Main Street from 1834 until 1846. The 1842 Directory states that Bailey was boarding with G. Bailey, Jr., who was at that time a journalist and editor of the *Cincinnati Philanthropist*. G. Bailey, Jr. left Cincinnati in 1847 and went to Washington, D.C. to become editor-in-chief of the *National Era*. Possibly his father went to Washington with him.

BANGS, JOHN .... (w. 1829)

The name John Bangs appeared only once in the Cincinnati Directories. This occurred in 1829, when he was listed as a silversmith boarding at D. Kautz's.

This John Bangs was most probably the John J. Bangs who worked at a later time in Chillicothe, Ohio. The Chillicothe newspaper, the *Scioto Gazette,* of May 23, 1839, carried an ad for the watchmaking and jewelry shop of E.P. Pratt and John J. Bangs (Pratt & Bangs). Pratt was in Cincinnati in 1828 and 1829, and the two men possibly met at that time.

By June of 1840 Bangs had opened his own shop in Chillicothe, and the *Scioto Gazette* of June 25th carried his ad. Bangs continued to work in Chillicothe and was still listed as a jeweler there in 1865.

Early spoons have been found with the mark:

J.J. BANGS

These were possibly made after he left Cincinnati, but since he was in Cincinnati briefly, his name is included in this book.

BEGGS, JOSEPH P. *(b. 1808, d. 1884)* .... (w. 1836-1861)

Joseph P. Beggs was born in 1808 near Pittsburgh, where he learned the trade of silversmithing. The *Pittsburgh Gazette* of December 28, 1829 carried an ad for Wallace and Beggs, clock and watchmakers.

The first confirmation of Beggs' arrival in Cincinnati is his appearance in the 1836 Cincinnati Directory, where he was listed as a watchmaker. In 1839 Beggs was listed as a watchmaker at W. McGrew's, his residence on Spring St. By 1842 the directory listing was J.P. Beggs & Co., silversmiths and jewelers, located on Main between 3rd and 4th.

Cincinnati Daily Gazette, September 10, 1843

In 1843 Wilson McGrew and J.P. Beggs became partners (McGrew & Beggs). We can see from the included ad that they carried a variety of silver articles, some of which were of their own manufacture.

By 1848 Beggs had changed partners and was working with Harry Smith (Beggs & Smith). The included ad appeared in the newspaper in 1849. The handsome tea set illustrated on page 10 bears the mark of Beggs & Smith. An illustration of this mark appears in the inset. The tea set was presented to Fenton Lawson in 1850.

This very elaborate ad shown on the following page for Beggs & Smith appeared in the *Ohio State Business Directory* of 1853-1854.

Cist's Weekly Advertiser, Aug. 8, 1849

The partnership of Beggs & Smith continued until 1861, when Beggs retired.

Beggs died in Pittsburgh in 1884. His obituary states that during his first years in Cincinnati Beggs had connected himself with the First Presbyterian Church and was ever after

BEGGS & SMITH,
No. 6 West Fourth Street, Cincinnati,

(One door east of the magnificent First Presbyterian Church,)

DEAL IN ALL KINDS OF FINE

WATCHES, DIAMONDS,

AND THE RICHEST DESCRIPTION OF

JEWELRY.

THEY KEEP A GENERAL ASSORTMENT OF FINE SILVER

Forks, Spoons, Cups, Pitchers, Tea Sets, etc.

And are Agents for the same style of Articles plated, and varying in price in proportion to the thickness of the Silver. They also have a general assortment of

GOLD, SILVER, & STEEL SPECTACLES,

AND A LARGE VARIETY OF

Fancy Goods,

Such as Gold and Silver head Canes, Fans, Fancy Clocks, Porte Monnaies; Gold Pens, Pocket and Table Knives, Vases, Razors, etc., etc. Those wanting

CHOICE GOODS,

Are invited to call and examine their Assortment.

P. S. Watches, Clocks, Music Boxes and Jewelry, repaired.

A maganificent four piece tea set bearing the inscription: To Fenton Lawson From the Cincinnati Independent Fire Engine and Hose Companies, Pilots, Rovers and Witches, Cincinnati 1850." The cream pitcher shows the fire engine in detail and the larger pieces depict scenes of fires. The finials are firemen carrying a fireman's trumpet. The set is very large, the coffee pot being 15 inches high. The set bears the mark Beggs & Smith in a cartouche and the pseudo hallmarks shown in the photograph.

Private collection.

The mark appearing on the four piece tea set.

An enlargement of the body of the tea pot, showing in more detail the scene depicted.

known as an earnest worker in the Church and Temperance cause.

Marks found on silver are:

J.P. BEGGS & Co.   **McGREW & BEGGS**

BEGGS & SMITH (incised)

Another Beggs & Smith mark is illustrated on page 10.

Illustrated on page 15 is a teaspoon marked J.P. Beggs & Co., and on page xii are a teaspoon and a butter knife marked McGrew and Beggs.

BEGGS & SMITH .... *(1848-1861)*

J. P. BEGGS & CO. .... *(1842-1843)*

BENSON, GABRIEL L. .... **(w. 1819-1825)**

In 1819 G.L. Benson, from New York, appeared in the Cincinnati Directory, listed as a silversmith at 148 Main. In June of 1819 the included ad for G.L. Benson & Co. appeared in a Cincinnati newspaper. For a short time Benson was associated in business with Jeffrey Seymour and Othniel Williston (Seymour, Williston & Benson).

The notice of the marriage of Gabriel Benson to Abigail Mills was carried in *Liberty Hall* newspaper in 1820.

The last listing of G.L. Benson in Cincinnati appeared in the 1825 Directory, where he was listed as a watchmaker, residing at 157 Main.

> **G. L. Benson & Co.**
> *Watchmakers, Silversmiths, & Jewellers,*
> No. 148, Main-street, opposite the Presbyterian Church,
> CINCINNATI,
> HAVE on hand a handsome assortment of Gold and Silver Watches, Fine and Jewellers' Gold Watch Chains, Seals and Keys, elegant Gold Ear and Finger Rings, Breast Pins, Necklaces, Bracelets, Gold, Cornelian, and Gilt Vest Buttons.
> *Gilt and Silver Wares.*
> Ladies' elegant Reticule Clasps, Chrystalized Purses, Amulet Beads, Bracelets, and Ear Rings— a general assortment of Gilt Watch Chains, Seals, and Keys, Silver and Plated Table and Tea Spoons, &c. &c.
> ☞ All kinds of Gold and Silver Ware manufactured on the shortest notice. Watches of every description repaired and warranted. Orders punctually attended to.
> *** Hair work of every description handsomely braided and mounted. Cash given for human hair from 20 to 30 inches in length.
> June 22.   53 tf

The Inquisitor & Cincinnati Advertiser, June 22, 1819.

BERTLING, ERNST *(b. 1811, d. 1866)* .... **(w. 1842-1866)**

Ernst Bertling was born in Germany in 1811. The record of his marriage in 1841 to Johanna Buring, also from Germany, was found in the Hamilton County, Ohio Court House.

Bertling first appeared in the Cincinnati Directory in 1842, where he was listed as a goldsmith. In succeeding directories he was listed as a jeweler and goldsmith at 426 Walnut. The 1850 Cincinnati Census listed Bertling's occupation as goldsmith. Also included in the Census listing were his wife and three children.

Bertling died in 1866, his will leaving everything to his wife Johanna, who must have been a very enterprising woman for her day, since she continued the business until 1879.

BEST, ROBERT *(b. 1790, d. 1831)* .... (w. 1812-1819)

Robert Best was the youngest son of Thomas and Sara Greenham Best. He was born in Ilminster, England in 1790, and came with his family to Cincinnati in 1803.

> *Robert Best,*
> **WATCH & CLOCK-MAKER,**
> SILVERSMITH & JEWELLER,
> RESPECTFULLY informs the public, that he has commenced the above business at his shop, opposite *Hough & Blair's Store,* in
> **HAMILTON, BUTLER COUNTY.**
> If unremitting attention to business, united with a wish to please his employers, are qualifications requisite to ensure success, he flatters himself he shall not be idle.
> Hamilton, March 20, 1811.
> N. B. Old Gold, Silver, Copper, Brass or Pewter, will be received in payment for Goods or Work.   R. B.

Liberty Hall,
March 20, 1811

When he was twenty-one years old, in 1811, he opened a shop in Hamilton, Ohio, and the above ad appeared in a Cincinnati newspaper. Business in Hamilton must not have been good, however, as in July of 1812 Robert was back in Cincinnati and had formed a partnership with his brother Samuel (see S. Best). Like so many of the partnerships of the time, this one did not last long, and in November of 1812 the included notice of dissolution appeared in the newspaper. The notice also included the information that Robert had become a partner of Jacob Deterly. In July of 1813 Best & Deterly were still advertising, but in December of that year the notice on the following page appeared, relating the dissolution of Best & Deterly and the formation of Best & Woodruff.

> THE FIRM OF
> **SAMUEL & ROBERT BEST**
> is this day dissolved by mutual consent.
>   S. & R. BEST.
> Cincinnati, Nov. 7, 1812.
> The business will be continued, as usual, at the same place in Main street, next door to I. C. Barker & Co's Drugstore, by
> **Robert Best & Jacob Deterly,**
> **WATCH & CLOCK MAKERS,**
> JEWELLERS, SILVER-SMITHS, &c.
> They choose rather to recommend themselves to the public by the execution of their work, and attention to business, than by a pompous advertisement, and doubt not of giving general satisfaction to those who favour them with their patronage.
> N. B. They keep on hand a constant supply of SADDLE MOUNTING of the best quality both silver and plated.
> DIRKS & SWORDS, neatly mounted with Eagle heads, or otherwise.
> The highest price will be given for old gold, silver, copper, brass, and pewter.
> ☞ Wanted to the above business 2 or 3 APPRENTICES (from 10 to 14 years of age) who can come well recommended.

Liberty Hall,
November 7, 1812

By 1815 the firm had a new name, R. Best & Co. This firm was the partnership of Robert Best, Enos Woodruff and Jacob Deterly. A very large ad appeared in the newspaper in 1815, as shown.

One interesting note is found in the ad, showing the English background of these men. The ad says, "Silver ware of every description (warranted to be Sterling silver)."

In 1817 the partnership existing under the name of R. Best & Co. was dissolved, a notice to that effect appearing in *Liberty Hall*

NOTICE.

THE partnership of BEST & DETERLY is this day dissolved by mutual consent. Those having unsettled accounts with the above firm are requested to call on them for settlement, as J. Deterly (one of the late firm) intends leaving this place in a few days.

ROBERT BEST.
JACOB DETERLY.

Cincinnati, September 27, 1813.

E. WOODRUFF having purchased of J. Deterly his interest in the above concern the business will be continued at the same place under the firm of

BEST & WOODRUFF.

They intend, in addition to their former business, to carry on that of SILVER-PLATING extensively, and have now on hand an assortment of *Bridle-bits, Stirrup-irons*, &c. of the newest patterns. Also, a quantity of *Saddle mounting* and *Carriage moulding*. Carriage mounting and other articles in their line will be plated on the shortest notice.

They have just received a large and elegant assortment of the best Philadelphia *Jewelry*, with an assortment of *Miniature Glasses*.

They have also received an addition to their former stock of *Watch materials*, among which is a handsome assortment of *Dials*, &c.

They have also, & intend keeping on hand, a general assortment of SILVER WARE, among which are the following articles—*Soup or Milk Ladles, Cream or Jelly Spoons, Table Desert, Tea, Salt and Mustard ditto Sugar Tongs, Tumblers, Saddle Mounting, &c.* All of which they will sell as low as can be purchased in the western country.

N. B. The highest price in cash will be given for old Gold, Silver, Copper, Brass and Pewter.

Western Spy, September 27, 1813

Western Spy, February 18, 1815

REMOVAL.
ROBERT BEST &CO.

HAVING removed their shop to the centre of the three Brick Houses lately erected on Main between Columbia and lower Market streets.— They return their sincere thanks to their friends and the public in general, for the liberal encouragement they have received in the

WATCH & CLOCK MAKING JEWELLER & SILVERSMITH

business, and having added the

HOLLOW WARE MAKING

and manufacturing of all kinds

PLATED WARE,

branches of importance and new in this place, they feel the greatest confidence of meriting the future support of the public. As they have on hand an extensive assortment of the best materials for *Watch Work*, and are determined to pay particular attention to that branch, likewise on hand a number of *eight-day clocks*, of the best materials and workmanship, (warranted.) And an extensive assortment of

Mourning & Fancy Jewelry, Tortoise Shell Combs, &c.

SILVER WARE

of every description, (warranted to be Sterling silver,) which they will sell as low as can be purchased in any part of U. States; consisting of the following articles viz: all kinds of *Urns, Coffee and Tea Pots, Sugar and Slop Bowls, Cream Ewers, Pitchers, Goblets, Tumblers, Salt Cellers, Castors, Soup and Sauce Ladles, Cream, Mustard, Salt, and Marrow Spoons. Table, Desert & Tea* do. of the three last mentioned articles, they have constantly on hand from 50 to 100 setts of various patterns, Silver and Gilt mounted Swords and Dirks, Belt mounting &c.

Also an extensive assortment of PLATED WARE, consisting of Men and Women's Stirrup Irons, Bridle bits, Spurs, Martingale Hooks, &c. all of the newest patterns and of a quality equal to any manufactured in the United States, which they will retail low and make a handsome allowance to those who purchase by the quantity.

Swords, Dirks, Watches &c. neatly gilt. They will give constant employ to 2 or 3 Journeyman Platers who are good workmen.

Also wish to take 2 or 3 Boys from 14 to 16 years of age, who can come well recommended as apprentices to the Plating business. The highest price will be given for old Silver, Brass, and Pewter.

February 18th, 1815.   33 3m.

newspaper of that year. We cannot help but wonder why the early silversmiths changed partners so frequently. Was it professional jealousy, differences in temperament, or what? It often seems like a continuous game of "musical partners"!

In 1817, after the dissolution of the partnership of R. Best & Co., Robert Best again became a partner of his brother Samuel (see S. Best). By 1818 Robert was again working alone, but in 1819 he gave up his business and the included notice appeared in the newspaper:

> **ROBERT BEST,**
> HAVING engaged with the managers of the Western Museum Society to devote a considerable portion of his time in that institution, found it necessary to close his business in Main-street; he has therefore transferred his establishment to Messrs. *Seymour, Williston, & Benson*. He with pleasure returns his grateful acknowledgments to the public for their liberal support, which he hopes will be continued to his successors, as they are gentlemen he can recommend to his former customers.
> NB. Those having left Watches or other articles with him to repair, will please to call for them at the old stand.
> Aug. 31.   63 tf

Cincinnati Inquisitor & Advertiser, Aug. 31, 1819

> **ROBERT BEST,**
> *Curator of the Western Museum.*
> WILL repair all kinds of *Philosophical* and *Mathematical Instruments*—all the higher order of *Time Keepers*, and in short, every species of delicate and *Complicated Machinery*.—He will also execute Seals of office and Dies of every description in steel or any other metal. He may be applied to either at the Western Museum, in the Cincinnati College, or at his dwelling nearly opposite, on Walnut Street.
> Cincinnati, Dec. 30, 1820.   190-tf

Liberty Hall, Dec. 30, 1820

On December 1st, 1819 Deterly notes in his diary *"Museum.* Mr. Robt. Best & Thos. Dover set out for Fort Wayne. The object of this expedition is to collect curiousities for the Western Museum."

By 1820, when the included notice appeared, Robert Best had become the curator of the Western Museum, which was a repository of fossils, minerals and antiquities of the Western Territory. The notice also informs us that Best was holding other jobs while acting as curator.

In 1820 Robert Best lost his young son Samuel in a drowning, and the account shown was carried in the *Western Spy*.

> DROWNED, on Tuesday afternoon, the 3d inst. in the Ohio river at this place, SAMUEL BEST, in the 10th year of his age, son of Mr. *Robert Best*, Curator of the Western Museum. The body was recovered in less than 30 minutes, and every exertion used to resuscitate it, but without effect. The loss is severely felt by his parents, with whom this community deeply sympathize, as he was an only son, and a child of great promise.
> It is hoped that this melancholy occurrence will prove a warning to parents and guardians, not to suffer children to bathe in the river, unless accompanied by some person capable of taking care of them.

Western Spy

By 1823 Robert Best had discontinued his lectures at the Museum and the newspaper carried the included notice.

Not too long after this, Best left Cincinnati and went to Lexington, Ky., where he became an Assistant Professor of Chemistry. The notice on the following page appeared in a Cincinnati newspaper, copied from the *Lexington Republic*.

> **R. BEST,**
> HAVING discontinued his Lectures in the Western Museum, will for the present devote his whole attention to repairing the higher order of Time Keepers, Mathematical and Philosophical Instruments, and to engraving Seals of Office, &c.
> He will be found at present, at the Museum, corner of Main and Columbia streets.
> Feb. 17, 1823.   13tf

Liberty Hall,
February 17, 1823

> ROBERT BEST, A. M. has been chosen by the Trustees of Transylvania, assistant Professor of Chemistry, to lecture to the MEDICAL CLASS twice a week on Pharmaceutical Chemistry, and to take ¼ of the product of the tickets. We congratulate the public on this prominent accession to our Medical School of a gentleman so amply qualified to give instruction on those applications of Chemistry which are peculiarly important to physicians. *Lex. Rep.*

National Republican & Ohio Political Register, August 13, 1825

Robert Best became a licensed physician in 1826, but he did not practice as a doctor for long. His health failed, melancholia set in, and he died in 1831 at the age of forty-one.

Marks found on silver spoons in private collections are:

BEST & DETERLY

R. BEST   **R. BEST & Cº**

Appearing in the illustration below is a teaspoon marked R. Best.

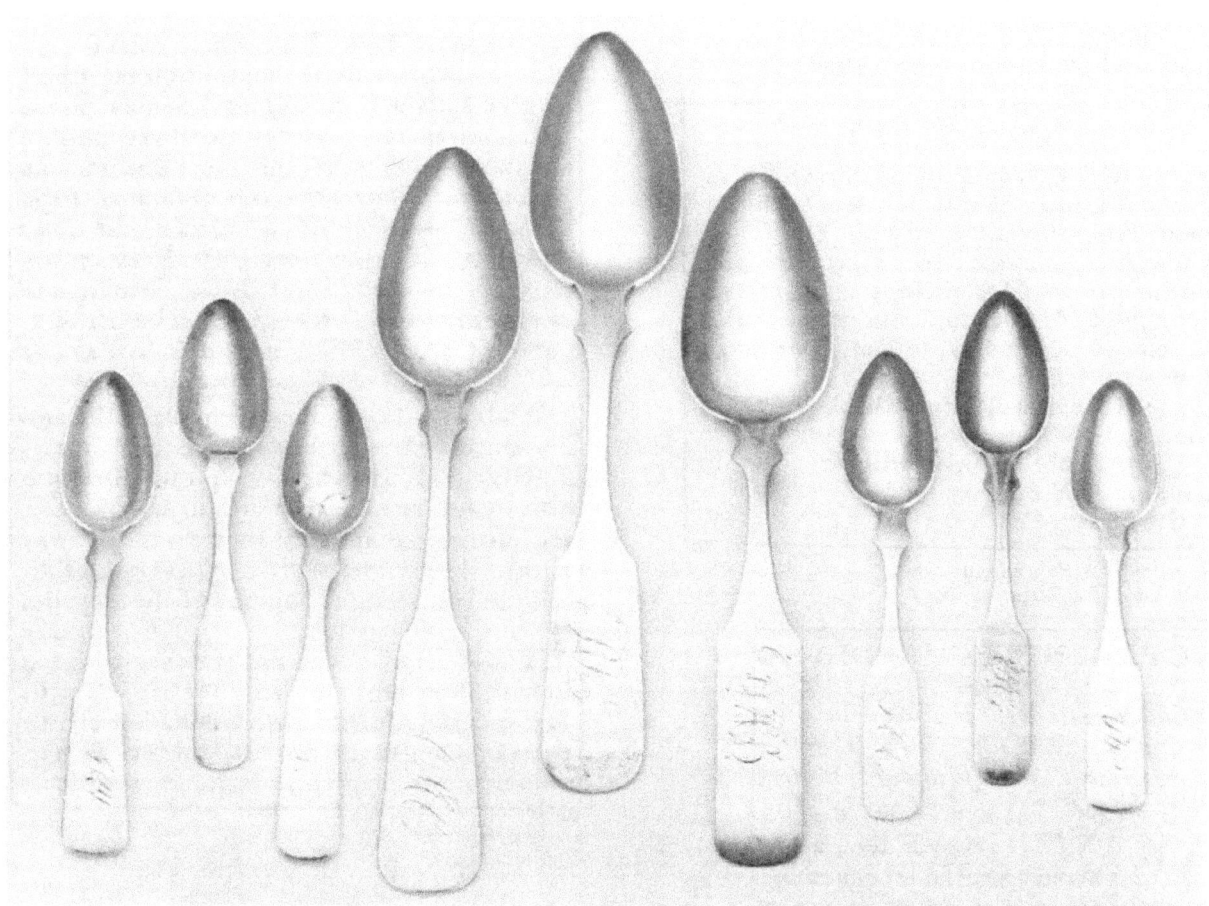

A group of early fiddle handled spoons by Cincinnati makers bearing the following marks, left to right: Hazen, R. Best, P. Collins, J. Draper, A. Palmer, A. McGrew, P. Scovil, J.P. Beggs & Co., and F. Droz. These marks all appear in a cartouche with the exception of F. Droz, whose mark appears in a banner.

Private collections.

BEST, SAMUEL (b. 1776, d. 1859) .... (w. 1802-1818)

Samuel Best was born in Ilminster, England in 1776, the eldest son of Sara Greenham and Thomas Best, Sr. The Best family came from England to Philadelphia in 1801.

A picture of Cincinnati in 1802 included Samuel Best's house, a log structure at the corner of Front and Walnut, where he began repairing watches and making clocks and silver spoons.

In 1804 Best married Eunice Winkler, and in 1805 the first ad found for his shop appeared in the newspaper. Best advertised again in 1806, this time for an apprentice to the silversmithing business, and whether he needed another apprentice or his earlier ad had brought no results, he was advertising again in 1807 for an apprentice, this time appealing to parents and guardians. (See ad below)

Samuel Best,

CLOCK & Watch Maker, Silver-Smith, &c, next door to Mr. Anderson's tavern, Front-street, returns his greatful acknowledgments to his friends, and the public in general, for their paſt favors; he hopes by a ſtrict attention in point of execution and punctuality, to meet their future ſupport.

☞ Has on had, a few Clock glaſſes for ſale.

N. B. A liberal price will be given in caſh, for good country ſugar.

Cincinnati, Feb. 13, 1805.

Western Spy, February 13, 1805

TO PARENTS & GUARDIANS.

"Children like tender Osiers take the bow,
"As first they're fashioned, so they grow."

WANTED immediately, a Boy from respectable connexions of about 14 or 15 years of age, as an apprentice to the CLOCK AND WATCH MAKING and SILVERSMITH'S business.

SAMUEL BEST.

Cincinnati, June 3d, 1807.

Western Spy, June 3, 1807

SAMUEL BEST,

Watch & Clock Maker, Jeweler Silversmith, Engraver, &c.

TENDERS his thanks to the citizens of Cincinnati, and the public generally, for the liberal encouragement bestowed on him since his commencement in this place, which will be gratefully remembered. He wishes also to inform them that he has removed his shop into Main street; in the Store lately occupied by Jacob Baymiller, next door to T. C. Barker & Co's Drug Store, where the business will in future be carried on more extensively under the firm of

SAMUEL & ROBERT BEST;

No endeavors will be wanting on their part to give satisfaction to all who may please to call on them. They intend keeping a constant supply of the most fashionable *Jewelry & Silverwork, Watch Chains, Keys and Seals—Dirks &c.—Clocks and Time Peices of the best materials & workmanship, warranted—Pad, Chest, Desk, Drawer and small Furniture Locks fitted with Keys.*

☞ Litherland, Whiteside, & Co's. PATENT LEVER WATCHES, for sale.

All those having open accounts with Samuel Best are requested to settle them immediately, and those who have left watches with him to be repaired, more than one year, are informed, that unless they are taken away within three months from this date, they will be sold for the amount of the repairs.
S. BEST.

Those persons who left watches with me in Hamilton, are informed they are left with Dr. Samuel Milikin who is authorised to deliver them to the owners and receive the amounts due on them. ROBERT BEST.

Western Spy,
July 4, 1812

In 1812 Samuel's brother Robert closed his shop in Hamilton, Ohio, and the two brothers became partners. The in-

> **SAMUEL BEST,**
> *Clock & Watch-Maker, Jeweler, Silversmith, &c.*
>
> Respectfully informs his former customers and the public generally, that he has again commenced business, as above, in all its various braches, and on a scale far more extensive, at his OLD STAND, *corner of Front & Walnut streets, opposite Edson and Carleten's Brick Tavern;* where every article in those lines may be had on LIBERAL TERMS;—such as
>
> **Silver Tumblers and Rummers, Milk and Soup Ladlers, Sauce and Cream do. Mustard, Marrow, Table and Tea Spoons, Sugar Tongs, &c.**
> ALSO,
> Swords, Dirks, Mounting for Belts, and other Military Equipments; Clocks, Watch Seals and Keys, &c. &c. together with Saddlery Mountings of every description, Silver or Plated.
>
> ☞ Having for the last 18 months, been much engaged in engraving and printing for the Banks, he has not been able to pay that attention to matters more immediately within the scope of his business, which his duty to the public required—and disappointments have, in consequence ensued. He now can assure his friends, that nothing in future, shall divert his attention from meeting their demands with promptness and dispatch.
> Cincinnati, Jan. 18, 1814.   77 6m.

Western Spy, January 18, 1814

cluded ad appeared in the newspaper in that year. This partnership was brief, for what reason we do not know, as in November of the same year it was dissolved (see Robert Best for notice of dissolution).

Samuel Best continued to advertise, and in 1814 the ad shown above appeared in the newspaper, enumerating the items of silver carried in the shop.

By 1817 Robert and Samuel Best had again become partners and *Liberty Hall* newspaper carried the included ad that year. This partnership lasted until 1818. Shortly after that time, Samuel left for Rising Sun, Indiana, as his name does not appear in the 1819 Cincinnati Directory.

Samuel Best lived in Rising Sun and continued working as a watchmaker and silversmith until his death there in 1859.

From Samuel's will we learn that he had five children by his first wife, Eunice, three by his second wife, Mary Green, and also a stepson, the son of his third wife, Mary Crouch.

> **Samuel & Robert Best,**
> WATCH AND CLOCK MAKERS, JEWELLERS, SILVERSMITHS, ENGRAVERS, &c.
> *Main street a few doors below the United States' Branch Bank,*
> RESPECTFULLY tender their services to their friends and the public, from whom, by their attention to business, they hope for support. To those who may have favored either of them with their custom, they would deem any thing farther unnecessary; to strangers they beg leave to add, that *S. Best*, having learnt and followed the Watchmaking Business many years in Europe, and they being furnished with every Tool and Material necessary for prosecuting that branch in a proper manner, they can make or repair any kind of Horological machine whatever; and to remove any doubt from Ladies or Gentlemen having delicate pieces, as Lever, Musical, Repeating or any other Watches, Musical Seals, &c. to repair, they can, by calling at their shop, see a *Patent Lever Watch*, MADE AND FINISHED by R. Best, and thereby judge of their ability.
> They will execute on the shortest notice, and in the best manner, all kinds of *Masonic Jewels and Medals, Seals of Office*, &c.
> Watch Cases and other articles Gilt in a neat and durable manner, either with Yellow or Jewellers' gold.
> S. & R. BEST intend keeping constantly on hand, a handsome assortment of
> **Jewellery and Silver Ware**
> of every description. As the beauty of the latter depends much on the style of the engraving, they trust, the manner in which they can execute that part of the work, will be an inducement for Ladies and Gentlemen, who may want articles of that kind, to favor them with their custom.
>
> ☞ R. BEST offers for sale, the HOUSE lately occupied by R. Best & Co. and where Messrs. Woodruff and Deterly now do business.
> Also, for sale, an OUT LOT, and a BUILDING LOT near the bottom of Broadway. The latter, if not sold shortly, will be leased for a few years. It is a good situation for either a Blacksmith or Cooper's Shop.
> Cincinnati, May 5th 1817.   57-70

Libery Hall,
May 5, 1817

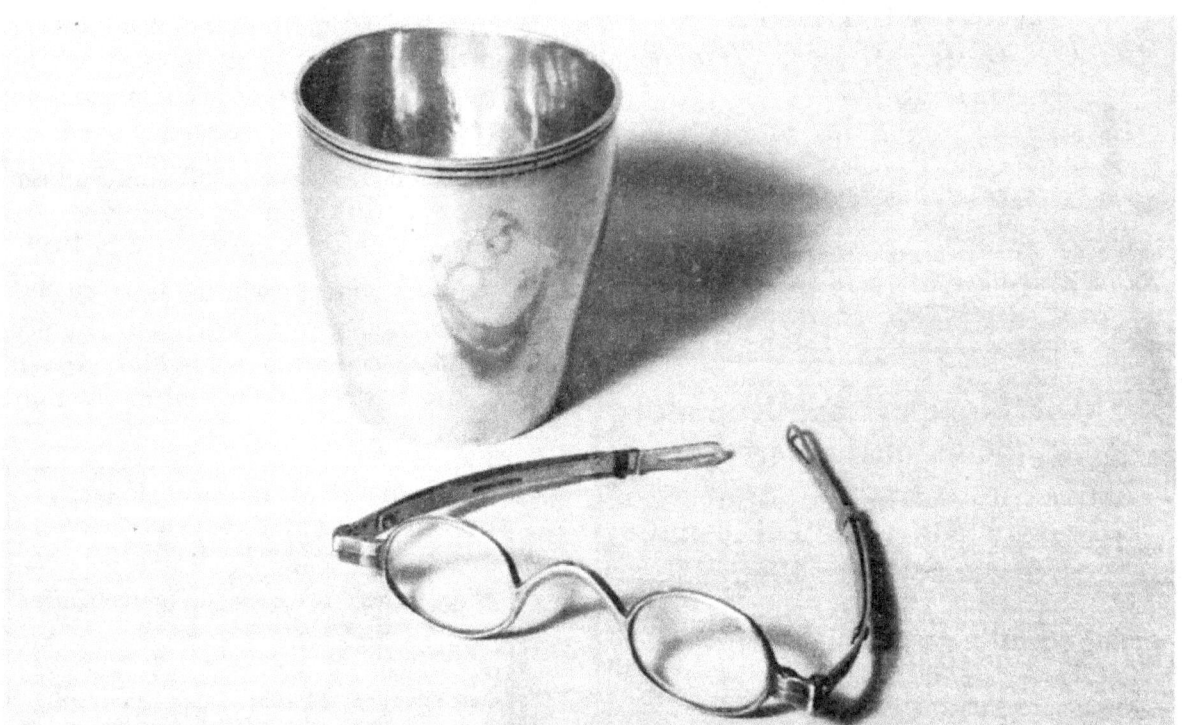

An early Cincinnati beaker bearing the mark S. Best in a cartouche, and the only known pair of spectacles by Cincinnati makers, bearing the mark Scovil & Kinsey as illustrated below. *Private collection.*

An enlargement of the mark which appears on the spectacles illustrated above.

Examples of the fine silver by S. Best include a sugar tongs in the Cincinnati Art Museum, the lovely cup illustrated above, as well as a teaspoon by S. & T. Best in the Ohio Historical Society collection.

The following are reproductions of the marks used:

| S. & T. BEST |

(Actual mark unavailable for reproduction.)

Several beautiful clocks made by Samuel Best are in existence, one of which is in the Cincinnati Art Museum. The reader is referred to Jane Sikes' article, "The Best Family of Silversmiths," in *The Magazine Antiques* of July 1974 for a more detailed discussion of Best's clocks.

BEST, THOMAS, SR. *(b. 1747, d. 1813)* .... (w. 1803?)

Thomas Best, Sr. was born in Ilminster, England in 1747 and died in Cincinnati in 1813. In 1775 he was married to Sarah Greenham. There were five children of this union, three sons, Samuel, Robert and Thomas, Jr., who are included in separate articles, and two daughters, Sarah and Ann.

Thomas was a silversmith and it was undoubtedly he who taught the trade to his sons. He came from England to Philadelphia in 1801, then moved on to Cincinnati in 1802. His three sons all worked as silversmiths, clock and watchmakers in Cincinnati, but by 1820 Thomas, Sr. had died and two of his sons had left the city and the third was no longer working as a silversmith. But these men left behind examples of their work to become part of our heritage.

Thomas' daughter Sarah married John Prell and they lived in Lebanon, Ohio. His daughter Ann married James Dover; after Dover's death she married Joshua Lawton and they also lived in Lebanon. Thomas' widow Sarah lived in Cincinnati until 1820, then moved to Lebanon, where she died in 1828.

A private collection includes a very early spoon, circa 1800, marked:

T. BEST

This was most probably made by Thomas Best, Sr., and was possibly made when Best was in Philadelphia.

For a more complete study of the Best family readers are referred to Jane Sikes' article, "The Best Family of Silversmiths," in *The Magazine Antiques* for July, 1974.

BEST, THOMAS, JR. *(b. 1781, d. 1844)* .... (w. 1806-1808)

Thomas Best was born in 1781, in Ilminster, England, the son of Thomas and Sara Greenham Best. He came with his family to Cincinnati in 1802. Since he was twenty-one years old at the time of his arrival, we can suppose that he started working as a silversmith shortly thereafter.

The first notice found for Thomas Best, Jr. appeared in the newspaper in 1806. Best at that time was a partner of Isaac Van Nuys (Van Nuys & Best) and the two men advertised for an apprentice.

The partnership did not last long, as in 1807 the included notice of dissolution was published in the newspaper. Thomas Best continued working in the same shop on Sycamore

> Wanted Immediately,
>
> A smart active LAD, about 14, or 15 years of age, as an apprentice to the Clock & Watch making, Silver-Smith & Jewelry bufinefs.
>
> A boy that can come well recommended, will meet with good encouragement.
>
> VAN NUYS & BEST.
>
> Cincinnati, Sept. 23d, 1806.
>
> N. B. The highest price will be given for old Gold & Silver.

Western Spy, September 23, 1806

Street, until, in 1808, he moved to Lebanon, where he continued to work as a silversmith, clock and watchmaker until his death in 1844.

Portraits of Thomas and his wife, Margaret Mannly Best, hang in the Glendower Museum in Lebanon, Ohio.

One of Thomas and Margaret's sons, Henry, born in 1804, moved to Dayton, Ohio and went into the jewelry and watchmaking business in that city. He became one of Dayton's most reliable and worthy citizens and died there in 1873.

Marks found on flat silver are:

T. BEST

S. & T. BEST

(Actual mark unavailable for reproduction.)

Dissolution of partnership.

THE Co-partnership between Isaac Van Nuys and Thomas Best, Silversmiths, Jewellers, Clock and Watch-Makers, being dissolved, by mutual consent—all persons indebted to that firm, will please to make immediate payment to the latter, and those who have demands against the said firm are requested to bring them in, as above, for settlement.

Thomas Best,

BEGS leave to solicit the patronage of the public in the above line, who will continue to carry on in the same shop, in Sycamore Street—His endeavours to serve them will be unremitting, and such, he presumes to say as will give entire satisfaction.

N. B. An apprentice is wanting.
Cincinnati, June 5th, 1807.

Western Spy,
June 5, 1807

BEST & DETERLY .... *(1812-1813)*

BEST & WOODRUFF .... *(1813-1815)*

R. BEST & CO. .... *(1815-1817)*

S. & R. BEST .... *(1812) (1817-1818)*

BEST & DOVER .... ?

Spoons marked:

DOVER & BEST

are in a private collection.

BISHBEE, ISAIAH .... (w. 1817)

> **Watches, Rich Pearl Jewellery, and Silver Spoons.**
>
> THE subscriber informs his friends and the public, that he has taken a shop in *Main-street third door above the U. S. Branch Bank*, where he intends to carry on the Watch Making and Jeweller's Business, and now offers for sale a good assortment of ENGLISH WATCHES, warranted to perform well, a few French Watches, good quality, and low priced. Gold Filigree Seals, Keys, Plain Gold & Gilt Chains, Keys and Seals, Silver Table and Tea Spoons, of the latest patterns, from the Boston manufactory. Also, an elegant assortment of rich
>
> *PEARL JEWELLERY,*
>
> which will be sold below Philadelphia prices.
> WATCHES of every description cleaned and repaired in the best manner, and warranted;— every favor duly received and promptly attended to.   ISAIAH BISBEE.
> Cincinnati, Aug. 21.   63 tf.

The included ad appeared in the *Western Spy* in 1817. Isaiah Bisbee was not listed in the 1819 Cincinnati Directory and no other record of him was found.

Western Spy, August 21, 1817

BLAKESLEE, EDWARD .... (w. 1840-1866)

Although E. Blakeslee's name did not appear in a Cincinnati Directory until 1846, the included ad appeared in the newspaper in 1840.

By 1846 Blakeslee was also selling looking glasses and the ad which appears below was found in the Cincinnati Directory of that year.

Charles Cist's book on Cincinnati in 1851, described Blakeslee's looking glass factory, and also included the following information about Blakeslee's marine time pieces. "Mr. Blakeslee's marine time pieces, or patent lever

> **CLOCK STORE,**
> No. 280, MAIN STREET,
> *Between Sixth and Seventh streets.*
>
> THE subscriber has on hand a splendid assortment of Eastern made, 8 day and 30 hour Brass and Wood Clocks, selected expressly for the city retail trade. All Clocks sold at this establishment will be put up and warranted to keep correct time.
> All persons in want of good time keepers are respectfully invited to call and examine his assortment. Dealers furnished by the case or hundred, at reduced prices. All kinds of Clocks carefully cleaned and repaired.
> A share of the public patronage is respectfully solicited.   E. BLAKESLEE.
> nov 30   4S-3m

Cincinnati Daily Gazette, December 11, 1840

E. BLAKESLEE'S

CLOCK AND LOOKING-GLASS STORE,

283 Main street, between Sixth and Seventh,

CINCINNATI.

Brass and Wood Clocks of all kinds, and Looking-Glasses, wholesale and retail. Clocks of all kinds repaired and warranted.

clocks, are a curiosity. These are of various sizes, the case shaped like that of a watch, and adapted accordingly, to steamboat, canal-packet, or railroad car use. They can be carried either horizontally or perpendicularly, being no more affected by the roughest motion, than a pocket watch would be. They are in fact, admirable chronometers."

Blakeslee continued to be listed as a clock dealer until 1866, when the last listing occurred. At that time Edward took his son Lyman W. into the business, and the listing was Blakeslee and Son. For the next two years the company was listed as L. W. Blakeslee, but in the years following was no longer listed.

BLAKESLEE, GARRET S. *(b. 1819, d. ?)* .... (w. 1842-1853)

We find the first Cincinnati listing of Garret Blakeslee in the 1842 Directory, where he was listed as a clock dealer on Main between Sixth and Seventh. This was the shop of E. Blakeslee, most probably Garret's brother. Garret continued to work at the aforementioned shop until 1853, after which time his name no longer appeared in the directories.

BLAKESLEY, HARPER (BLAKESLEE, BLAKSLEY) .... (w. 1829-1836)

Several private collections of silver include cups as well as flat silver marked Willey & Blaskley. Some of these pieces are also marked Cincinnati. Although the names of these two men were never listed together in a directory, and no ad was found to verify the partnership, it is self-evident that they worked together.

Harper Blakesley was first listed in the Cincinnati Directory of 1829, as a clockmaker boarding at Pickering's. (John Pickering was a clockmaker.) From 1831 until 1836 Blakesley was listed as a clockmaker at various addresses. Brooks Palmer, in this book *A Treasury of American Clocks,* includes a picture of the label of a clock by H. Blakeslee, Cincinnati.

Assuming that H. Blakesley was actually the Blaksley who worked with Willey, we can say that they probably worked together between 1831 and 1836, since by 1836 Willey had become a partner of Pulaski Scovil (Scovil & Willey).

Possibly the financial crisis of 1837 forced Blakesley out of business. His name was not listed in the 1840 Directory, but from 1842 to 1844 he was listed as a machinist.

Several other Blakeslees worked in Cincinnati as clockmakers, including Garret S. and Edward Blakeslee. These two men did not work in Cincinnati until the 1840's, and since Willey's name never appeared in a directory in the 1840's, it seems logical to conclude that silver marked Willey & Blaksley was made in the 1830's. The shape of spoons made by these two men, typical of the 1830's, attests to this fact.

Illustrated on page 147 is a cup marked:

WILLEY & BLAKSLEY

Also included is an illustration of the mark which appears on the cup.

BLANCHARD, JOSHUA .... (w. 1829)

Joshua Blanchard, from Massachusetts, appeared in the 1829 Cincinnati Directory, his occupation listed as clockmaker, his address 3rd between Sycamore and Broadway. Later directories listed him with first no occupation, then as a laborer, and in 1840, when the last listing occurred, as a painter and glazier.

BLISS, HENRY .... (w. 1849-1862)

Henry Bliss' name appeared in the 1849 Cincinnati Directory where he was listed as a clerk at 157 Main. This was the shop of N. L. Hazen. Hazen died in 1851 and Bliss undoubtedly took over the business, as in 1852 his name appeared in the Business Directory, his shop at 157 Main. Bliss also married Hazen's widow, Hannah Jeanette Twitchell, born in Connecticut in 1815, the daughter of John and Hannah Twitchell.

The following ad appeared in a Cincinnati Business directory of 1853.

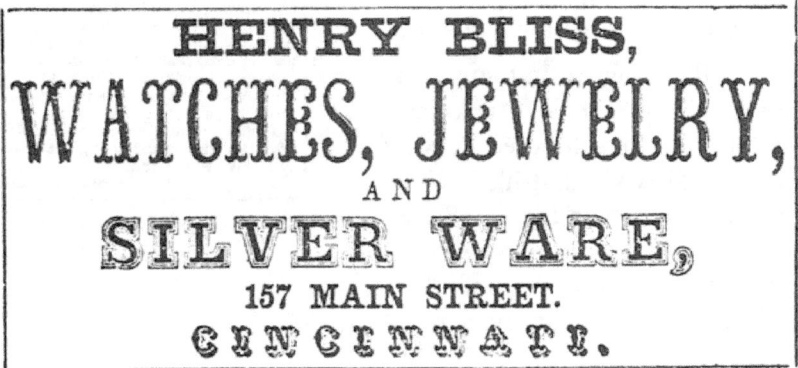

(W.H. Fagin, Publisher)

Bliss continued to work as a jeweler and silversmith until 1862. He died before 1869, as in that year Jeanette is listed in the Cincinnati Directory as a widow. Bliss' wife H. Jeanette and his son Henry are buried in Spring Grove Cemetery.

Private collections of silver include flat silver marked:

H. BLISS

BOERNER, CHARLES *(b. 1821, d. ?)* .... (w. 1850-1863)

The 1850 Census listed Charles Boerner as a watchmaker, twenty-nine years old, from Germany.

The 1850 Cincinnati Directory listed Boerner as a watchmaker at Palmer & Owen. He continued to work for Palmer & Owen for several years, but by 1858 he was working for

Beggs & Smith. In 1861 Joseph Beggs retired and Boerner became a partner of Harry Smith (Smith & Boerner).

Smith & Boerner seem to have remained partners only until 1863, and by 1865 Boerner is no longer listed in the Cincinnati directories.

Several private collections include flat silver marked:

> SMITH & BOERNER

BOYD, JOSEPH B. *(b. ? , d. 1854)* .... (w. 1840-1844)

Joseph B. Boyd was born in New York and died on March 13, 1854 in Maysville, Kentucky. When Boyd came to Cincinnati in 1839 he worked as a watchmaker at J. Draper's. In 1843 a Cincinnati newspaper carried the included notice stating that he was working as a watch and clockmaker at W.H. Allen's. The 1844 Directory also listed him as a watchmaker.

From Boyd's will, we learn that some time after 1844 he went to Maysville, Kentucky, and opened a jewelry shop. When he died in Maysville in 1854, his will directed that his business be carried on by Robert Adair for the benefit of Boyd's wife and children. It also provided that his property in Cincinnati be sold, if it were in the best interests of his family.

Cincinnati Daily Gazette, December 13, 1843

BRANDT, FELIX .... (w. 1817)

Felix Brandt, from Switzerland, worked in Cincinnati briefly. This ad appeared in the *Western Spy* in November of 1817. His name also appeared on the 1817 tax lists. The 1819 Directory, however, did not carry his name, and no additional information was found.

Western Spy, November 6, 1817

BROCKMAN, CHRISTIAN F. *(b. 1814, d. 1898)* .... **(w. 1839-1858)**

Christian F. Brockman first advertised in Cincinnati in 1839 (see included ad). Brockman worked as a clock and watchmaker and jeweler in Cincinnati from 1839 until 1858.

The Cincinnati Directory of 1850-1851 carried the ad below for Brockman.

Christian Brockman was born in Germany in 1814. In 1841 he married Margaretha Meuthe, also from Germany. Cemetery records show that the Brockmans lost a young daughter, Dorothea, to typhoid in 1857.

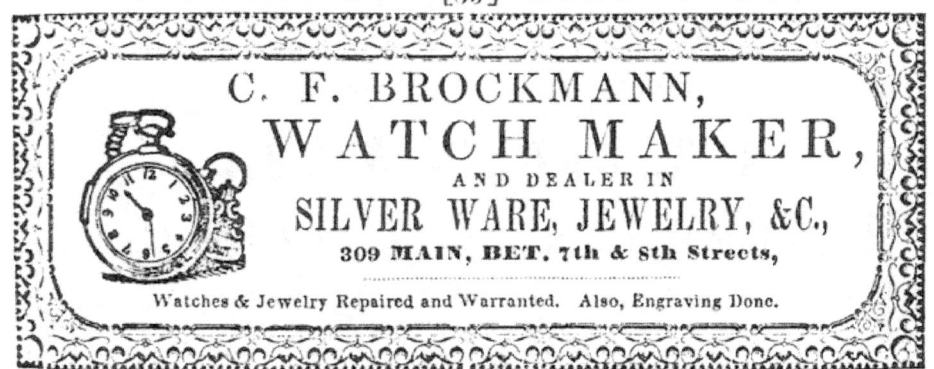

Cincinnati Advertiser & Journal, 1839

Christian Brockman died in Lynchburg, Ohio, in 1898. He and his wife and a daughter, Anna, are buried in Spring Grove Cemetery. Cemetery records also include those of Brockman's father, Ernst, showing the death of Ernst in 1851. The cause of death was listed as "old age and hardship", the place of death the Ohio River near Evansville. We can't help but wonder what "hardship" contributed to his death.

Several private collections include spoons marked:

F. BROCKMAN

Possibly this was the mark of C. F. Brockman.

BUSH (BUSCH), HENRY *(b. 1800, d. 1866)* .... **(w. 1836-1856)**

Henry Bush was a watchmaker, clockmaker and jeweler from Germany. He worked at these trades in Cincinnati from 1836 until 1856, his place of business for most of these years on 13th Street. The 1850 Census listed Bush, his wife Mary, and a daughter Elizabeth. Bush died in Cincinnati in 1866.

CARLEY, SAMUEL T. *(b. 1810, d. ?)* .... (w. 1837-1865)

Samuel T. Carley was born in New York in 1810. The first information found on Carley's arrival in Cincinnati, was an ad which appeared in the *Western Address Directory* of 1837 for Rhodes, Anthony & Carley, manufacturers of jewelry and silverware, at 50 Main St. In 1839 Carley's name appeared in the Cincinnati Directory where he was listed as a jewelry manufacturer on the north side of Fourth between Main and Walnut. In 1842 he moved his manufactory to Third, between Main and Walnut.

William Owen and S.T. Carley became partners in 1846 (Owen & Carley), and although the partnership only lasted two years, flat silver made by these two men is in private collections.

In 1849 Carley became associated in business with Henry Wray, and the directory listing for that year was Carley & Wray. This partnership did not last long, as the following ad appeared in Gray's *Cincinnati Business Mirror and City Advertiser* of 1851-1852:

---

40   CINCINNATI BUSINESS MIRROR

S. T. CARLEY & CO.,

MANUFACTURING JEWELERS,

WALNUT ST., 5th DOOR SOUTH OF 4th,

CINCINNATI.

Diamonds Set in the Newest Styles,

And every variety of Jewelry made to order.

The Census of 1850 listed Carley as a silversmith, and New York was listed as the place of birth of Carley and his wife Fay. Two daughters, Eliza and Susan, and two sons William and Oliver, were also listed.

In 1850, Carley & Co. entered "a lot of silver ornaments" in the Ohio Mechanics Institute Annual Fair. Quoting from the report of that year, "The committee consider the articles of superior workmanship."

The last listing of Carley in Cincinnati occurred in 1865, when he was listed as a jeweler at Fourth and Walnut.

There is only one Carley buried in Spring Grove Cemetery, a Sara Gano Carley, born in New York in 1785, died in 1877. Her parents were Sarah J. and Samuel Thane. If Sara was Samuel's mother, as seems likely, he was undoubtedly named Samuel Thane Carley after his grandfather.

In her booklet on Ohio silversmiths, Rhea Knittle listed a combination of silversmiths, Carey & Anthony as having worked in Cincinnati in 1837. She was undoubtedly referring to Carley & Anthony.

Illustrated on page 29 is a tablespoon from the 1830's marked:

CARLEY

Spoons marked

OWEN & CARLEY

are illustrated on page xii.

CARLEY & WRAY .... *(1849)*

CAZELLES, PETER .... **(w. 1815-1825)**

In July of 1815 a Cincinnati newspaper carried the included ad for Peter Cazelles.

Pleasants and Sill in their book of Maryland silversmiths, include the following notice of apprenticeship: "September 18, 1803: Peter Cazelles from Bordeaux, his father is living and now in France, for 5 years to Louis Poncet, gold and silversmith."

Peter Cazelles came from Baltimore to Cincinnati to open his own shop. He took a bride in Cincinnati, as *Liberty Hall,* January 28, 1815, carried a notice of the marriage of Peter Cazelles to Clarissa Mennesier.

Included in the household of Peter Cazelles in the 1817 tax list were one male over 21 (Cazelles), two women over 21, one male child and one girl between 12 and 21. Cummins' book on Hamilton County Court Records includes a record of a sale of property by Cazelles; the property, at 109 Main Street, was sold on September 30, 1817 to John Sutherland for $1,900.

In June of 1817 the ad on the following page appeared in a Cincinnati newspaper. Cazelles was listed in the 1819 Cincinnati

---

ELEGANT JEWELRY.

THE subscriber most respectfully informs the ladies and gentlemen of Cincinnati and vicinity that he has lately arrived from Baltimore and now opening on Main-street, next door to Mr. Philips' book-store on the hill, a large assortment of the most fashionable JEWELRY, consisting of

First rate gold Watch Seals
    Do.   do.   Chains
    Do.   do.   Keys
Rich mounted Pearl Ear-rings
    Do.   Topaz   do.
    Do.   Cornelian do.
With a number of other Ear-rings suitable for Ladies and Children.
A great variety of Ladies' and Gentlemen's Breast-pins, real Pearl, Cornelian, Topaz and Mock mounting—Ladies' finger Rings of every discription.
Hair Bracelets of the richest gold mounting
Gold and Silver Watches of all descriptions
Silver Soup Ladles
    Do. Table, Desert and Tea-spoons
    Do. Sugar Tongs and Mustard do.
Suspender Buckles, Ladies' Silver and Gilt Clasps.
Silver Sleeve Buttons and Pencil Cases
Silver Thimbles and Coral Beads.
                 PETER CAZELLES.
Cincinnati, July 28.   62-4

Liberty Hall, July 28, 1815

> **P. CAZELLES**
>
> Thanks his friends, and former customers for their patronage, and informs them that he has just received from Baltimore,
>
> A GENERAL ASSORTMENT OF
> **Jewellery and Silver Ware,**
> of the latest and most fashionable kinds, which he will dispose of low for cash.— He has removed from his former stand on Main Street, to the brick building on Upper Market near the corner of Main street.
>
> All work in his line will be done in the neatest manner and at the shortest notice.
>
> The highest price given for old GOLD and SILVER.
>
> Four Barrels best CORDIALS for sale for cash, as above.
> Cincinnati, June 18, 1817. 65-7

Liberty Hall, June 18, 1817

Directory as a silversmith, and in the 1825 Directory as a goldsmith and jeweler on Main Street.

On February 21, 1821 J. Deterly noted in his diary, "between 11 and 12 O'clock Peter Cazelles house took fire, was however extinguished without destroying the whole building."

Cazelles continued to advertise and ads were found for his shop in 1818 and 1822. In 1825 the included ad appeared in the West Union, Ohio newspaper.

> **Peter Cazelles,**
> WATCH MAKER, SILVER SMITH AND JEWELLER,
> (No. 113, Main Street, Cincinnati.)
> WILL keep constantly on hand, an elegant assortment of the most fashionable
> JEWELRY AND SILVER WARE.
> All kinds of Jewelry repaired.
> ☞The highest price given for old Gold and Silver.
> June, 1825. 2-6t

West Union Village Register, June, 1825

Later in the same year, Peter Cazelles' business came to an abrupt end. In the included notice we find that the court had appointed a guardian for Cazelles. Probate Court records of that year reveal that Cazelles was insane.

> **Notice.**
> ALL Persons indebted to Mr. P. Cazelles, of this place, are requested to make immediate payment to the undersigned, duly appointed guardian of said Cazelles by the Hon. the Court of Common Pleas; and any person having any demands against him prior to the 23d of August last, will please present their claims, legally authenticated, for settlement. Proprietors of watches and jewelry, left with him for repair, are also requested to come forward, prove property, pay charges, and take them away.
> J. DORFEUILLE, Guardian.
> Cin. Sept. 8, 1825. 73-tf

Cincinnati Advertiser, September 8, 1825

Although he worked in Cincinnati for 10 years, no example of Peter Cazelles' work has been seen.

CHOATE, STEPHEN .... (w. 1836-1840)

Stephen Choate, from Delaware, appeared in the Cincinnati Directory in 1836, listed as a silversmith boarding at C. Coffin's. In 1840 he was listed as working as a silversmith at J. Draper's.

From Cincinnati Choate went on to Louisville, and worked there from 1841 until 1852. (Hiatts, *The Silversmiths of Kentucky*)

Flat silver marked with Choate's name and also marked Louisville is in private collections.

CLARK, FRANCIS (b. 1800, d. ?) .... (w. 1848-1850)

The 1850 Census listed Francis Clark as a silversmith from New Jersey. It also listed his wife Martha and children Mary J. and James, born in New Jersey, and Francis, seven years old, born in Ohio, so we can assume that Clark came to Ohio before 1843. The 1844 Directory listed a Francis Clark as a grocer, and the 1846 Directory listed a Francis Clark, bookkeeper. Then, in 1848, the included ad for Francis Clark, dealer in watches and jewelry, appeared in the newspaper.

Cist's Weekly Advertiser, December 3, 1848

Daily Cincinnati Commercial, October 29, 1849

Clark does not seem to have made a success of his business, as a newspaper carried the included notice in November of 1849. In the 1850-1851 Directory Clark was listed as a clerk at J.F. Rhodes, the silversmith. Clark was listed in 1852 with no occupation given, and then his name disappeared from the Directories.

Although Clark worked as a silversmith for a very short time, there is some record of his work, as the Cincinnati Art Museum collection includes a spoon marked:

F. CLARK

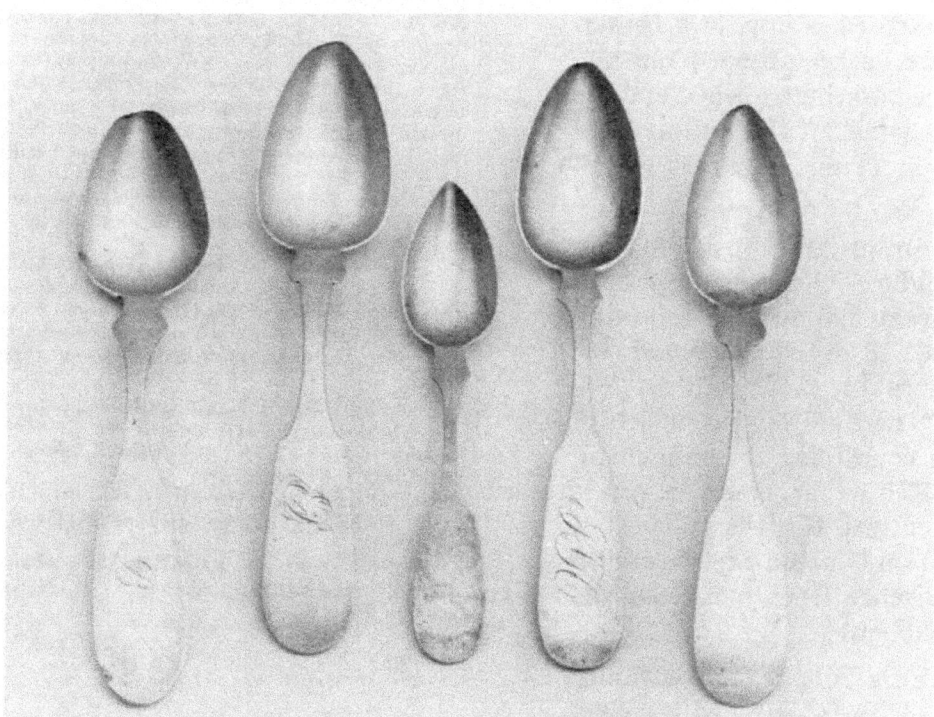

Typical spoons of the 1830's by Cincinnati makers. All of the marks found on these spoons appear in a cartouche. From left to right: Allen, Rhodes & Co., N. L. Hazen, Scovil, Willey & Co., Carley, and Scovil, Willey & Co.

Private collections.

CLAYTON, RICHARD *(b. 1811, d. 1878)* .... *(w. 1834-1859)*

Richard Clayton was Cincinnati's most colorful watchmaker and silversmith. In one of his first listings in the Cincinnati directories Clayton appeared as a watchmaker and aeronaut, a most intriguing classification that led one to wonder what would qualify a man in the 1830's as an aeronaut.

Many months later, in the course of reading the old newspapers, the answer was found, complete with wonderful illustrations. Clayton was a balloonist. He had become interested in ballooning as a boy in his native England.

In 1834 a balloonist named Thomas Kirkby made several successful balloon flights from an ampitheatre he had construced in Cincinnati on Court Street, between Race and Elm. Kirkby's flights inspired Clayton to attempt one, and in March of 1835 the included interesting ad appeared, announcing Clayton's first flight.

Later the *Cincinnati Gazette* reported that Clayton made a "splendid ascent". While still over the city Clayton dropped the "living animal" he had advertised, a dog, in a basket. At first the basket dropped quickly, but then the parachute opened and the dog landed safely. Within twenty minutes the Star of the West was out of sight.

Clayton's flight took place on April 8, but by April 15 there had been no word from him and the following notice appeared in the *Cincinnati Advertiser,* April 15, 1835, entitled "Mr. Clayton": "There are various reports in circulation concerning the gentleman, none of which as far as can be ascertained are correct. His friends have not yet heard from him, but expect soon to have intelligence from him from the Atlantic seaboard."

GRAND ÆRIAL VOYAGE!
WITH THE LARGEST AND MOST SPLENDID SILK BALLOON IN THE UNITED STATES, AND THE FIRST EVER CONSTRUCTED WEST OF THE MOUNTAINS!

MR. CLAYTON,

RESPECTFULLY informs his friends and the public, that he intends making an *ASCENSION*, with his stupendous Ærial Machine, from Cincinnati, on Wednesday, April 8th, from an Amphitheatre on Court Street, (between Race and Elm Streets,) and that when he has ascended to the altitude of a mile, be will let down a Parachute, 125 square feet in surface, containing a Living Animal, which will descend with safety to the earth. He will afterwards ascend to a great altitude, and, if the wind be favorable, continue in the atmosphere the whole of the night, and perform a voyage of unusual length.

This stupendous Machine is nearly fifty feet in height; is formed of 4,500 square feet of silk; occupies a space, when fully inflated, of **18,000** Cubic Feet, and has upwards of 1,000 pounds ascensional power, which will enable Mr. C. to accommodate *two or three passengers.*

☞ At half after 1 P. M. the doors of the Amphitheatre will be opened; at 3 o'clock Mr. Clayton will take his seat in the Car, and at 4, he will launch his Ærial Vessel into the atmosphere.

Several small Balloons will be sent up during the inflation of the large one—an excellent Band of Music will attend.

Tickets, 50 cents—to be had at the principal Hotels, and at the Amphitheatre on the day of the Ascension.
march 25

Cincinnati Republican, March 25, 1835

Clayton's voyage had actually been very successful. He had travelled 350 miles in nine and one half hours and had landed in a tree in Monroe County, Virginia. The area was later named Clayton, West Virginia in his honor. The voyage had set a distance record and was carried as a major news item all over the world.

Cincinnati accorded Clayton much acclaim and on May 9, 1835 the *Cincinnati Advertiser* carried the following account of Clayton's second voyage, which was to be launched on May 13.

> **Mr. Clayton's Second Ascension.**
> MR. CLAYTON.—This most successful and determined Æronaut, it will be observed, intends taking another excursion in the air on Wednesday next, his intended destination one of the cities on the Atlantic seaboard, *wind and weather* permitting. Mr. C. was remarkably successful in his first ascension from this city, having accomplished the *greatest feat* on record in the history and since the invention of the Balloon, and with such facility and ease that we can hardly ever expect to find its parallel. A majority of the eastern papers express their astonishment and admiration at his wonderful and successful attempt at navigating the "viewless regions of the air" at the rate of nearly 400 miles in nine or ten hours. His own exertions as an Æronaut have been crowned with a reputation and a fame that shall be as enduring as the principles of his science—but it is to be regretted that in a pecuniary point of view Mr. Clayton indeed has been but indifferently remunerated:— the great expense attending the construction of his Balloon—the vast cost of its inflation and the apparatus necessary therefor —his loss of time on his voyage and on his return, with other items which could be mentioned, should, altogether considered, induce the scientific, the philosophic, and the curious inquirers into the arts and sciences generally to extend to him that meed of support of which he is so eminently deserving. The munificence of the public at large it is to be hoped will be liberally granted on Mr. C.'s next ascension.

Cincinnati Advertiser,
May 9, 1835

But the second voyage met with disaster. As the Star of the West ascended, the car struck the eaves of a house. The concussion tore the netting and the balloon disengaged itself from the car. Thus Clayton, instead of landing on the shore of the Atlantic, found himself on a Cincinnati rooftop. Fortunately, the aeronaut was not injured.

Friends helped with donations for a new balloon, and on July 4th Clayton launched his third flight, but again he had troubles. He encountered a storm and developed a gas leak and so was forced to land about one hundred miles east of Cincinnati.

By 1837 Clayton was advertising his tenth voyage (see *Cincinnati Daily Gazette,* April 21). And in 1838 an ad for his sixteenth aerial voyage appeared. In June of 1838 the *Daily Evening Post* carried the included notice that he would ascend in company with a lady from Cincinnati.

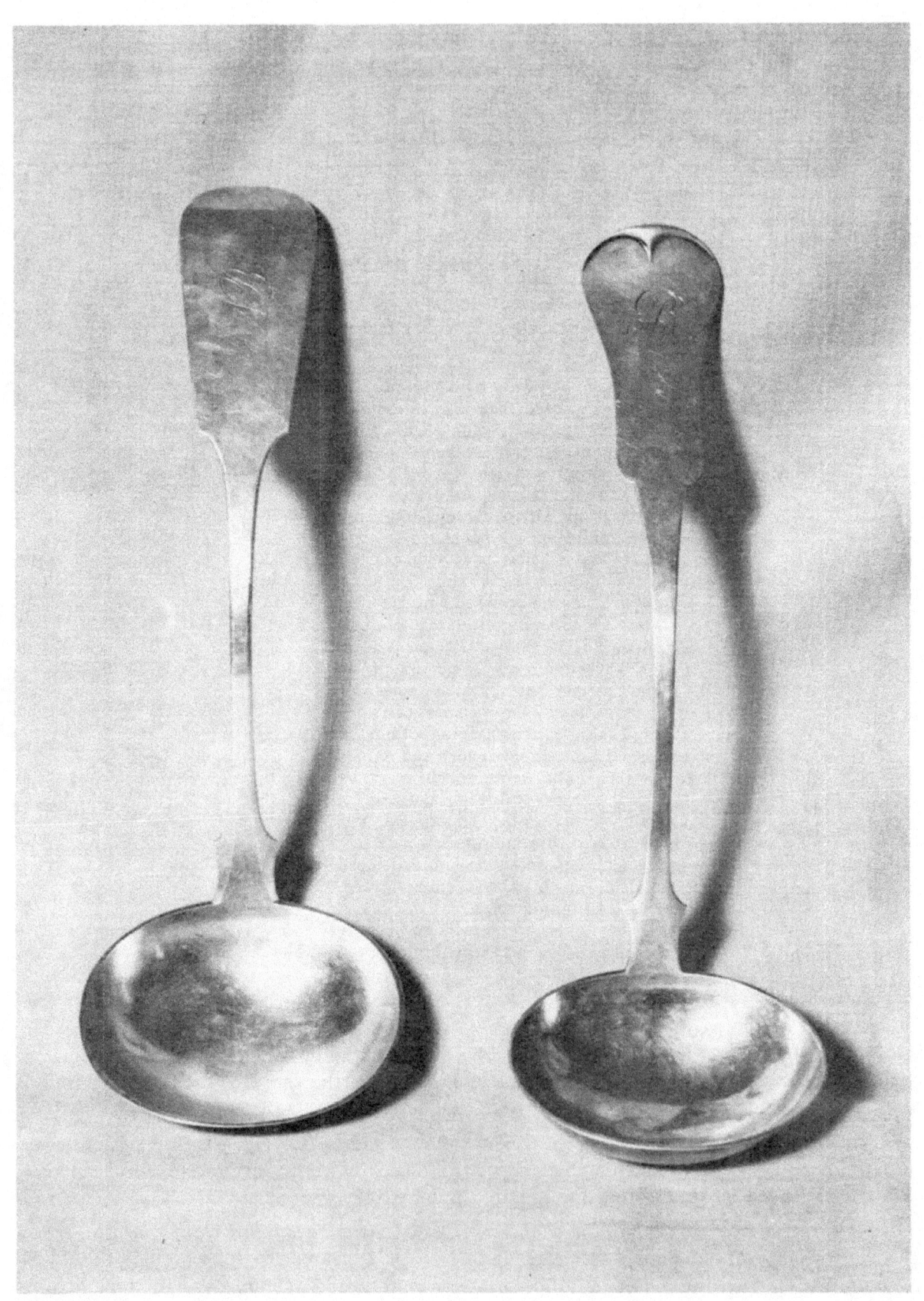

A pair of Cincinnati 13 inch coin silver punch ladles, the ladle on the left from the 1830's is marked Scovil & Co. in a cartouche, the ladle on the right is from the 1850's and is marked Clayton in a cartouche.

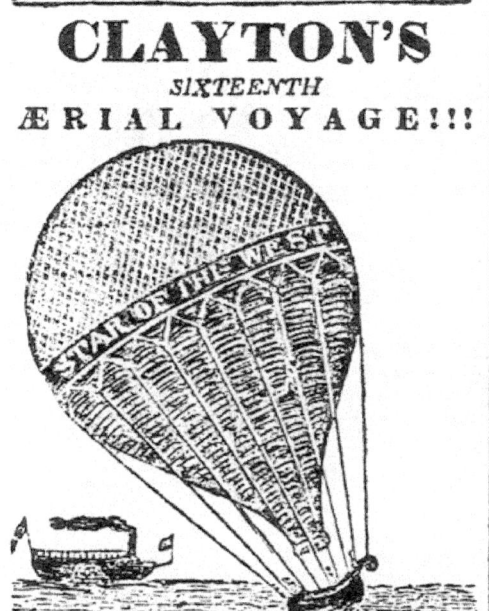

Daily Evening Post, June 22, 1838

In 1844 a notice of still another ascension appeared, but this was the last record found of a flight by Clayton. He continued, however, to use the balloon in his business ads for a number of years.

The ad below appeared in the *Daily Gazette* of 1846. It shows the famous balloon, and also carries a very interesting dissertation on the evils of credit.

Clayton was first listed in the Cincinnati Directory in 1834 and he continued to be listed until 1859, mainly as a wholesale dealer in watches and jewelry, with his shop located at the corner of Second and Sycamore.

Liberty Hall carried the following account of this flight on July 12, 1838:

"In the afternoon a very large concourse assembled to witness the ascention of Clayton. It was announced that he was to be accompanied by a lady, and great interest was manifest.

About six o'clock Clayton and his fair companion, nothing daunted, took their car. The balloon, amid shouts of the multitude, ascended with them gracefully into the upper air and floated off in an easterly direction."

No further account of this trip was found, but apparently it was successful, for in 1840 Clayton advertised his twenty-fourth voyage and in 1841 his twenty-seventh.

In January of 1843 Richard Clayton married Jane Jenkins, but Jane apparently died shortly thereafter, since in March of 1844 Clayton married Mary Ann Jenkins, possibly his first wife's sister. From Clayton's will, however, we can conclude that his second wife did not live a long life either, as his daughter Charlotte "was educated and brought up by her two aunts, Fanny and Martha Jenkins."

At some time prior to 1874 Richard Clayton had moved to Brooklyn, New York, as he was residing there when his will was written. He died in Brooklyn on May 29, 1878.

In his will Clayton left everything to his daughter Charlotte, or if she did not survive him the income of his estate was to go to her aunts, Fanny and Martha Jenkins of Cincinnati, and on their deaths to the Protestant Orphan Asylum situated on Mt. Auburn in Cincinnati.

From the amount of flat silver which is seen marked

CLAYTON

we must conclude that Richard Clayton made quite a bit of silver during the years he worked in Cincinnati. Hopefully this account of the colorful Mr. Clayton will bring more interest and appreciation to owners of silver marked with his name.

Illustrations of Clayton's work included are a salt spoon on page 3 and a soup ladle on page 32.

A private collection includes a spoon marked R. Clayton in a cartouche, but this is not a common mark.

COATES, WILLIAM .... (w. 1840-1850)

William Coates was listed by Cutten as a watchmaker in Buffalo, N.Y. from 1835 until 1839. The included ad for Coates appeared in a Cincinnati newspaper in August of 1840. Coates had a rather unusual combination of trades, being not only a watch and clockmaker, but an ornithologist, or what modern usage would call a taxidermist, as well!

The ad on the following page was carried in the 1844 Cincinnati Business Directory.

Coates was listed as a watchmaker or watchmaker and ornithologist through the 1850 Directory, but it would seem that he was unable to make a success of his varied businesses, since the directories from 1851 until 1858 listed him as a clerk, after which his name disappeared altogether from the directory listings.

> WILLIAM COATES, Clock & Watch Maker, Ornithologist, &c., Begs leave respectfully to announce to the citizens of Cincinnati, and vicinity, that he has opened a Shop at the corner of Walnut and Third streets, where he hopes to meet a share of public patronage and support, in the different branches of his profession—where the most prompt attention will be paid; and from his long experience in the manufactures in England, he has no doubt but giving universal satisfaction, Clocks and Watches, Musical Boxes, and Jewelry of every description, carefully executed by himself and warranted.
>
> QUADRUPEDS, BIRDS, INSECTS, &c.,
>
> Preserved and stuffed, and placed in their natural attitudes, and fitted with cases to order, for private ornaments on moderate terms.
>
> Any gentleman wanting an assortment of skins for exportation is informed that he has a collection on hand, and the best of qualities, in proper preservation, and also, some rare specimens in fine plumage. Birds bought or exchanged. Brands cut on the shortest notice. aug 24-tf

Spirit of the Times, August 24, 1840

> # WM. COATES,
> ## CLOCK AND WATCH MAKER,
> ### ORNITHOLOGIST &C.
> ## WALNUT STREET, SECOND DOOR BELOW THIRD,
> ### CINCINNATI,
>
> Clocks and Watches, Musical Boxes, and Jewelry of every description carefully executed by himself, and warranted.
>
> Quadrupeds, Birds, Insects, &c., properly stuffed, and put in their natural attitudes.—An assortment of dried skins for exportation.—Rare specimens in fine plumage.—Cases neatly fitted up to order, &c.

Coates was never listed as a silversmith, so there is very little likelihood of any silver marked with his name existing, but perhaps someday a bird or quadruped stuffed by Mr. Coates will be discovered.

COBB, ZACHARIAH B, *(b. 1800, d. ?)* .... (w. 1842-1864)

Zachariah Cobb was born in New York in 1800. He worked for years as a clockmaker and clock repairer in Cincinnati. His first Cincinnati Directory listing occurred in 1842 and he continued to be listed in the directories until 1864.

The 1850 Census listed Cobb as a carpenter and also included his wife Nancy A., and a son Charles.

COLLINS, PELEG *(b. 1799, d. ?)* .... (w. 1820-1850)

Peleg Collins and his wife Nancy were born in Rhode Island, he in about 1799, she a year later. The 1820 Census listed Collins in Cincinnati; perhaps he brought his new bride to try his luck in the fast-growing city of Cincinnati.

In 1825 the Cincinnati Directory listed Collins as a watchmaker at 166 Main. By 1829 he had become a partner of S.A.M. Shipp (Shipp & Collins), watchmakers and jewelers at 44 Main. (See Shipp)

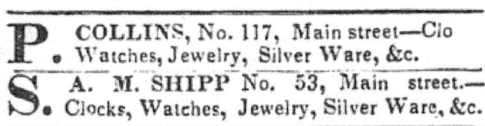

Cincinnati Daily Gazette, April 3, 1834

Although Shipp and Collins were still listed as partners in the 1834 Cincinnati Directory, in April of 1834 a Cincinnati newspaper carried separate listings (which see). In March of the following year, the ad on the following page appeared in the newspaper.

Collins continued to work alone in the silversmithing and watchmaking business until 1843, when he formed a partnership with N.L. Hazen (Hazen & Collins). An 1844 Directory carried the included ad for these two men. The partnership of Hazen & Collins was dissolved in January of 1847.

P. COLLINS, No. 53, Main street, Cincinnati, the old stand of Shipp & Collins, and recently by S. A. M. Shipp, where I offer to my friends, and those of the former concerns, a handsome assortment of Watches, (all descriptions,) Jewelry, fancy goods, Plated and Brittania Ware, Clocks, Silver Ware, &c. &c. Watches and Clocks repaired in the best manner, and warranted.
P. COLLINS.
jan 17   33-2m

Cincinnati Daily Gazette, March 14, 1835

HAZEN & COLLINS'
STORE OF
CLOCKS, WATCHES, JEWELRY,
AND
FANCY GOODS,
No. 177, Main Street.

Kimball & James' Business Directory for the Mississippi Valley, 1844.

NEW WATCHES AND JEWELRY.
At the corner of Main and Pearl streets, under the Museum.

P. COLLINS, has just returned from the East and is now opening a stock of Watches, manufactured by M. I. Tobias, Jos. Johnson, Hide & Sons, and other celebrated makers, together with a splendid assortment of Jewelry, consisting in part of Diamond, Garnet and other Set Pins, Finger and Ear Rings, Pencils, Pens, Pen Holders, Chains, Miniature Cases, Gold and Silver Specks and Thimbles, Lockets, Bracelets, Bead and Silk Bags and Purses, Card and Cigar Cases, Cutlery, Microscopes, &c. &c.; all of which will be sold for cash at the lowest prices.
mar 14

Cincinnati Daily Gazette, March 14, 1848.

One of the last ads found for Collins' shop, was this interesting ad which appeared in the newspaper in 1848, and listed the variety of articles Mr. Collins carried in his ship at the time.

The Census of 1850 listed Collins, his wife Nancy, a daughter Mary, and a son, age 25, a silversmith. The name of the son was illegible, but it may have been Edwin or Charles Edwin, since an Edwin, silversmith, boarding at P. Collins', was listed in the 1844 Directory, and a Cincinnati newspaper carried the following ad in 1849.

C. E. COLLINS,
Watches, Jewelry and Silver Ware,
NO. 121 MAIN STREET, BETWEEN 3D AND 4TH.
nov5-tf

The last listing of Collins in Cincinnati appeared in the 1850 Business Directory, where he was listed as a jeweler on the north side of Fifth between Elm and Plum.

The following mark appeared in Currier's *Marks of Early American Silversmiths*.

Illustrated on page 15 is an early teaspoon marked 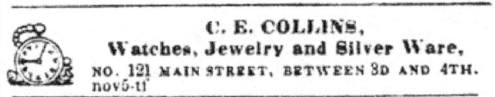 and spoons marked

HAZEN & COLLINS

are in private collections.

CONWAY, THOMAS A. *(b. ?, d. 1871)* .... (w. 1825-1848)

Pleasants and Sill, in their book on Maryland silversmiths, listed Thomas A. Conway as a watchmaker in Baltimore from 1819 until 1824. Undoubtedly Conway came directly from Baltimore to Cincinnati, since he was listed in the 1825 Cincinnati Directory as a watchmaker from Maryland. The same listing appeared in the 1829 Directory.

In 1832 Conway formed a partnership with Dennis McHenry, also from Baltimore (Conway & McHenry), and the included ad appeared in the newspaper. This partnership was dissolved in 1834.

The 1836 Directory listed Conway as a watchmaker on Sycamore between 7th and 8th. In 1840 Conway was working as a watchmaker for N.L. Hazen. By 1844 he was in business for himself again, and Williams' Business Directory listed Thomas A. Conway under watchmakers and silversmiths, his place of business Main between 6th and 7th.

The last listing of Conway as a watchmaker occurred in 1848. By 1853, and in succeeding directories, he was listed as a carpenter and then as a builder.

Thomas Conway died in 1871. Trying to piece together information from census and cemetery records, it would seem that Conway and his first wife, Catherine, had three sons, Wilton, Mason and James, and one daughter, Mary. Conway was married to his second wife, Sara Light, in 1835. Laura, Margot and Thomas, possibly children of this marriage, were listed in the 1850 census. But Sara was not listed, so Conway undoubtedly had lost another wife.

Cincinnati Daily Gazette, September 18, 1832.

Conway was always listed as a watchmaker, so it would seem that if silver exists marked with his name, it would most probably have been made during the Conway & McHenry partnership.

CONWAY & McHENRY .... *(1832-1834)*

COOPER, ARCHIBALD .... (w. 1836-1837)

Archibald Cooper was listed in the 1836 Cincinnati Directory as a gold and silversmith at Cooper & Saulnier's, boarding at William Borland's. The partnership of Cooper & Saulnier was dissolved in February of 1836, however, (see W. Cooper) and Archibald became a partner in the firm of W. & A. Cooper. Shortly after the new partnership was formed, the beautifully illustrated ad on the following page appeared in the newspaper.

The brothers continued to advertise in 1837, but it must have been toward the end of 1837 or the beginning of 1838 when they left Cincinnati for Louisville. The Hiatts' book on Kentucky silversmiths lists the Coopers as working in Louisville; Archibald is listed there from 1841 until 1848, also advertising in Frankfort in 1842.

The mark found on silver by the Cooper brothers is:

W. & A. COOPER.

Cincinnati Daily Gazette,
February 24, 1836

COOPER, WILLIAM .... **(w. 1835-1837; also w. 1846)**

William Cooper was a fine silversmith who worked in Cincinnati for several years. The first ad found for Cooper's silverware manufactory appeared in 1835; the ad listed the many articles of silver available at the shop.

Daily Evening Post, August 14, 1835

By 1836 Cooper had become a partner of W.H. Saulnier, and the included ad which appeared for the partnership carried very similar copy to the ad appearing above (see following ad).

SILVERWARE MANUFACTORY.

COOPER & SAULNIER,
Walnut, between Second and Pearl streets,
CINCINNATI:

MANUFACTURES to order, also keeps for sale, wholesale and retail,

SILVER WARE

Of all kinds, warranted equal to Spanish Dollars; among which are the following articles of the newest fashions, viz:
SILVER COMB,
TEA SETTS,
TABLE, DESSERT, & TEA SPOONS, of different patterns,
MUGS, TUMBLERS, GOBLETS, &c.
FORKS, FRUIT & BUTTER KNIVES.
Together with every article in his line, executed in the most workmanlike manner, at the shortest notice, and on the most reasonable terms.
☞Dealers in any of the above articles may depend upon having their orders executed with despatch and to their entire satisfaction.
aug14—1y

Daily Evening Post, February 10, 1836

SILVER WARE MANUFACTORY.

W. & A. COOPER, Walnut, between Second and Pearl streets, Cincinnati, manufactures to order, also keeps for sale, wholesale and retail, SILVER WARE of all kinds, warranted equal to Spanish Dollars; among which are the following articles of the newest fashions, viz:
SILVER COMBS,
TEA SETTS,
TABLE, DESERT, and TEA SPOONS, of different patterns,
MUGS, TUMBLERS, GOBLETS, &c.
FORKS, FRUIT and BUTTER KNIVES.
Together with every article in his line, executed in the most workmanlike manner, at the shortest notice, and on the most reasonable terms.
☞Dealers in any of the above articles may depend upon having their orders executed with despatch and to their entire satisfaction
feb 24   74tf

Cincinnati Daily Gazette, February 24, 1836

On February 22, 1836 the partnership of Cooper & Saulnier was dissolved by mutual consent; the *Daily Evening Post* carried the notice of dissolution.

William Cooper then became the partner of his brother Archibald, and the included ad appeared in the newspaper for the new partnership. The Cooper brothers continued to advertise in 1837, but then some time toward the end of that year or the beginning of the next, they left in search of greener pastures in Kentucky.

In their book on Kentucky silversmiths, the Hiatts list the Coopers as working in Louisville from 1838 until 1841 and advertising in Frankfort in 1842. Also, the 1843 and 1844 Louisville Directory carried William's name.

William Cooper returned to Cincinnati in 1846 and opened a silverware manufactory, as the included ad indicates. This ad was the only information found concerning William Cooper's return to Cincinnati. A William Cooper, who was born in Baltimore in 1809, died in Cincinnati in 1847 and is buried in Spring Grove Cemetery. Whether this was William Cooper the silversmith is difficult to determine, as William Cooper is not an uncommon name.

MISCELLANEOUS.
SILVER WARE MANUFACTORY.--W. COOPER, Manufactures all kinds of *Silver Ware.* Entrance from Third street, (in the court adjoining Franklin Bank,) Cincinnati.   sep 7   35-1y

Daily Cincinnati Gazette, September 7, 1846

The Cooper brothers made beautiful silver. My Old Kentucky Home in Bardstown, Ky. has a set of beakers made by them. The beakers are marked W. & A. Cooper, Louisville.

The following are reproductions of the marks used by William Cooper:

W. COOPER   **W. & A. COOPER**

COOPER & SAULNIER .... *(1836)*

W. & A. COOPER .... *(1836-1837)*

COX, RUDOLPHO (b. 1819, d. 1854) .... w. 1839-1851)

Rudolpho Cox was born in Wheeling, Virginia in 1819, the son of Jesse and Catherine Cox. In 1839 he appeared in the Cincinnati Directory as a silversmith at Musgrove's. He was listed in succeeding directories up until 1851 as a silversmith or jeweler.

The 1850 Census listed Cox as a jeweler; it also listed the names of his wife, Lucy B., and those of his children, Marion, Kate and Eugene. Cox died in Cincinnati at thirty-five years of age; we can't help but wonder what happened to his young widow after his death.

The directory listings, except for 1839, give no clue as to whether Cox worked for another silversmith or had his own shop.

DALLER, JOHN (b. 1815, d. ?) .... (w. 1837-1868)

John Daller came from Germany and in 1837 established a watchmaking and jewelry business in Cincinnati at 391 Vine. The 1850 Census listed him as a jeweler, thirty-five years old. Also listed are his wife Theresa, a son Joseph, and a daughter Mary.

In 1868 Daller retired from the business. He was succeeded by his son who continued the business until 1895. A contemporary article, appearing in the Centennial Review of Cincinnati of 1888, states that "... the Dallers have enjoyed the highest repute, and have earned the favor and confidence with which they are regarded...."

DAUMONT, PETER .... (w. 1840)

Peter Daumont, from New York, was listed only once in a Cincinnati directory. This occurred in 1840, when he was listed as a jeweler located on West 4th near Main, his residence 4th between Vine and Race.

Daumont went on to Louisville, working there from 1843 until 1846, according to the Hiatts' *The Silversmiths of Kentucky*. He was one of the many men who went from Cincinnati to Kentucky or St. Louis or elsewhere to try their luck.

We know that while Daumont was in Cincinnati he had at least one other man working for him, as William Feltmann was listed as a goldsmith at Daumont's in the 1840 Directory.

DETERLY, JACOB (b. 1786, d. 1848) .... (w. 1812-1833)

Jacob Deterly was born in Maryland in 1786, the son of Johann Ludwig Deterly and Mary Elizabeth Keither. Little was actually known of Deterly until his diary was printed in 1972. Through this diary a wealth of hitherto unknown information about other Cincinnati silversmiths was obtained, also a much broader look at the friendships which existed between men in the same trade. Most of Deterly's friends were of the same trade and they corresponded with one another when separated, visited one another on trips, and even took care of one another when sick. Actual quotes from Deterly's diary have been used throughout this book, when pertinent. Deterly began making notes in 1819 and continued until his death in 1846, but it is his years in Cincinnati, between 1819 and 1833, with which we are most concerned.

The exact date of Deterly's arrival in Cincinnati is unknown, but in 1812 the announcement of the formation of his partnership with Robert Best appeared in the newspaper (see R. Best).

Several months later this partnership was dissolved and Best became the partner of Enos Woodruff. By 1815 R. Best & Co. was advertising. This company was composed of Best, Woodruff and Deterly. This partnership lasted only two years, and in 1817 was dissolved.

Enos Woodruff and Jacob Deterly then became partners and in 1817 the included ad appeared in the newspaper.

The 1819 Cincinnati Directory listed Woodruff & Deterly as silversmiths at 58 Main. This was the year in which Deterly began his diary. Regretfully he never mentioned watches or silverware that he worked on, but he did mention the following items. In February of 1821 he stated, "Made a pair of large hand bellows, being the 1st I ever made". Later the same month he said, "Hydrometer, finished the first one today for Mr. Harvey". (A hydrometer is an instrument for finding the specific gravity or density of liquids.) In November of the same year Deterly stated, "Graduated a Thermometer for Davees Embree engraved scale and so forth." (According to Greve, Davis Embree was the founder of the brewery business in Cincinnati, and in 1811 his establishment was on the river at the foot of Race Street.)

> **WOODRUFF & DETERLY,**
> East side of Main-street,
> Opposite Saml. Lowry's Store, have just rec'd
> *DIRECTLY FROM ENGLAND*
> A quantity of
> **Gold and Silver Watches,**
> *Of a very superior quality,*
> Which they offer for sale on reasonable terms.—Among them are the following:
> Gold PATENT LEVERS, detached scapement,
> do. Watches,   common   do.
> do. LADIES'   do.   do.
> (the above are Cased in a very superb style.)
> SILVER PATENT LEVERS,
> do.   common scapement, cap'd & jewel'd;
> And a variety of low priced ones, making a much better assortment than can be found elsewhere in this place—all of which they warrant to perform well.
> They continue the WATCH REPAIRING as usual. This branch is conducted by one of the firm, who, although he cannot boast of "having learnt the Watch *Finishing* business in London," nor even "having learnt his business in Europe," yet he can boast of having repaired [*not botched*] more watches in this town, within the last six years, than any other person—the humiliating fact of his having learnt the business in the back-woods to the contrary notwithstanding.
> They have always for sale almost every article of SILVER WARE used in this country, not inferior in quality or workmanship to any made in, or brought to the Western Country.—They have likewise a very general assortment of JEWELLERY.
> Also, a large quantity of PLATED BRIDLE BITTS, STIRRUP IRONS, &c. &c. which they offer unusually low.
> Cincinnati, Nov. 19, 1817.   77 tf

Western Spy, November 19, 1817

In February of 1821 the diary relates that Woodruff and Deterly began dividing their wares. The included dissolution of partnership appearing on page 43 was published in the newspaper in April of that year. By October of 1821 Deterly had set up shop at 92 Main, then in 1822 he moved to 2½ Front Street. The 1825 Cincinnati Directory listed his clock and watchmaking shop at 2 West Front.

In May of 1825 General Lafayette paid a visit to Cincinnati and Deterly's diary contains a detailed account of the activities.

Deterly's entry in his diary for September 22, 1826, states: "MONEY, advanced Mr. S.A.M. Shipp five hundred dollars: a part of stock for a connection in business." In October of that year he moved to Shipp's shop.

The following interesting notation appears in Deterly's diary in October of 1828: "JACKSON CANES, Hickory canes are getting much into fashion, there are a great many

In the center, a magnificent coffin end 13 inch ladle, belonging to the descendants of an early Cincinnati family and bearing the mark W & D in a cartouche (Woodruff & Deterly). The cup on the right bears an identical mark. The cup on the left is inscribed "Pacing Premium Awarded by the Hamilton County Agricultural Society to William Parker. 1835." This cup is marked N. L. Hazen in a cartouche. The miniature spoon in the foreground is 4 inches long and is marked McGrew & Beggs in a cartouche.

Private collections.

to be mounted with silver heads, one in particular is to be mounted with a fine gold head in style, which is intended to be presented to Genl. Andrew Jackson."

> **DISSOLUTION.**
>
> THE partnership heretofore existing under the firm of WOODRUFF & DETERLY, was dissolved on the first of February last, by mutual consent. All business pertaining to the late firm will be settled by Enos Woodruff who is legally authorised for that purpose.
>
> ENOS WOODRUFF,
> JACOB DETERLY.
>
> **ENOS WOODRUFF,**
> No. 58, Main street,
>
> CONTINUES the business as usual—he has on hand, in addition to his former assortment of *Silverware, Jewellery, &c.* an assortment of Swords, Epaulets, Gold and Silver Lace, with a variety of other military equipments. Also, a quantity of PLATED CASTERS—all of which will be sold low for cash.
>
> ALL those indebted to the firms of *Robert Best & Co.* or *Woodruff & Deterly*, are requested to pay the same without delay to the subscriber—further indulgence cannot be given.
> ENOS WOODRUFF.
> Cincinnati, April 7, 1821.   57-9

Western Spy, April 7, 1821

By November of 1828 Deterly had sold his interest in Shipp's shop and from that time until he left Cincinnati for the last time in 1833, he spent his time between Cincinnati and Marietta, Ohio where his brother lived. During these years, while he was in Marietta he worked for D. B. Anderson, and while in Cincinnati for Shipp & Collins.

While Deterly was in Cincinnati in October of 1831, he recorded in his diary: "Theft, J. D. was busy in repairing a Theodolite for a Mr. Given, turnpike surveyor and engineer, the said Given was left alone near the Bench where lay J.D.'s watch tools, Mr. Given was very good to pilfer J.D.'s watch screw driver and take it with him!!"

Deterly lived in Marietta from 1833 until 1839, when he moved to a farm near Athens, Ohio. He remained on the farm until his death in 1846.

The following was written by Amos Miller, the husband of Deterly's niece, Louisa, on February 10, the day of his death, and on February 11, the day of his funeral.

"This day Jacob Deterly the Author of the foregoing miscellania and Memoranda departed this life & was numbered with those who finished their earthly course & entered the land of the spirits. ..... Thus closed the earthly career of Jacob Deterly a name dear to & never to be forgotten by the author of this article. During a period of some seven years he was a boarder in this family and after an intimate acquaintance with the deceased he can truly and unhesitatingly say that he was an honest man, a scholar and a gentleman. He was a man who loved & sought retirement from the noise & bustle of the world & having a well disciplined mind he turned aside from idle conversation & chose those subjects which require & call into exercise intellectual strength.

The last years of his life were spent in the study of mathematics & astronomy. By day he might be found solving difficult problems & by night when the weather was favorable contemplating & studying the different constellations as they made their majestic & silent journey through the skies.

Jacob Deterly was when he died in the 62nd year of his age & would have completed the same had he lived until the 16th day of March following. His funeral was attended on Friday the 11th of Feb. 2 o'clock P.M. by a large concourse of neighbors & friends who listened attentively to a plain practical & excellent sermon delivered by the Rev. Mr. Welsh from these words of divine inspiration. Thus saith the Lord, set thine house in order; for thou shalt die and not live."

The Cincinnati Art Museum has in its collection, a spoon bearing the following mark:

BEST & DETERLY

It is reasonable to assume that the mark:

W & D

found on spoons in the Cincinnati Art Museum and also on the ladle illustrated on page 42, belonging to the descendants of an early Cincinnati family, could very well be the mark of Woodruff & Deterly.

DE YOUNG, RALPH (RAPHAEL) .... (w. 1837-1840 ?)

Ralph De Young came from England. The Cincinnati Directory of 1837 listed him as a jeweler and silversmith, located on Front between Sycamore and Broadway. The 1840 Directory listed him as a watchmaker at William Pyne's, although the same directory listed William Pyne as a tailor.

De Young was not listed in the directories from 1842 to 1846, but a *Richard* De Young was listed in the 1848 Cincinnati Business Directory under watches and clocks, located on the north side of George between Western Row and John. The 1850 Directory listed a Richard De Young as a clock cleaner at the same address on George St. Whether Raphael or Ralph De Young changed his name to Richard or whether they were two different people is not known, and no further information on De Young was found.

DOLL, FRANCIS (FRANZ) .... (w. 1850-1872)

Francis Doll is included in this book because of his work with gold and silver, being a manufacturer of gold and silver watchcases from 1850 until 1872, when the company was sold out to Duhme and Co. Watchcases marked with his name may be in existence and this listing will make identification possible.

DOLL, WILLIAM .... (w. 1850-1851; w. Covington, Ky. 1855)

The 1850 Cincinnati Census listed William Doll as a twenty-five year old silversmith from Germany. He is also listed in the 1850 Directory as a watchmaker. In 1851 we find Doll listed as a watchmaker at R. Clayton's. He is not listed in the next two directories, but in 1855 he appeared in the Cincinnati Directory under watches and jewelry, his address Madison between 5th and 6th, in Covington, Kentucky.

Doll is included in this book because the mark

W. DOLL

is recorded in Currier's *Marks of Early American Silversmiths*.

DORAN, JOHN .... (w. 1829-1831)

A John Doran worked in Cincinnati briefly as a silversmith. He was listed in the 1829 and 1831 Cincinnati Directories as a silversmith, boarding at D. Kautz's. No other information is available concerning Doran, but we can suppose that he may have worked in the shop of another silversmith, since no shop address was listed under his name.

DORNSEIFER, HENRY .... (w. 1848-1863) (also w. 1875-1884)

Henry Dornseifer, 38, a silversmith from Germany, was listed in the 1850 Cincinnati Census. Also listed were his wife and a son, Charles.

Dornseifer had arrived in Cincinnati a few years before 1850 as he was listed under watch and clockmakers in Williams' 1848 Business Directory, his shop on the east side of Main between Hunt and Abigail. By 1852, the address listed was the west side of Main between Canal and 12th (445 Main), where he remained until 1863.

His name did not appear in the directories from 1865 until 1875, when it reappeared listed under jewelers, the address Colerain Pike, Cumminsville. This listing continued until 1884.

DRAPER, JOSEPH *(b. 1800, d. 1864)* .... (w. 1832-1856)

The book *Silversmiths of Delaware*, by Jessie Harrington, states that "very little information concerning Joseph Draper has been found". Included in the book was an ad which appeared in the *Delaware Journal* of February 3, 1832:

> "The Subscriber intending to leave the state requests all persons indebted to him to call and discharge their bills, ... etc.
>
> > Joseph Draper,
> > Silversmith and Jeweler."

Joseph Draper arrived in Cincinnati in 1832 and reproduced here in its entirety is an article which relates his life and career in the city. The article appeared in a book called *Memorial Associations* which was published in Cincinnati in 1888.

> Joseph Draper
>
> The subject of the following sketch was born near Trowbridge, England, in 1801. He came to this country in 1810, accompanied by his father,

who, remaining with him only for a short time, started back to England to bring his wife and other children to this wonderful El Dorado, but was drowned just before the vessel reached England, thus leaving his young son, at the early age of nine years, alone in a strange land. But circumstances like this often make our very best men, necessitating self-reliance and diligence in their very earliest, formative years. Thus it proved with Joseph Draper, who went to Wilmington, Delaware, and apprenticed himself to an old citizen in the silversmithing business, making enough to clothe and educate himself, by working before and after ordinary hours; so that we are not surprised, in a few years, to find success so crowning his labors as to enable him to open a silversmith and jewelry store in the little Quaker settlement of Wilmington, Delaware. In this place Mr. Draper made three very important steps in life. First, and certainly we must say the best, he became a Christian, connecting himself with the Baptist Church; next, he became a member of the Masonic Order, that all through his subsequent life proved such a source of pleasure to him; and last, he wooed and won a pretty English girl, who came with him to Cincinnati in 1832. He was the first manufacturer of silverware in this city, and the first jeweler on West Fourth Street, where he began his business in what is now No. 19 West Fourth Street. He subsequently removed to the west side of Main Street, between Third and Fourth Streets, midway of the square, now No. 129.

Subsequently removing to No. 16 West Fourth Street, he remained in the same calling until 1856, a period of about thirty years. During his residence in Cincinnati he was, at different times, a director in one of our old banks, president of the Queen City Fire and Marine Insurance Company, a trustee of the Cincinnati College of Medicine and Surgery for many years, one of the original stockholders of the Cincinnati and Covington Suspension Bridge Company, and a director of our City Infirmary. In the latter position he made many friends among the helpless and neglected poor, who greeted his visits at the Infirmary with unfeigned joy. An old blind woman used to say of him there, "We never had so kind a director as Joseph Draper since I've been here." And, indeed, all through his life his heart went out in tenderest sympathy to the orphan and widow, who came confidently to him for advice and help.

Immediately upon coming to Cincinnati, in 1832, he connected himself with the Lafayette Lodge of Free Masons, of this city, and continued one of its most influential members until failing health prevented his taking a part in active lodgeroom work. The trust reposed in him by his brother Masons was practically shown in their electing him their treasurer for twenty consecutive years.

Of his private home and social life, we need only say that he was very affectionate and thoroughly devoted to the interests of those most intimately associated with him. Indulgent almost to a fault, his children remember him with tenderest reverence, while hosts of friends recall his name as that of one very precious to memory.

Joseph Draper died in his sixty-fourth year, wonderfully upheld by the consolations of the religion he sought and found in youth. A member for thirty-two years of the Ninth Street Baptist Church of this city, he was buried from its sacred altar with Masonic honors. He left a wife, two sons, and four daughters, all now surviving him, while he himself lies beside four little ones in the beautiful cemetery of Spring Grove.

Joseph Draper's wife was Martha Inskip, born in England in 1811; their children who lived to maturity were Martha, Anne, Louise, Harrisonia, John and George. The memorial article mentions the four Draper children who died as babies; checking cemetery records of the early smiths, we realize the high rate of infant mortality at that time.

The included rather interesting notice appeared in the newspaper in 1837. It is not know how common it was to have women burnishers, but one other listing of a woman silver burnisher was found. The Cincinnati Directories from 1842 until 1846 listed a Mrs. Elizabeth Martin as a silver burnisher. This may have been a way for a widow to earn a living.

> LOST.
> A SMALL Sheep Skin Memorandum Book, containing a list of Spoons and other Silver work, burnished by Mary Hoffman, for J. Draper. The finder will be liberally rewarded by returning it to the subscriber, on Main street, opposite the Commercial Bank.
> J. DRAPER.
> june 9 2t

Daily Evening Post, June 9, 1837

> **JOSEPH DRAPER,**
> NO. 15 WEST FOURTH STREET,
> Keeps constantly on hand, and for sale, a new and select stock of
> **WATCHES, JEWELRY,**
> And other articles in his line, which he offers at the lowest CASH PRICES, and requests those wishing such articles to give him a call.

Gray's Cincinnati Business Mirror & City Advertiser, 1851-1852.

The earlier directories (1832-1845) listed J. Draper as a silversmith, watchmaker and jeweler, but the only ad found for Draper was the ad included here, which appeared in Gray's Business Directory of 1851-1852.

Most of the Draper flat silver seen is fairly early in shape, but occasionally a piece made in the late 1840's or early 1850's is seen. The following is the mark used:

J. DRAPER

Illustrations of silver by Draper include a tablespoon on page 15, a salt spoon on page 3, and a sugar tongs on page 78.

DROZ, FREDERICK .... (w. 1819-1831)

The name of Frederick Droz, from Switzerland, first appeared in the addenda of the 1819 Cincinnati City Directory, where he was listed as a silversmith at the corner of 7th and Main. In 1822 Droz ran the included ad. His name appeared in succeeding directories as a watchmaker or silversmith. The last directory listing of Droz occurred in 1831, when the business address given was the corner of 7th and Main, his residence Walnut between 6th and 7th.

In her booklet on Ohio silversmiths, Rhea Knittle listed a John Droz as working in Cincinnati. She undoubtedly meant Frederick since no mention of a John Droz was found in early records.

Early spoons by Droz are in a private collection and the mark used was:

Frederick Droz,
Watch & Clock Maker, & Jeweller,
No. 11, Lower Market street,

OFFERS his services to the public in all the branches of his business; and particularly the repairing of *Clocks, Watches,* and *Jewellery,* and making all kinds of surveying and mathematical instruments.

☞ The highest price paid for old GOLD and SILVER.
Cincinnati, May 18, 1822.   15

Western Spy & Literary Gazette, May 18, 1822

An illustration of a teaspoon with the above mark appears on page 15.

DUEBER, JOHN C.

Included is an illustration from Kenny's *Illustrated Cincinnati of 1875* that should be of interest to watch collectors who own watches with coin silver watch cases made by the Dueber Co.

INTERIOR OF THE DUEBER WATCH CASE MANUFACTURING CO.'S ESTABLISHMENT.

The following article appeared in the same publication:

> The Dueber Watch Case Manufacturing Company's Establishment is situated in the building on the south-west corner of Fourth and Race Streets.

Mr. John C. Dueber established this business in 1864. The business grew steadily ever since, and the Dueber Watch Case Manufacturing Company was incorporated in 1873. The floor-space now occupied by their manufactory exceeds 12,000 square feet.

The accompanying engraving illustrates one of the main rooms of their manufactory, where about 60 skilled workmen are employed. They manufacture all kinds of Gold and Silver Watch Cases, and the reputation the "Dueber" Watch Cases have made for themselves, in all the States, from Maine to California, is abundant proof of their superiority and intrinsic value.

Long years of experience enables the Dueber Watch Manufacturing Company to turn out watchcases of great beauty, and in those of high cost great elaboration of detail. It has always been supposed — owing to the want of experience, great skill required, and the high price of labor in America — that the business of watch-case making, and particularly the finer descriptions of these articles, would be confined almost exclusively to Switzerland; but the American energy and enterprise have supplied ingenious machines and expert workmen, whose efforts have been crowned with success; and many of the beautiful cases made by this company vie in costliness, workmanship, and finish with the finest productions of the best foreign artists.

The Dueber Watch Case Co. continued in business in Cincinnati until 1888 when the company moved to Canton, Ohio.

DUFFNER, VINCENT *(b. 1797, d. ?)* .... (w. 1836-1851)

The 1836 Cincinnati Directory listed an L. Dafner as a clockmaker. As the early directories contained many mistakes, we can assume that this was probably V. Duffner, whose name appeared in the next directory (1840) as a clockmaker.

The Cincinnati Directory of 1843 carried the included ad. Duffner was also building organs! Duffner continued to be listed in the directories until 1851.

The 1850 Census listed Duffner as a cabinet maker owning $13,000 in property. The listing also included his wife Anna, two sons and four daughters. His son John is listed as having been born in Ohio in 1831, so we do know that Duffner had come to Ohio by that time.

VINCENT DUFNER,

CLOCK AND MUSICAL-CLOCK MAKER,

And Organ Builder,

South east corner Vine and Twelfth Streets,

CINCINNATI.

☞ Repairing promptly attended to.

DUHME, HERMAN *(b. 1819, d. 1888)* .... (w. 1842-1888)

Herman Duhme was born in 1819 in Osnabruck, Germany. He himself was not a silversmith or a jeweler, but he employed many silversmiths and jewelers, and his shop, from very humble beginnings, was to become the "Tiffany" of Cincinnati and the midwest.

The included ad, and the first listing of Herman Duhme in Cincinnati, appeared in the Cincinnati Directory in 1842.

Duhme Herman, dealer in watch tools and materials, jewelry, fine cutlery, and fancy goods, 4th b. Main and Wal.

```
VARIETY STORE.
HERMAN DUHME,
Fourth, between Main and Walnut Streets,
CINCINNATI,
DEALER IN WATCH TOOLS & MATERIALS,
Jewelry, Fine Cutlery and Fancy Goods.
```

It was from this little variety store that the great store, illustrated below was to grow.

INTERIOR VIEW OF DUHME & CO.'S

The following excerpts and picture of the interior of Duhme's store were taken from Kenny's *Illustrated Cincinnati of 1879.*

DUHME & CO.'S

In all large cities it appears that some business houses become so thoroughly noted and prominent that they become features of the city itself. Such a house is that whose name heads this article, and it may be further stated that this house has for nearly half a century been closely identified with the growth and prosperity of Cincinnati. For many years it has been not only the great representative house of Cincinnati, but the West. It was to this house that the fathers and mothers of the past generation resorted when they desired to adorn themselves with jewelry, a custom which has been practiced in all countries from time immemorial . . . .

. . . . The visitor who desires to see one of the finest displays of jewelry on the continent will not be disappointed in visiting Duhme's. The arrangements of the great double warehouse are of the most admirable order, and show off to advantage the costly displays. Upon many pieces of the finer description of silverware, great expense is incurred in order to give them the character of art productions. The term jewelry means so much of late years, that nothing less than a catalogue could convey an idea of the great assortment of articles exhibited. Prominent, however, will be the decorative gold and silver plate, such as racing cups, testimonials, centerpieces, salvers, candelabra, etc.; table plate, such as soup and sauce tureens, dessert services, claret jugs, wine coolers, cruit (sic) frames, water pitchers, etc.; gold and silver plated goods, electro-plated goods, gilt and ormolu work for table and personal decoration, jewelry containing precious stones, epergnes, cake and fruit baskets and table cutlery in silk and satin lined boxes.

In particular branches of manufactures, there may be and doubtless are larger houses than Duhme & Co., but in the regular work of the gold and silver smiths' profession there is none more extensive. Every department, such as designing, engraving, chasing, enameling and electro-plating, is fully represented by workmen whom none can excel. . . . Many of Duhme & Co.'s own designs in spoons and other articles are preferred to all others. Their silver ware is now altogether made of sterling silver. . . .

. . . . The retail department, with its choice display of diamonds, jewelry, silver-ware, both solid and plated, valuable watches of gold and silver, is well worth examination. Among their useful specialties they carry a full line of jeweler's tools, at wholesale, and also clocks, watches and chains of every design, manufactured by themselves. The wholesale department is in the rear part of the ground floor, where the heavy solid silver ware is manufactured. It may be well to mention that while this house carries full lines of all standard plated goods, none of that work is done by them. They make only the solid article. All of their flat silver and gold wares, which embrace everything except the table sets, are made by hand and hammered out. This method is preferred to the rolling process as securing better work, the artificer being by this means enabled more readily to detect flaws and imperfections. For the same reason no hot work is allowed, but everything is

A beautiful little engraved condiment set bearing the mark of Duhme & Co., incised.

Private collection.

wrought and cut. In the second basement are the steam engines and the process by which every particle of gold and silver is washed, is by the use of quicksilver here collected and eventually separated one from the other. . . .

Herman Duhme died in 1888, and the following sketch of his life appeared in Greve's *Centennial History of Cincinnati and Representative Citizens:*

> Herman Duhme, one of the old, reliable and prominent business citizens of Cincinnati, proprietor of the great jewelry house of Duhme & Company, one of the largest and best equipped in the West, died at his home in St. Clair, Michigan, August 21, 1888. Mr. Duhme was born in the ancient dukedom of Osnabruck, Hanover, Germany, June 14, 1819, and was a son of Herman H. and Margaret Duhme.
>
> Herman H. Duhme was a man of influence and prominence in his native country. In August, 1834, he brought his family to America, and was also accompanied by some 100 other emigrants, the voyage being made from Bremen to New York in a small vessel chartered for the purpose by Mr. Duhme. They proceeded to Ohio and settled in a colony at Springfield, becoming some of the most worthy people of that locality, their habits of thrift and industry soon enabling them to acquire means and a high standing in the community.
>
> At this time our late subject was a youth of 15 years. He had been educated both in public and religious schools in his native country, and began his business life with Griffith Foos, an old pioneer of Clark County. Mrs. Foos took a motherly interest in the bright, ambitious, pleasant young

This magnificent soup tureen bears the following inscription:
Designed and Manufactured
by
Herman Duhme
of Duhme & Co.
for the
Cincinnati Exposition
1872

Private collection.

man and devoted much time to him, teaching him the English language and training him in social usages. When this admirable woman died, 20 years later, her surviving husband came to Cincinnati and found a home and filial care with Mr. Duhme, — surely a case of "bread cast upon the waters."

In 1840 our subject came to this city and became a salesman in a dry goods store, but one year later accepted a similar position in a jewelry store, beginning an interest that lasted through his life. He remained in this position three years, devoting careful attention to all of its details and methods and also saving his earnings. During the depression of business in 1841-42 his salary, with that of thers, was reduced, and he concluded as he was then 21 years of age that he would be in a better financial position if he embarked in a small, safe business for himself. He considered the matter well and ended by investing his savings in a few first class goods, and opening a store, which in later days expanded into one of the greatest jewelry emporiums in the West, a manufacturing plant that to-day, in its line, has few equals, and it is a fact that the value of the dust and sweepings from its workrooms is more in one year than the whole original capital invested. When the great exposition was opened in 1851 at Hyde Park, London, Mr. Duhme visited it in the interest of his trade and became acquainted with the leading manufacturers of England, France, Germany and Switzerland, and entered into arrangements with them for importing direct. From 1857 to 1861 disaster fell upon Mr. Duhme on account of the business depression all over the country, and, like many other business men of this city, he witnessed the loss of his capital. However, his reputation for business integrity was such that unsolicited assistance came to him, and in a few years he was again prosperous and his business continually advanced. The plant requires 300 skilled workmen of every nation, who turn out their choicest productions for the house of Duhme & Company.

Mr. Duhme was married in April, 1847, to Mary Ann McNichol, daughter of Peter McNichol, an old pioneer of this city; the two sons of this union, Herman and Frank, are prominent in business. In August, 1865, he was married to Mary C. Galbraith, who with two children, Lottie and Albert, survives. Mr. Duhme was a man of highest personal character, and was valued in every circle where he was known.

The Duhme Company continued in business after Herman's death until 1896, when we find the name changed to The Duhme Jewelry Co. By 1899 there were two Duhme listings, one of Duhme Brothers, which was operated by Frank and Herman, sons of Herman, Sr., and The Duhme Jewelry Co., run by Herman and Oscar Keck.

The last listing found of the Duhme Brothers was 1904; The Duhme Jewelry Co. continued in business until 1910.

A large amount of beautiful hand made flat silver and holloware made by Duhme & Co. exists today. Duhme & Company was undoubtedly one of the few companies in America still making handmade silver after the Civil War. The *Cincinnati Graphic News* of 1884 carried the large ad shown on page 55 picturing the Duhme shop and telling of the products it offered.

Illustrated on page xiii are examples of twist flatware made by Duhme & Co., on page 53 a magnificent soup tureen made for the Cincinnati Industrial Exposition of 1872, on page xiv an elaborate pitcher, goblets and tray presented to the mayor of Cincinnati in 1880, and on page 52 a charming little condiment set.

Some of the marks found on silver made by Duhme & Co. are:

DUHME & CO. (incised)

This is the most common mark found.

Not included are later marks including 925/1000 and the word "Sterling".

SCENE IN THE GOLDSMITH SHOPS OF DUHME & CO., CARLISLE BUILDING, FOURTH & WALNUT STS.

 STERLING SILVER TABLEWARES

All Silverwares made by **DUHME & CO.** bear the mark ⟨STERLING 925 DUHME&CO⟩ and are guaranteed 925/1000 **Fine,** the standard for English sterling.

DUHME & CO. are among the few prominent manufacturers of Sterling Silverwares in the United States who do not produce rolled or machine-made wares, their entire product being hand-made, hand-engraved and hand-burnished, by which processes, only, can the best results be realized.

Fourteen styles of Spoons and Forks, complete lines of larger pieces, also chests of Silver, constantly in stock or made to order, at

DUHME & CO. - **Fourth and Walnut.**

Cincinnati Graphic News, 1884.

DUHME, JOHN H. *(b. ?, d. 1853)* (w. 1844-1853)

John H. Duhme, the brother of Herman Duhme, was born in Osnabruck, Hanover, Germany, the son of Herman H. and Margaret Duhme.

The family came to America in 1834 and settled first in Springfield, Ohio. John Duhme came to Cincinnati, and the first directory listing found of him was in 1843; the listing reads: "Duhme, John H., Clothing Stores, Landing between Broadway and Ludlow — Ludlow between Second and Congress."

The supplement of the 1844 Directory carried the included listing and ad. As we can see, Herman Duhme was boarding with his brother John at this time.

Duhme & Co. dealers in fancy goods, 4th bet Main and Walnut

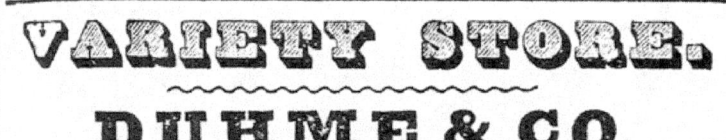

Duhme Herman, (D. & Co.) boards John Duhme
Duhme John (D & Co.) Gano st.

The 1851-1852 Directory carried the following listing: "Duhme & Co. (John H. and Herman D.), importers of watches and fancy goods, 130 Main." It would seem from this that at that time John was a partner in business with his brother Herman. But John died in 1853, and Herman continued the business, which was to grow and prosper and become Cincinnati's finest jewelry store.

DUNLEVY, WILLIAM D. (w. 1849-1853)

William Dunlevy worked as a silversmith at J. Draper's in 1840. In 1843 and 1846 he was listed as a barkeeper at William Luck's. In 1849 he formed a partnership with William Ryland (Dunlevy & Ryland), and they were listed as silversmiths, located on the north side of Sixth between Walnut and Vine. This partnership seems to have lasted about one year.

The 1850 Census listed William Dunlevy as a barkeeper, thirty-seven years old, from Pennsylvania. In 1853 William Dunlevy was listed in the Directory under Jewelry, Silverware and Watches, his address 19 W. Sixth. This was the last directory listing found for him.

DUNLEVY & RYLAND (1849)

EAVES, WILLIAM T. .... (w. 1836-1840)

William Eaves was born in England. He and James H. Martin formed a jewelry company in Cincinnati in 1836 (Eaves & Martin).

The 1840 Cincinnati Directory listed Eaves as a jeweler residing on W. Front between Elm and Plum. This was the last directory listing of Eaves in Cincinnati.

The Hiatts' book on Kentucky silversmiths listed William Eaves as advertising in Lexington in 1842, where Eaves had formed a partnership with A. Falize (see Falize). But Eaves did not stay in Lexington long. Mrs. Roach, in her book on St. Louis silversmiths, reported that Eaves was working as a silversmith in St. Louis from 1845-1848, and with Herbel in 1849 (Eaves & Herbel).

No silver marked Eaves & Martin is known, but a ladle marked Eaves & Herbel is in the St. Louis City Art Museum.

EAVES & MARTIN .... *(1836-1837)*

EVANS, WILLIAM R. .... (w. 1844)

William R. Evans was listed in the Cincinnati Directory in 1844 as a silversmith located on Main between 3rd and 4th. There was no other listing of a William R. Evans until 1855, when the Cincinnati Directory listed a William R. Evans under jewelry, watches, etc. and located him on the west side of Scott between 5th and 6th in Covington, Kentucky. This is undoubtedly the man listed by the Hiatts in their book on Kentucky silversmiths.

EVANS, WILLIAM M. .... (w. 1850-1863)

A William M. Evans appeared in the Cincinnati Directory in 1850. He continued to be listed as a clock or watchmaker or both at 206 John St. until 1863. Little else, however, is known of him.

FALIZE (FALLIS), ALEXANDER .... (w. 1840; also w. 1842-1846)

Alexander Falize, from Belgium, appeared in the 1840 Cincinnati Directory as a manufacturer of jewelry at S.T. Carley's. We can surmise that he went briefly to Lexington, as the *Lexington Advertiser and Reporter* of April 20, 1842 carried an ad that W. Eaves and A. Falize had opened a shop on West Main, according to the Hiatts' book on Kentucky silversmiths.

Falize was also listed in the 1842 and 1843 Cincinnati Directories as a jeweler boarding at S.T. Carley's. The last listing in Cincinnati of Alexander Falize appeared in the 1846 Cincinnati Directory, when he was listed as a jeweler located on the north side of 3rd between Walnut and Vine.

FELTMANN (FELDMANN), WILLIAM, WILLIAM H., OR H.W. ...... (w. 1840-1851; also w. 1857-1863)

As can be seen, Mr. Feltmann appeared in the Cincinnati Directories under a variety of listings. In 1840 Feltmann was listed as a goldsmith at Daumont's; in 1842 the listing was silversmith; in 1846, jeweler.

Old Hamilton County marriage books record the marriage of William H. Feldmann to Mary Schmidt in June of 1843.

In 1849 and 1851 Feltmann was listed as a spectacle-maker, but from 1852 through 1856 his name did not appear in the directories. Feltmann's name reappeared in 1857 and continued to be listed until 1863, with varying occupations including spectacle-maker, silversmith, and goldsmith. Some later directories listed a William Feldmann in occupations other than those with which we are here concerned.

FISHER, EBENEZER ...... (w. 1842-1844)

The 1842, 1843 and 1844 Cincinnati Directories listed Ebenezer Fisher as a watchmaker. The only clue to his later whereabouts was a listing found in the 1850 Ohio Census of an Ebenezer Fisher in Brighton, Lorain County, Ohio. This may have been the same man.

GARNER, JOHN *(b. ?, b. 1832)* ...... (w. 1829-1832)

B.H. Caldwell Jr. in his article on Tennessee silver, lists John Garner as having worked in Knoxville from 1809 until 1813. The first directory listing of John Garner in Cincinnati occurred in 1829, when he was listed as a silversmith on Front Street. The 1831 Cincinnati Directory listed him as a watchmaker on Fifth Street. He must have been a partner of N.L. Hazen for a short time, as J. Deterly's diary entry for March 26, 1832 mentioned Hazen & Garner's shop. The partnership could not have lasted for long, as Isaac Covall's list of cemetery records includes John Garner's name, and the information that he died in 1832.

GILMORE, ROBERT ...... (w. 1834-1838)

The 1834 Cincinnati City Directory listed Robert Gilmore as a silversmith on Main. In 1836 he was listed as a watchmaker, at 117 Main.

The included notice concerning a lost watch and mentioning Gilmore appeared in a Cincinnati newspaper in 1837.

Cincinnati Daily Gazette, April 29, 1837

```
                    LOST.
ON Race street, between Fourth and Fifth,
   on Sunday afternoon, the 23d inst. (April)
a plain English WATCH, new—marked Wm.
Green, Liverpool, No. not recollected; chain
black figured ribbon, with two keys. If left
with R. Gilmore, Watch-maker, the finder will
be liberally rewarded.         ap 29—39†41
```

A year later, in 1838, Gilmore announced that he was retiring to the country and turning over his business to Owen & Read, as the included ad indicates. A clock made by Robert Gilmore is in a private collection in Cincinnati.

Daily Gazette, June 30, 1838

> **OWEN & READ,**
> WATCH AND CLOCK MAKERS,
> *SILVERSMITHS AND JEWELLERS,*
> No. 117 Main Street, Cincinnati,
> (Nearly opposite Commercial Bank,)
>
> RESPECTFULLY inform their customers and the public generally, that they have removed from their former stand to the above-named place, where they are prepared to execute all work in the various branches of their profession, which may be intrusted to their care, in the best manner.
>
> They have at this time, and will keep constantly on hand for sale, a general assortment of *superior Watches, Jewelry, Spectacles, and Silver Wares,* of the newest fashion, and most approved workmanship.
> july 9   5tf
>
> A CARD.
> Having declined my profession, and retired to the country, I take pleasure in recommending my old friends and customers to Messrs. Owen & Read, as above, having every confidence that they will give general satisfaction to all who may favor them with their custom.
>   ROBERT GILMORE.
> Cincinnati, June 30, 1838.

GOLDSMITH, DAVID .... (w. 1840)

The only year during which we know with certainty that David Goldsmith was working in Cincinnati was 1840, as he was listed in the 1840 Cincinnati Directory as a jeweler, his residence Race between Front and Columbia. He was also listed in 1842, 1843 and 1844 Directories at the corner of Symmes and Pike, but no occupation was given.

Silver spoons marked

D. GOLDSMITH

are in a private collection, and the shape of the spoons is typical of Cincinnati spoons of the 1840 period.

GORDON, JONATHAN B. *(b. 1802, d. 1874)* .... (w. 1824-1831)

According to Hamilton County records compiled by Robert D. Craig, Jonathan B. Gordon was born in Monmouth, New Jersey in 1802 and came to Cincinnati in May of 1810. In July of 1824 a notice of the marriage of Jonathan B. Gordon to Miss Jane Harsha appeared in the *Cincinnati Advertiser.* In December of the same year the *Cincinnati Emporium* carried the included ad.

Gordon was listed as a silversmith in the 1825 and 1829 Directories, but he does not seem to have been successful as a silversmith, as in later directories he was listed as a laborer, engine finisher and news carrier. By 1853 he is listed as a railroad agent and this listing continued for many years.

Jonanthan Gordon died in Cincinnati in 1874. His will mentioned his wife, his daughters Eliza and Margaret, and sons Henry and Charles.

Cincinnati Emporium, December 2, 1824

> **Gunsmithing,**
> *Walnut street, opposite the West end of the Upper Market House.*
>
> SILAS BRYANT has commenced the Gunsmith business next door below the corner of 5th street, opposite the Market and corner, where he is ready to receive orders for Rifles, Guns, Pistols, &c. and to do all kinds of smithing in that line of business, or repairs that may be wanted.
>
> ALSO—AT THE SAME PLACE,
> **J. B. GORDON,**
> *Silversmith and Jeweller,*
> Carries on his business in all its branches. All orders will be thankfully received and promptly attended to.
> J. B. Gordon will purchase old Gold and Silver, for which he will pay the highest price.
> Dec. 2.   43-6§

GORDON, L.

This ad, which appeared in the *Western Spy* in September of 1816, is included because it is typical of the ads of itinerant salesmen of the time. Business must have been good, since Mr. Gordon advertised again eight days later that he would stay a week longer than planned.

Western Spy, September 5, 1816

GOULD, J.

Several J. Goulds are listed in the Kovels' book on silversmiths. One could possibly have been the J. Gould who placed the included ad in the newspaper in 1819.

J. Gould stayed in Cincinnati a little longer than the few days he advertised, and on the evening of January 23rd his store on Main Street was broken into.

The notice of the robbery which appears on the following page was carried in the newspaper in early February. This notice was also carried by newspapers in Louisville, New Orleans, St. Louis, Nashville, Lexington, New York and Pittsburgh.

In his diary J. Deterly had some wonderful comments on the robbery.

August 30, 1815, 8 3w

L. GORDON.
(*Of New-York.*)

IN passing through this town, has the honor to inform the ladies and gentlmen, that he offers for sale, Wholesale and Retail, at the New-York prices, an elegant assortment of

Fine Jewellery,
CONSISTING OF

Patent Lever, Musical, Repeating, Horizontal, Plain, Single, and Double Cased GOLD and SILVER WATCHES, Chains, Keys, Musical, Fancy and Plain Seals.

A GENERAL ASSORTMENT OF

Ladies Watches, Chains, Seals, Keys, &c. Also, Diamond, Pearl, Filligree and Plain Gold Earrings, Rings, Broaches, Bracelets, Hair, Coral, and Cornelian Necklaces, Pearl Hair Dresses, Miniature Settings, Fancy Scent Boxes, Silver Snuff Boxes, Tea Spoons, Thimbles, and all kinds of Fancy Pencil Cases, Gold Buttons, Cornelian Beads for Buttons, all of the latest importations and fashions.

☞ Old SILVER, GOLD, and all kinds of valuable stones taken in exchange.

Ladies and Gentlemen who wish to supply themselves with any articles in the above line, may depend on the most reasonable terms.— Also Gold and Silversmiths can supply themselves with assortments to the best advantage.

This assortment is opened in the house lately occupied by Messrs. Ruffin & Oliver, opposite the Lower Market, where it will remain about 10 days.

Cincinnati, Sept. 5. 8 3w

SILVER-PLATED WARE,
AND FANCY ARTICLES.

Now opening and will be offered for sale,
FOR A FEW DAYS ONLY,

At No. 24, Main-street,
AN EXTENSIVE ASSORTMENT OF

WATCHES and Jewellery, Gilt and Marble Clocks, Silver-Plated Coffee & Tea Setts, Castors, Liquor Frames, Candlesticks & Branches, Bottle Stands, Snuffers and Trays, Waiters, Table and Tea Spoons, Jappan Waiters Dressing Cases, Bread and Cheese Trays, Britannia Ware, Gilt Goods, Ladies' Reticules, Shell Combs, Purses, and Morocco Work-Boxes, Gentlemen's Shaving Cases, Ivory Handle Knives and Forks, Penknives, Scissors, Razors, Curtain Pins, Hearth Brushes, Steel Snuffers, Paint-Boxes, Music-Boxes, Indelible Ink, Hair Netts, Beads, &c. Swords, Pistols, Dirks, Epauletts, Wings, Lace, Cord, Spurs, and other Military Equipments; at wholesale and retail.

The above goods will be offered for a few days only, the subscriber being on his way to the west. J. GOULD.

Cincinnati, December 24. 85-7

Liberty Hall, December 24, 1819

$1000 REWARD.

Daring Robbery ! ! !

THE Store on Main-street, occupied by J. GOULD, was broken open on the afternoon of January 23, & the following valuable articles were stolen therefrom, viz : 1 double case gold patent lever Watch, No. 34,446, one ditto 38,611, one ditto 38,610, one ditto 6,759, one ditto 6,767, one double cased Gold Watch 2,388, one ditto 6,763, one single cased 6,201, one ditto 6771, one ditto lever 9,564, one ditto not numbered, one ditto 1,971, five gold repeaters, ten single cased Gold Watches, three Silver patent levers 38,601, 38,602, 7,359, two jewelled Silver Watches 8135, 7108 three capped, with the day of the month, silver, 5280, 5252, 5230, two sets of real pearl ornaments, one ditto pearl and amethyst, from six to eight thousand dollars worth of pearl and gold jewellery, consisting of watch seals, chains and keys, bracelets, pins, ear-rings, finger-rings, diamond pins, jet jewellery, paste ditto, sets of pearl and topaz in Morocco boxes, and other articles.

Liberty Hall, February 7, 1820

"Sunday January 23rd. Robbery. A scamp who calls himself 'J. Gould' from Baltimore, and is a strolling watch and jewelry pedler has opened a shop on Main Street, No. 24, was robbed as he says of eight or ten thousand dollars worth. It is thought that he was the *theif* and robbed himself.

Friday, January 28th. Search. Mr. James Gould and suite made a general search thro the several Silver Smiths Shops, and more particular thro' Messrs. Perret & Mathey's Shop, but made no discovery.

A damnable charge & stigma on the profession!"

GRANDBECK, DANIEL *(b. 1800, d. ?)* .... (w. 1839-1860)

The included ad, which appeared in a Cincinnati newspaper in 1839, announced the shop opening of Daniel Grandbeck, from Sweden.

In 1842 Grandbeck married Charlotte Schenke, also from Sweden.

The directories from 1842 until 1860 listed Daniel Grandbeck as a watchmaker or jeweler at varying addresses, the last being 43 Sycamore. The 1850 Census listed him as a watchmaker, 50 years old, and also listed his wife Charolotte and two children, Oscar and Isabelle. After 1860 Grandbeck's name disappeared from the directories.

Watch & Clock Making.

D. GRANDBECK, RESPECTFULLY informs the Citizens of Cincinnati and vicinity, that he has opened a Shop in Lower Market street, near Broadway, for the purpose of repairing Watches, Clocks, and Jewelry, of every description. He respectfully solicits a share of patronage.

☞ Work warranted for twelve months.
june 14 -1m

Cincinnati Advertising & Journal, June 14, 1839

GRAVES, THOMAS .... (w. 1829)

In 1829, a Thomas Graves was listed in the Cincinnati Directory as a silversmith boarding at S. Graves'. There was no further listing until the early 1850's when a Thomas H. Graves was listed as a real estate broker. In 1856 Thomas H. Graves died; his will can be found in the Court House records. Whether this was the Thomas Graves who had worked as a silversmith in 1829 has not been conclusively proven.

GUINAND, EDWARD (F. EDWARD) .... (w. 1828)

F. E. Guinand was listed in Pleasants and Sill's book on Maryland silversmiths as working in Baltimore from 1814 to 1827. This book also stated that in 1817 Guinand married Frances Duon, doubtless the daughter of a French gold and silver lace manufacturer who occupied the same shop as Guinand from 1814 until 1823.

The included ad appeared in a Cincinnati newspaper in 1828.

Guinand was not listed in the 1829 or any succeeding directories, and we have no inkling of what became of him. But the ad is proof enough that he was in Cincinnati, if only briefly.

Again according to Pleasants and Sill, flat silver marked F. E. Guinand is occasionally seen.

Cincinnati Daily Gazette, September 12, 1828

HANKS, GEORGE L. *(b. 1813, d. 1859)* .... (w. 1835-1840)

George Lucius Hanks was born in New York in 1813, the son of Alpheus and Zeniah Hanks. His wife was Julia Bunce of Hartford, Connecticut.

The included ad, which appeared November 10, 1835, announced the opening of Hanks' jewelry store in Cincinnati. In the 1836 Cincinnati Directory Hanks was listed as a watchmaker. George Hanks was still advertising in 1837, as an ad for his company appeared in the Western Address Directory of that year.

By 1839 Hanks had become a partner of A. Palmer (Palmer & Hanks). The 1842 Cincinnati Directory listed Hanks as boarding at A. Palmer's, but he was no longer in the jewelry business, having become associated with McGraw in the operation of a bell and brass foundry. He remained in this business until his death in 1859.

Hanks, his wife Julia, and two sons are buried in Spring Grove Cemetery.

Although silver spoons are mentioned in the ad for Hanks' store, no silver made by G.L. Hanks or Palmer & Hanks has been seen.

Cincinnati Daily Gazette, November 10, 1835

HARRIS, CALEB K. *(b. 1816, d. ?)* .... (w. 1839-1853)

Caleb K. Harris worked as a silversmith in Cincinnati for fourteen years. His first listing in the Cincinnati Directories occurred in 1839, when he was listed as a silversmith working at E. Kinsey's. In the 1846 Directory he was listed as a silversmith boarding at D. Kinsey's.

The 1850 Census listed Harris as a silversmith from New York, with $2300 in property. From 1850 until 1853 his address was 273 Cutter Street; the property mentioned in the census may have been his house at that address.

After 1853 Harris' name disappeared from the directories.

HARRIS, WILLIAM .... **(w. 1839-1840)**

William Harris, from England, was in Cincinnati for a short time. In 1839 a Cincinnati newspaper carried the included ad. The 1840 Cincinnati Directory listed Harris as a silversmith and watchmaker at 289 Main, but he apparently changed occupations, since Harris is listed in the 1842 Directory as a dry goods merchant located at Main between 6th and 7th. The 1843 and 1844 Directories listed Harris at the same address with no occupation given.

Jewelry.

AT W. HARRIS', 289 Main, near Seventh, will be found a good assortment of Jewelry, consisting of Finger Rings, Ear Rings, Broaches, Spectacles, Silver Spoons, ever pointed Pencils, Thimbles, and a variety of other articles in his line of business, the greater part of which being of his own manufacture, he can warrant to be good, and can afford to sell at very low prices. The public are respectfully invited to call and inspect his goods before purchasing elsewhere.

Watch Cases and Jewelry of every description, made to order, or repaired in the best manner.

Watches, Clocks, and Musical Boxes repaired.

Old gold and silver taken in exchange.

june 27-3m dw

Cincinnati Advertiser & Journal, June 27, 1839

HAYNES, JOHN R. .... **(w. 1848-1859)**

The 1850 Cincinnati Census includes two listings for John R. Haynes: the first, a jeweler and watchmaker, 22 years old, from New York; the second, a jeweler and watchmaker, 25 years old, from New York, this listing also including his wife Mary E., 24 years old, born in Pennsylvania. Possibly during the course of the cenus-taking Haynes was married, moved, and consequently was listed twice.

Williams' 1848 Business Directory listed J.R. Haynes as a watchmaker and jeweler at 40 W. Fourth. This same listing continued in consecutive years until 1859.

Charles Cist's book, *Cincinnati in 1851,* contained the following information about J.R. Haynes, under the listing of Goldsmiths and Silversmiths:

> J.R. Haynes, 40 West Fourth Street, manufactures to order all kinds of jewelry and silverware. Value of product during the past year, $5000. He is also a dealer wholesale and retail in watches, jewelry, silverware, etc.

The included ad for Haynes appeared in the Cincinnati Directory of 1850-1851.

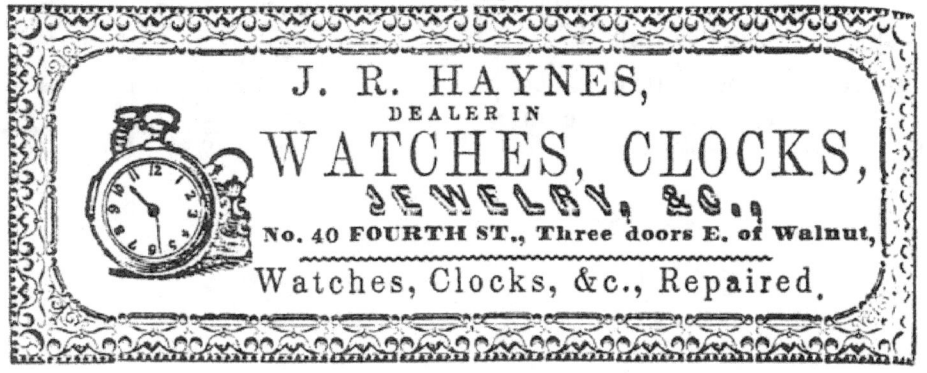

HAZEN, NATHAN L. *(b. 1809, d. 1851)* .... (w. 1831-1851)

Cincinnati Daily Gazette, May 7, 1831

Nathan L. Hazen was born in Worthington, Massachusetts in 1809, the son of Nathan L. and Phoebe Hazen. Cutten listed N.L. Hazen as a silversmith working in Troy, N.Y. from 1829 to 1830.

In 1831 Hazen arrived in Cincinnati and the Directory for that year listed him as a watchmaker. In May of 1831 he ran the above ad. Hazen must have been a firm believer in advertising, as he ran a great number of ads from the time of his arrival in Cincinnati until his early death in 1851.

The included ad, which appeared in 1838, gives a very good list of the many articles Hazen carried in his shop.

Liberty Hall, March 12, 1838

In 1843 Hazen became the partner of Peleg Collins (Hazen & Collins), and the included ad, which appeared in 1846, mentions all kinds of silver made to order. In January of 1847 the partnership of Hazen & Collins was dissolved, but Hazen continued to advertise often. In May of 1847 the included large ad appeared in the newspaper.

Cincinnati Daily Gazette, December 17, 1846

In December of 1851 Nathan Hazen died of apoplexy, at 42 years of age. He left his wife Hannah Jeanette, and two sons, John F., then six years old, and Nathan Lord, 4 years old. Hazen's son Nathan died at an even earlier age than his father, committing suicide at 23. The family are buried in Spring Grove Cemetery.

During the twenty years Hazen worked in Cincinnati he produced quite a bit of flat silver and holloware if we are to judge by the amount of silver which has been seen. He used a variety of marks; the earliest of his marks appears below and is found on the teaspoon illustrated on page 15.

Hazen

Later marks used were:

N L HAZEN

NLHazen

HAZEN & COLLINS

Other illustrations of Hazen's work included the handsome handled cup shown on the following page, the cup illustrated on page 42 and the sugar tongs on page 78.

Cist's Daily Advertiser, May 14, 1847

A beautiful embossed and engraved handled cup, bearing the mark N. L. Hazen.
Private collection.

HAZEN & COLLINS .... *(1843-1847)*

HELLEBUSH, CLEMENS *(b. 1832, d. 1893)* .... **(w. 1866-1893)**

    Although C. Hellebush did not commence his own business until 1866, his name is included in this book because of the frequency with which silver marked with his name is seen. Directories in the 1880's and 1890's include his name under Silverware Manufacturers.

    Hellebush had been a silent partner of Clemens Oskamp for sixteen years before he began his own business. He established his wholesale jewelry house at Pearl and Main in 1866, and in 1879 he added a high class retail department and moved to 77 West Fourth. He remained at this address until his death in 1893.

    The Centennial Review of Cincinnati of 1888 says of the business "Mr. Hellebush has a large and growing demand for his elegant and artistic line of fine diamonds, watches, silver watch cases, French clocks, watch materials, etc."

    Hellebush was born in Germany and came to this country when he was fifteen years of age. He died in Cincinnati in 1893.

    An article appearing in *The Industries of Cincinnati of 1886* related the following:

> Clemens Hellebush's residence in Walnut Hills is in one of the most
> beautiful suburbs of Cincinnati and is surrounded by large grounds (some

five acres), elegantly laid out, the whole being valued at over $75,000. Mr. Hellebush is the architect of his own fortune, and is emphatically a self made man. No one in the community stands higher and no business man is more respected. He was married in 1855 to Elizabeth Specker and is the father of an interesting family.

C. HELLEBUSH (incised)

appears on silver found in private collections, and illustrated on page xiii are examples of twist flatware marked C. Hellebush.

HILL, EDWARD H. *(b. 1814, d. 1873)* .... (w. 1839-1873)

Edward H. Hill, born in Virginia in 1814, started his career in Cincinnati in 1839 as a watchmaker at J. Owen's. By 1843 he was listed in the Cincinnati Directory as a watchmaker at 175 Main, and in 1845 he took over J.G. Joseph's old stand at 155 Main. He continued at this address until 1856, when he moved to 103 Main, where he remained until he retired, or died, in 1873.

Cincinnati Daily Gazette, July 3, 1845.

The 1850 Census listed Edward Hill as a watchmaker with $7500 in property, and also listed his wife Elizabeth, born in Pennsylvania, and three young sons, Edward, John and Samuel.

Undoubtedly Hill produced quite a bit of silver during his long career, as flat silver marked E.H. Hill turns up quite frequently. The mark found on his silver is:

E.H.HILL

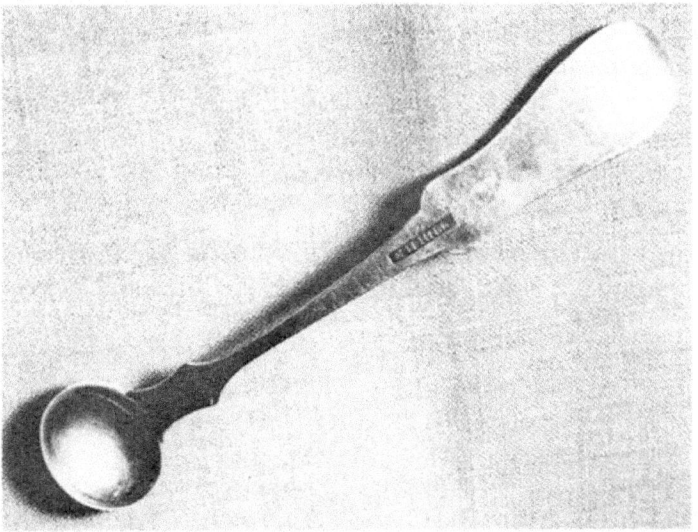

A mustard spoon by E. H. Hill. This is the only known piece of Cincinnati silver on which the maker's mark appears on the front of the piece.

In her booklet on Ohio silversmiths, Rhea Knittle listed E. Hill as working in Cincinnati. We can assume that she was referring to E.H. Hill.

HOLLAND, JOHN .... (w. 1842-1844)

John Holland was listed as a watchmaker in the 1842 through the 1844 Directories, but Holland's name did not appear again until 1858, when he was listed as a gold pen maker.

Kenny's *Illustrated Cincinnati of 1875* carried a very interesting article about the John Holland Pen Company, from which the included illustration and the following material were obtained.

The Exterior of the John Holland Pen Co. in 1875.

> John Holland's gold pen manufactory is situated at 19 W. Fourth Street. The business was established in 1842. Its beginning was small and it took years to reach the magnitude it has now attained. It now ranks as the second largest manufactory of this class of goods in the United States, and the house has branches in New York, San Francisco and other cities. For years it has received the contract for supplying the United States Treasury Department in Washington. The business extends over almost every state in the Union, and it has made several shipment of gold pens to Europe.
>
> The main productions are fine gold pens and pencil cases, mounted in gold, pearl, ivory, ebony, rosewood or silver; and gold, rubber and silver mounted toothpicks....

For Cincinnati collectors, this sounds like a fruitful field to explore. Although no longer a manufacturing company, the John Holland Gold Pen Co. is still in business today; the shop is at 127 E. Fourth.

HOLLEN, STEPHEN W. .... (w. 1842-1850. also w. 1855-1857)

In 1842 the Cincinnati Directory listed Stephen Hollen as a watchmaker on Vine between Court and Canal. This listing continued until 1850. Hollen was not listed in the directories from 1851 to 1854, but he reappeared in 1855 as a watchmaker at 367 Vine. This listing remained the same until 1857. Later directories listed him living at 34 Grant, with no occupation given.

HORTON, HENRY V. *(b. ?, d. 1871)* .... (w. 1837-1847)

Henry V. Horton, from New York, first appeared in a Cincinnati Directory in 1836, when he was listed as a watchmaker on Fifth between Vine and Race.

By 1839 Horton had his own store and a Cincinnati newpaper carried the included ad.

The 1840 Directory listed Horton as a watchmaker, but as we can see from the ad below which appeared in that Directory, he also listed himself as a silversmith:

Cincinnati Daily Gazette, November 12, 1839.

From 1842 until 1844, the directories continued to list Horton as a watchmaker, but in 1844 Horton advertised that he had resumed clock and watch repairing. He may have been working as a watchmaker for someone else from 1842 until 1844, since no shop address was given for him in the directories.

In 1846 the directory listing for Horton was watchmaker, located on the west side of

Daily Gazette, August 30, 1844.

Plum above Ninth. Cincinnati did not print directories in 1847 and 1848, and in the year 1848 we find Horton in Louisville. The Hiatts state that the Louisville Directory of that year listed H.V. Horton as a jeweler at Fifth and Walnut. In 1849 a Cincinnati listing of H.V. Horton was found, this time as a manufacturer of Sons of Temperance emblems.

The 1850 to 1853 directories listed several Henry Hortons but no H.V. Horton, but by 1855 H.V. was again listed, as a watchmaker at 147 Baymiller. Succeeding directories listed H.V. Horton with no occupation, as a canal inspector, boat inspector, insurance agent and canal collector. Horton seems to have had problems with his business career.

Horton died in 1871 and in his will leaves property in Cleves, Ohio, so in spite of his difficulties, he had at least acquired some real estate.

Horton's wife was Sophia Mathilda, born in 1811. She died in 1891 and is buried in Spring Grove Cemetery.

HUNTINGTON, WILLIAM C. *(b. 1826, d. 1904)* .... **(w. 1848-1857)**

W.C. Huntington was born in Norwich, Connecticut in 1826, the son of Erastus and Sarah Huntington.

The first appearance noted of Huntington in Cincinnati was in 1848, when his name appeared in the Williams' Business Directory listed under watches, jewelry and silverware. The address given was 123 Main. By 1850 Huntington had become a partner of Isaac N. Laboyteaux (Hungtington & Laboyteaux). This partnership lasted until 1857. The following ad appeared in the Cincinnati City Directory of 1855:

HUNTINGTON & LABOYTEAUX,
WATCH IMPORTERS,
—AND—
WHOLESALE DEALERS
—IN—
CLOCKS, JEWELRY & FANCY GOODS,
119 Main Street, between Third and Fourth,
CINCINNATI, O.

WESTERN SHOW CASE MANUFACTORY.

We also manufacture and keep constantly on hand, a full assortment of Silver, German Silver and Wood Counter Show Cases, suitable for Jewellers, Stationers, Druggists, Fancy Goods dealers, etc.

WARE ROOMS—Basement 119 Main Street.

In 1858 Huntington was associated with Huntington Brothers & Co., dealers in house furnishings and fancy goods.

Huntington died in Asheville, North Carolina in 1904, but he was buried in Spring Grove Cemetery in Cincinnati.

Flat silver made by Huntington & Laboyteaux is in private collections, and the mark used was:

HUNTINGTON & LABOYTEAUX

HUNTINGTON & LABOYTEAUX .... *(1850-1856)*

JAMISON, JACOB .... *(w. 1832)*

J. Deterly's diary revealed some information about the clockmaker Jacob Jamison who worked in Cincinnati for a brief time.

On March 17, 1832 Deterly noted: "J. Jamison late of Springfield, Ohio got the back room on second floor of Shipp & Collins' shop, fitted up for clock making. S. A. M. Shipp will have an interest in the Time Piece Manufacturing." Then on October 12, 1832, during the cholera epedemic of that year, Deterly noted: "Foggy and chilly — Mr. Elkins, clock maker to J. Jamison dies of the cholera."

The death of Mr. Elkins must have been too much for Jamison, as an October 15th Deterly noted: "Jamison and Woodbridge put off to the country yesterday."

Deterly's entry for October 16th was: "Cholera still raging, the city is pretty much deserted. J.D. (Deterly) feels uncomfortable takes medicine, 10 grams calomel and 1 opium, mixed."

In December of 1832 Jamison left Cincinnati for Dayton, as Deterly's entry for December 8, 1832 was the following: "Removal, Jacob Jameson clock maker removes his shop to Dayton."

Jamison continued to work in Dayton for many years and was still listed there as late as 1866.

JENKINS, HENRY *(b. 1820, d. 1877)* .... *(w. 1842-1874)*

The 1850 Census listed Henry Jenkins, 30, a jeweler born in Ireland, his wife Lucinda, 21, also from Ireland, and a baby daughter, Clara, born in Ohio.

Henry Jenkins worked for many years in Cincinnati, beginning as a watchmaker in 1842. By 1855 he was listed in the Cincinnati Business Directory under Jewelry, Silverware and Watches, at 36 Sycamore. This listing continued until 1860, when H. Jenkins & Co. was listed at the same address. In 1863 Jenkins formed a partnership with Samuel Hatch (Jenkins & Hatch), with their shop located at 51 W. 4th. This partnership lasted until 1874.

By 1856 Jenkins' residence had become Ludlow, Kentucky, but he continued to work in Cincinnati. Jenkins died in Ludlow in 1877 of malarial fever and is buried in Spring Grove Cemetery.

JOHNSON, WILLIAM M. .... (w. 1836-1840)

William M. Johnson, from Virginia, was the only black silversmith found working in Cincinnati. He was listed as a silversmith in 1836 and 1840. In 1842 a William M. Johnson was listed as a glazier. This may have been the same man, but since William Johnson is a fairly common name and there were several listed, it is only possible to speculate.

JONAS, JOSPEH (b. 1792, d. 1869) .... (w. 1817-1836)

Joseph Jonas was born in Exeter, England in 1792. He migrated to America in 1816 and arrived in Cincinnati in 1817. Shortly after his arrival in Cincinnati he became the partner of Alexander McGrew (McGrew & Jonas) and the included ad appeared in the newspaper.

Joseph Jonas was not the first Jew to come to Cincinnati, but he was the first permanent Jewish settler in Cincinnati.

> **ALEX. M'GREW & JOS. JONAS,**
> **Clock and Watch Makers**
> AND
> **SILVERSMITHS AND JEWELLERS,**
> [*Mr. Jonas being immediately from LONDON*]
> TAKE this method to inform the citizens of Cincinnati and the public in general, that they have commenced business in the above branches at their shop on Main-street, one door above the Post Office, where they hope by their strict attention to business to merit a share of public patronage.
> JOSEPH JONAS, having studied the Watch finishing business in London, they feel confident in assuring the public, that Clocks, Watches and Timepieces of every description, entrusted to them, shall be carefully repaired and duly attended to.
> Cincinnati, May 15th 1817.   48 tf

Western Spy, May 15, 1817

> **JOSEPH JONAS,**
> *Watch-Maker, Silversmith, & Jeweller,*
> BEGS leave to inform his friends and the public in general, that he has removed to No. 121, Corner of Main & Third streets,
> He has just received from New York, an elegant assortment of
> Gold and Silver WATCHES,
> Gentlemen and Ladies' Fine Gold Watch Chains, Seals, & Keys,
> Elegant Gold Ear and Finger Rings,
> Breastpins, Necklaces and Braceletts,
> Also, a handsome assortment of
> Jeweller's gold Chains, Seals, & Keys,
> Gold, Cornelian and Gilt Vest Buttons,
> He has also received a general assortment of
> **Steele, Gilt and Silver Ware,**
> CONSISTING OF
> Ladies Reticule Clasps, Bracelets,
> Earrings, Clasps for the waist,
> Watch-Chains, Seals and Keys.
> He also manufactures and keeps on hand,
> SILVER-WARE, of all descriptions,
> JOSEPH JONAS returns his sincere thanks to the citizens of Cincinnati and its environs for the very liberal encouragement he has already received, and hopes by his strict attention to the WATCH REPAIRING business, still to merit a share of their favors.
> Cincinnati, June 29, 1819.   33-8

Liberty Hall, June 29, 1819

In May of 1819 the partnership of McGrew and Jonas was dissolved (see A. McGrew). In June of the same year, Jonas advertised that he had opened his own shop. The 1819 Directory listed Jonas as a silversmith at 121 Main. This directory also listed him as an officer of the first Vail of the Cincinnati Royal Arch chapter of Masons, showing that he mingled frequently and honorably in the city's social life.

In the included ad, Jonas mentions that he manufacturers and keeps on hand silverware of all descriptions.

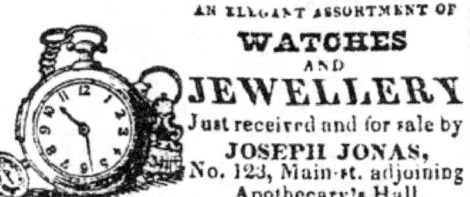

Cincinnati Emporium,
March 11, 1824

In 1824 Jonas advertised that he had *again* entered into business as a watchmaker (see ad above). What happened between 1819 and 1824 we do not know.

The 1825 through 1836 directories listed Jonas as a watchmaker and jeweler located near Third and Main.

The last ad of Jonas' that was found, appeared in the *National Republic* on May 6, 1828. The directory listings of J. Jonas from 1840 on, did not list his occupation.

An article entitled "Ancient Tombs," in the *Cincinnati* Enquirer of March 10, 1901, recounts this story of Mr. Jonas:

> "Being the first Hebrew seen in the settlement he was a great curiosity for some time, not only in the city, but in all the surrounding country. Great numbers of people would come to take a look at him. They had very peculiar ideas about Hebrews then. Among the callers was an old Quakeress. 'Art thou a Jew?' she asked. 'Thou art then one of God's chosen people. Wilt thou let me examine thee?' Turning him round and round to her entire satisfaction she at last exclaimed: 'Well, thou art no different from other people.'"

The same article carried the following additional information about Joseph Jonas.

Jonas's brother Abraham came to Cincinnati from England in 1819 and the two brothers married beautiful Jewish sisters from New York, the daughters of Rabbi Gershom Mendes Seixas. But the married life of both was brief, as Abraham's wife Lucia passed away in 1825 at the early age of twenty. She was followed in 1827 by Joseph's wife, Rachel, then twenty-six.

Jonas was one of the ten charter members of B'ne Israel Congregation, founded in Cincinnati in 1824, the oldest in the West. He was several times its president and always was active in promoting Jewish schools and charities.

Jonas served a year in the Ohio Legislature as a Democrat at about the commencement of the Civil War. When his second wife died in 1867, the pioneer gave up his residence and went to live with his daughter, Mrs. Moses, at Spring Hill, a suburb of Mobile. Jonas died two years later and was buried on his 77th birthday.

No silver marked McGrew & Jonas or J. Jonas has been seen, but hopefully some tucked away in some drawer or attic may yet come to light.

JOSEPH, JOSEPH G. *(b. 1812, d. ?)* .... (w. 1834-1844)

Although the first directory listing of J.G. Joseph occurred in 1834, when he was listed as a watchmaker on Main between 3rd and 4th, the included ad, which appeared in *1836,* claims that his was an "Old Established Spectacle Store"! As can be seen, Joseph's store also carried a large assortment of articles.

The 1840 Cincinnati Directory carried the included full page ad (see page 76) for Joseph, in which he includes silversmithing as one of his trades.

From 1842 until 1844 Joseph was listed as a silversmith. In 1846, however, the listing was clerk, and by 1850 Joseph was operating a clothing and jewelry store at 49 Front St. After 1850 Joseph is listed at various occupations, but no longer as a silversmith or jeweler.

OLD ESTABLISHED

SPECTACLE STORE,
169, *Main street,* 4 *doors north of the Two Steeple Church, and nearly opposite Dennison's Tavern.*

J. G. JOSEPH begs leave to return thanks to his friends and the public generally, for the liberal encouragement he has received for many years past, and would state that he has just returned from the East with a large assortment of goods in his line, which he is enabled to sell as low, wholesale and retail, as any house west of the mountains; consisting of all kinds of Spectacles, mounted in Gold, Silver, Tortoise, Pearl and Steel Frames, with the best Brazil pebbles and newly improved glasses, adapted to every sight within the reach of artificial assistance. Ladies' new fashioned and improved folding Spectacles: gold and silver Eye Glasses: white, green and blue Preservers, to avert the dust, and glare of the sun, and for persons who have never habituated themselves to wear glasses: Cataract glasses for persons who have been couched; prospect, opera, and reading glasses, variously mounted; mineral and flower do., day and night Telescopes and Spy Glasses, Microscopes of various descriptions: Surveyor's Compasses and Chains: Theodolites: Mathematical and Drawing Instruments: Brewers' bath and botanical Thermometers: concave and convex Glasses, for short sighted persons: ladies' and gentlemen's gold and silver lever, horizontal, vertical and plain Watches: gold watch and neck Chains: Seals, Keys, Ear and Finger Rings, Broaches, Pins, Silver Tea, Table, Soup, and Cream Spoons, of all descriptions; plated Castors, Candlesticks, Tea Setts, &c. &c.; a good assortment of Pistols, and every other article of his vocation.

june 10   66-1w—66-9

Liberty Hall & Cincinnati Gazette, June 21, 1836

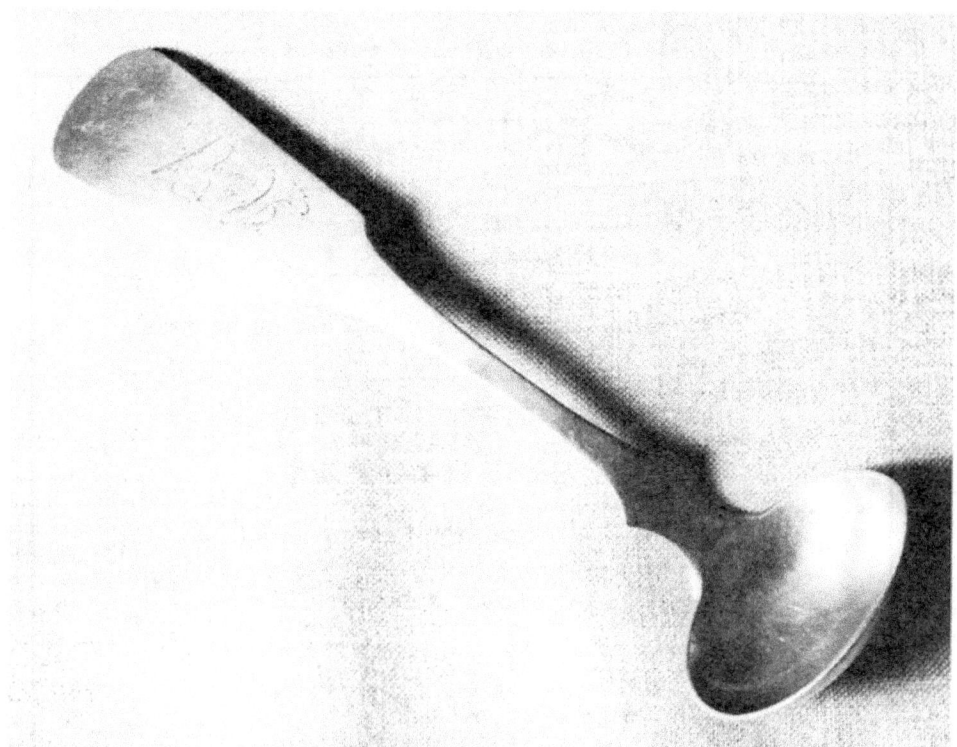

A gravy ladle from the 1830's, bearing the mark which appears in the enlargement below.
Private collection.

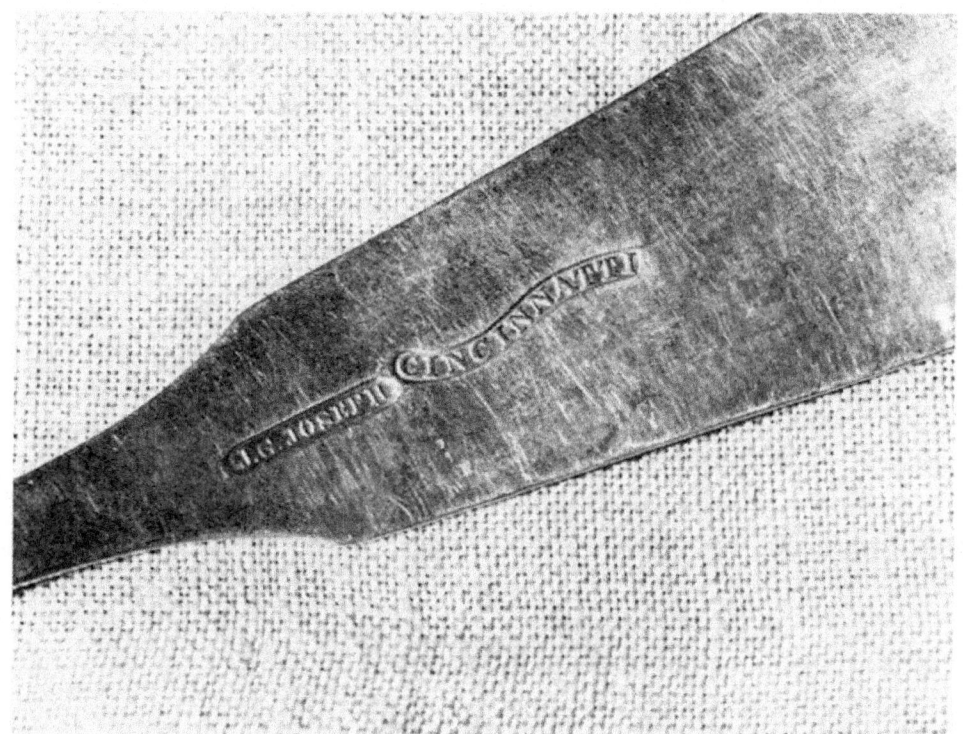

Mark which appears on the above gravy ladle. J.G. Joseph is the only known maker who used the above Cincinnati mark, spelling Cincinnati incorrectly.

Advertising Directory. 9

OLD ESTABLISHED

SPECTACLE STORE.

J. G. JOSEPH,

Optician, Jeweller, Silversmith, Watch and Clock Maker,

175, MAIN STREET,

West side, 2 doors above Fourth,

CINCINNATI.

Where may be had all kinds of Spectacles, mounted in **Gold, Silver,** and **Steel Frames**, with the best **Brazil Pebbles** and **newly improved Glasses**, adapted to every sight within the reach of artificial assistance. **White, Green,** and **Blue Preservers**, to advert the dust and glare of the sun, and for persons who have never habituated themselves to wear Glasses. **Catarac Glasses** for persons who have been couched; **Reading Glasses,** variously mounted; **Mineral** and **Flower Glasses; Day and Night Telescopes and Spy Glasses;** Surveyors' Compasses and Chains; Mathematical and Drawing Instruments; Theodolites and Levels; Brewers' Bath, and Botanical Thermometers; Concave and Convex Glasses, for short sighted persons; Ladies' and Gentlemen's Gold and Silver, Lever, Horizontal, Vertical and Plain Watches; Gold Watch and Neck Chains; Seals; Keys; Ear and Finger Rings; Broaches; Pins; Silver Tea, Table, Soup, and Cream Spoons, of all descriptions; and every other article in his vocation.

The highest price given for Gold and Silver.

3

Joseph Joseph did make silverware in his early years, and several private collections include spoons marked:

Notice the spelling of Cincinnati; no other Cincinnati smith has been found who used this particular stamp of "Cincinnatti".

An illustration of the above mark appears on page 75, as does the gravy ladle on which the mark appears.

KELLER, CHARLES .... (w. 1848-1892)

Charles Keller's name first appeared in the 1848 Cincinnati Business Directory, under Watches, Clocks and Silverware; his address was given as the south side of Court between Main and Walnut. The 1850 Directory listed him as a watch and clock manufacturer at the same address.

From 1851 until 1874 Keller was listed as a watchmaker, clockmaker or jeweler at 43 W. Court, in both the regular and the business directories. From 1874 until 1892 he was listed in the regular directory as a watchmaker with no business address given, so one can surmise that he might have been working for another company during those years.

KELLY, CHARLES *(b. 1814, d. ?)* .... (w. 1842-1889)

Charles Kelly was born in New York in 1814. He first appeared in the Cincinnati Directory in 1842, listed as a silversmith. He continued to be listed until 1889 as a silversmith and in various allied trades, including spectacle-maker, watchmaker, and jeweler. In the 1850's the address given was 192 W. Front, and in the 1860's and 1870's a 4th St. address was given.

The 1850 Census listed Charles Kelly as a silversmith, and also recorded his wife Lydia, born in Maryland, and a son and a daughter.

From 1869 until 1889 Kelly seems to have concentrated on spectacle-making. Anyone interested in finding examples of Cincinnati craftsmen might do well to examine old spectacles for the Mark of C. Kelly, since some of his unrecognized work may still be in existence.

KENT, LUKE SR. *(b. ?, d. 1842)* .... (w. 1813-1842)

When Luke Kent arrived in Cincinnati in 1813, he opened a shop on Main Street, and the included ad appeared in the newspaper. This was the beginning of a business which was to continue under the Kent name for many years.

The following article, which appeared in the *Proceedings of the Memorial Association,* etc. in 1881, gives a resume of Luke Kent's life:

```
LUKE KENT,
WATCH & CLOCK MAKER,
      MAIN-STREET, CINCINNATI,
On the hill, opposite the court-house, where he
will carry on the business in all its branches. From
his long experience at the city of Washington, he
hopes to give satisfaction to his employers here.
   Cincinnati, July 19, 1813.           56tf
```

Liberty Hall, July 19, 1813

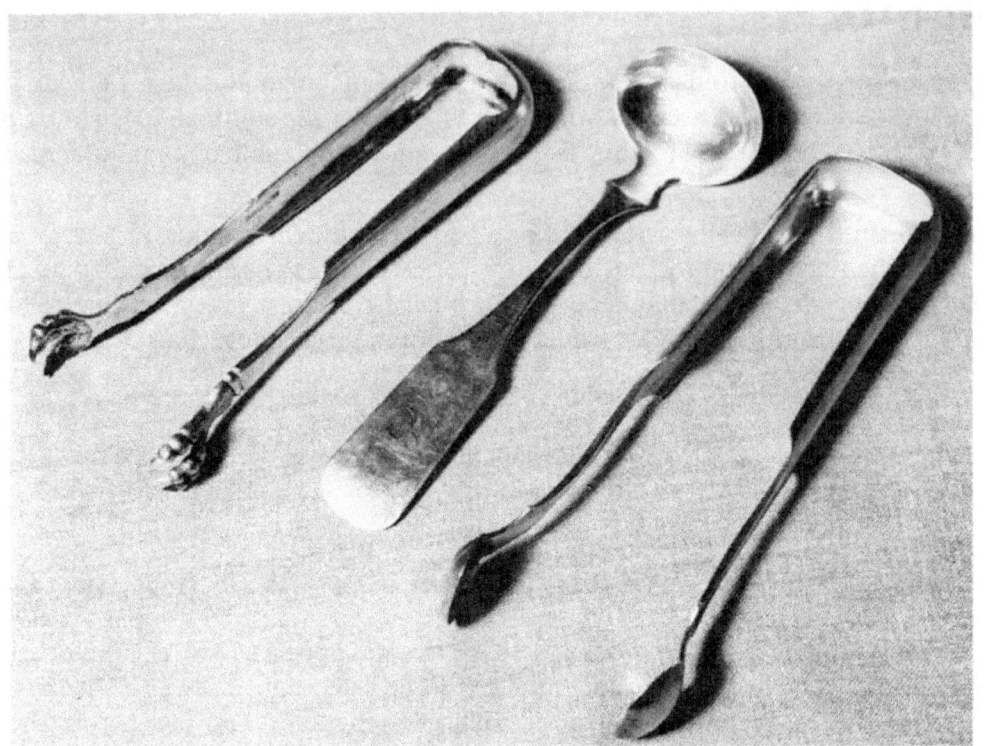

Examples of serving pieces by Cincinnati makers, on the left a claw end sugar tongs by N. L. Hazen, in the center a gravy ladle by L. Kent, Sr., and on the right a spoon end sugar tongs by J. Draper.

Private collections.

LUKE KENT

was born in Portsmouth, England, and came to this country, locating first in Washington, D.C., thence to Cincinnati in the latter part of 1813 with his wife and two children, traveling over the mountains by wagon to Marietta, and then by flatboat to Cincinnati. He opened a jewelry store on the east side of Main, between Fourth and Fifth Streets, remaining there four years, and then moving to the west side, below Allen's drugstore, and some years afterward above Fifth. He then again moved to the east side, between Fifth and Sixth Streets, taking his son (the present Luke Kent), then but sixteen years of age, in partnership. He remained there twenty-one years, until his death in 1842. He was an open-hearted, genial old gentleman, and both he and his wife were faithful members of the Radical Methodist Church. Many of our old-time citizens will remember their good and happy faces.

Kent's wife was Eliza Douglas, born in England in 1783; she died in Cincinnati in 1841.

From Luke Kent's will, written in 1842 and found in the Court House records, the following information was learned: Kent had four sons, William, Thomas, Luke and Asbury, and three daughters, Mary Disney, Martha Allen, and Elizabeth Lyon. To his son Luke he bequeathed "all the tools and materials of the watchmaking and jewelry business, remaining on hand at my death, and I hereby relinquish and will to him all my right and title of the house and business we now jointly occupy in Main Street, and hereby give him full possession of said business or my joint half of same."

Luke Kent, Jr. was to continue that business for many years.

An early gravy ladle bearing the mark

L. KENT

is illustrated on page 78; this mark is assumed to be the mark of Luke Kent, Sr.

For the convenience of readers, the following is a listing of the various business names used by the Kent family over the years:

1813-1839 Luke Kent (Senior)

1840-1842 Luke Kent & Son

1843-1864 Luke Kent (Junior)

1865   Kent & Michie

1866-1869 Luke Kent & Co.

1870-1877 Kent & Michie

1878-1879 Luke Kent & Co.

1880-1891 H.T. Kent

KENT, LUKE, JR. *(b. 1812, d. 1895)* .... **(w. 1838-1879)**

Luke Kent, Jr. was born in Washington, D.C. in 1812, the son of Luke and Eliza Kent. He was still an infant when he arrived in Cincinnati with his parents in 1813. He entered business at a very early age, as he was only sixteen when he began to work in his father's shop. The business was willed to him upon the death of his father in 1842 (see Luke Kent, Sr.).

As the table above shows, the Kent business continued for many years under many different titles.

The following beautifully illustrated ad appeared in Williams' Cincinnati Directory of 1864:

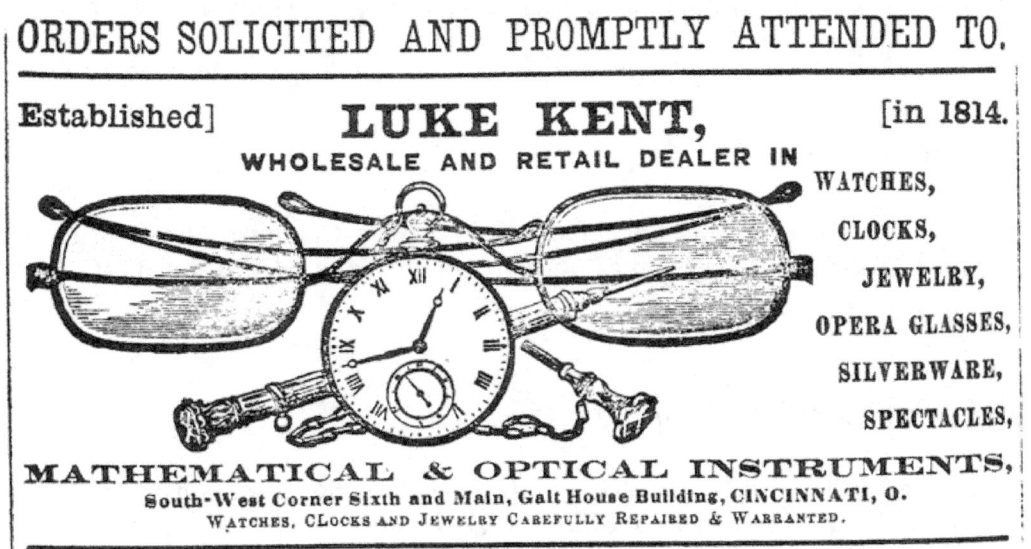

The Centennial Review of Cincinnati, published in 1888, carried an article on H.T. Kent (Luke, Jr.'s son), and included the following information on the Kent business:

> "The record of this house, covering a period embracing three-quarters of the century comprising the history of the city, is one of uniform reliability and fairness in dealing, and it enjoys a steady and prosperous trade and a deservedly high place in public confidence."

Luke Kent, Jr. married Adeline E. Ernst, daughter of Andrew and Elizabeth H. Ernst. Luke and Adeline Kent are buried in Spring Grove Cemetery, as are three of their children who died in infancy, and four children who lived to maturity, namely a daughter, Amelia, and sons Walter, Luke, and Herbert Townsend, the H.T. Kent mentioned above.

Flat silver in private collections bear the following marks:

L.KENT

LUKE KENT (incised)

KENT & MICHIE (incised)

KENT, THOMAS .... (w. 1836-1844)

Luke Kent, Sr., had a son Thomas who is mentioned in his will. This was undoubtedly the Thomas Kent who worked as a watchmaker and jeweler in Cincinnati from 1836 until 1844, first at 54 Main and later on Sycamore between Second and Lower Market.

B.H. Caldwell Jr. in his article on Tennessee silversmiths lists Thomas Kent as having worked as a silversmith in Nashville from 1845 until 1853.

Several Thomas Kents were listed in the Cincinnati Directories after 1855 but none were listed as silversmiths or jewelers. Also, Spring Grove Cemetery records include a Thomas Kent who was born in England in 1802 and died in Cincinnati in 1890. This Thomas Kent however, is not buried in the Luke Kent lot, so there is some doubt as to whether this was Luke Kent's son.

We have been told that flat silver exists marked T. KENT, CINCINNATI.

KERDOLFF, WILLIAM .... (w. 1842-1844)

William Kerdolff's name appeared briefly in the Cincinnati Directories. The 1842 through 1844 Directories listed him as a jeweler boarding at Mrs. J. Kerdolff's.

KINKEAD, GEORGE L. *(b. 1800, d. 1852?)* .... (w. 1836-1839)

According to the 1850 Census, George Kinkead was born in Pennsylvania in 1800. He worked briefly as a clockmaker in Cincinnati, and the included ad appeared in the 1836

Cincinnati Directory. The 1839 Directory also listed him as a clockmaker, but later directories listed him at various other trades. His wife Elizabeth was listed alone in the 1853 Directory, so it is farily safe to assume that he died in 1852.

GEORGE L. KINKEAD,
CLOCK MAKER,

Seventh street, between Main and Sycamore.

Keeps constantly on hand Clocks of every Pattern, which he will sell on accommodating terms, and warrant to keep good time.

Clocks of all descriptions neatly repaired and warranted. Old Clocks taken in exchange for new ones.

KINSEY, DAVID *(b. 1819, d. 1874)* .... **(w. 1840-1870)**

David Kinsey was born in Wales on October 18, 1819, the son of Thomas and Ann Kinsey and the brother of Edward Kinsey. The date given in some books for David Kinsey as a working silversmith is 1817. This seems to be completely erroneous.

In November of 1816 *Liberty Hall* published a list of names of men who had purchased land, and five years having elapsed without full payment being made, were liable to forfeiture. A David Kinsey was on this list, but he was not the father of David Kinsey, David's father being Thomas. This David Kinsey was never listed elsewhere, and no evidence is available to substantiate that he was a relative of David Kinsey the silversmith.

David Kinsey, the silversmith, was first listed in the Cincinnati Directory in 1840 as a silversmith at E. Kinsey's. At this time he was 21 years old. According to a biography appearing in *Ohio The Future Great State* published in 1875, David had been brought by his parents from Wales to New Jersey when he was six months old, and had come to Cincinnati at fourteen to learn the trade of silversmithing from his brother, Edward. In 1843 David purchased his brother Edward's business and the included notice appeared in the newspaper.

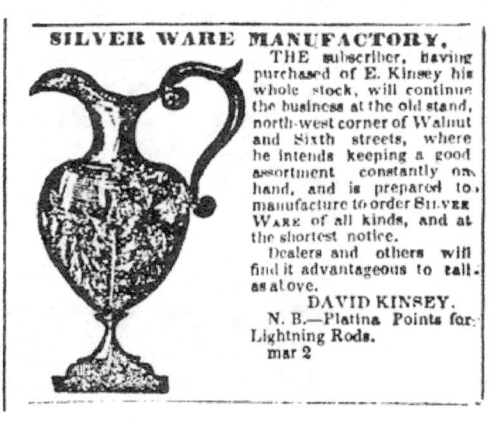

Cincinnati Daily Gazette, March 2, 1843

What happened to cause Edward to sell out (if only temporarily) remains a mystery. By July of 1843 Edward was advertising again, and by January of 1844 ads began to appear for E. & D. Kinsey (see E. Kinsey).

According to the aforementioned biography, in 1849 David Kinsey left Cincinnati for California in search of gold, but returned to Cincinnati in 1850, after an unsuccessful trip.

The combination of Edward and David working together lasted until 1861, when Edward retired. The business was then listed under David Kinsey until his death in 1871. The ad on the following page appeared in the 1872 Cincinnati Directory.

An unusual three piece tea set, the tea pot 11½ inches tall, bearing the mark D. Kinsey, incised.

Private collection.

From 1874 until 1878 the business was listed as D. Kinsey & Co., and David's son Louis A. Kinsey, in partnership with John B. Callahan, continued the business. In 1879 the name was changed to L.A. Kinsey. Louis seems, however, to have been unable to continue the success of the business since the last listing occurred in 1882. Louis Kinsey eventually moved to Indianapolis where he was engaged in the grain business.

In 1843 David Kinsey married Julia A. Peacock, born in Terre Haute in 1820. David and Julia lost a son and a daughter before 1850, but three sons lived and were mentioned in Kinsey's will, Edward W., Charles S., and Louis A. Julia Kinsey most probably moved to Indianapolis with her son Louis as she died there in 1903. She and her husband are buried in Spring Grove Cemetery.

The 1875 biography says of David Kinsey, "His life was an eventful one. He always directed his conduct by principles based on the soundest morality. There is not a word of reproach against his character, nothing to dim the luster of his life, still left shining as a bright example to be followed. And now that his spirit has calmly glided from this earth his honored name will not be forgotten."

When the name Kinsey passed from the list of silversmiths and jewelers in Cincinnati, the most prolific of the silversmiths of the pre-Civil War period were gone.

Edward and then Edward and David Kinsey had a silverware manufactory, and had produced the bulk of the handmade holloware and flatware of Cincinnati of their time. Much silver by these men remains, including tea sets, cups, pitchers, ladles and other flatware.

Many other silversmiths were employed in the Kinseys' shop and all of the silver produced was of a high quality. Cincinnatians can be justly proud of the handmade silver produced by these men.

Marks found on silverware are reproduced below.

E. & D. KINSEY (incised)

D. KINSEY (incised)

KINSEY (incised)

Picture of David Kinsey, courtesy Cincinnati Historical Society.

A lovely three piece tea set by David Kinsey is illustrated on the preceeding page and a group of cups by E. & D. Kinsey on page 85. Included in the illustration on page xiii are twist butter knives, one marked David Kinsey, the other E. & D. Kinsey.

KINSEY, EDWARD (b. 1810, d. 1865) .... (w. 1834-1861)

Edward Kinsey, son of Thomas and Ann and brother of David Kinsey, was born in Wales in 1810. His father Thomas was a silversmith and undoubtedly taught the trade to his son.

The first proof of Edward's arrival in the Cincinnati area was found in the 1834 Cincinnati Directory, which listed residents of Newport, Kentucky. Edward Kinsey appeared in this directory as a silversmith boarding at the Newport Hotel. By 1836, the Cincinnati Directory listed Edward Kinsey as a silversmith at Third and Walnut, his residence Fourth near Race.

Very probably Kinsey moved to Cincinnati late in 1834, or lived in Newport and worked in Cincinnati, since an ad of 1844 stated that Edward had had ten years of business in Cincinnati (see 1844 ad on page 86). It was undoubtedly during this period that Edward Kinsey worked with P. Scovil; the shape of the spoons marked Scovil & Kinsey would substantiate this.

By 1836 Edward Kinsey had his own silverware manufactory, and the included ad appeared in the newspaper in that year.

In 1838 Kinsey moved his manufactory and the notice below appeared in February of that year.

> **SILVER WARE MANUFACTORY.**
> E. KINSEY, corner of Walnut and Third streets, Cincinnati, manufactures to order, and offers for sale, Silver Ware of all kinds, warranted equal to Spanish dollars, among which are
> TEA AND COFFEE SETTS,
> Soup Ladles, Table, Dessert, and Tea Spoons, Mugs, Tumblers and Goblets, Candle Sticks, Forks, Fruit and Butter Knives, together with every article in his line.
> Any of the above articles will be furnished to order, at short notice, wholesale or retail.
> june 13   68tf

Cincinnati Daily Gazette, June 13, 1836

> **SILVER-WARE MANUFACTORY REMOVED.**
> EDWARD KINSEY has removed his Silver-ware Manufactory from the corner of Third and Walnut streets, to the corner of Sixth and Walnut, where all orders in his line of business will be thankfully received and executed with punctuality and despatch. A good assortment of Silver Spoons kept constantly on hand, and will be disposed of at the very lowest prices. His customers, and the public generally, are respectfully invited to call and examine for themselves.
> feb 2   72tf

Cincinnati Daily Gazette, February 2, 1838

Also in 1838 the Ohio Mechanics Institute began what was to become an Annual Fair, with exhibits in many classifications. The Report of the Committee on Silverware of that year had the following to say of E. Kinsey, "The subscribers, having examined the specimens of silver ware by Mr. E. Kinsey, consisting of a beautiful silver pitcher, a cup, table and tea spoons, silver and pearl handled knives, etc., adjudge, that Mr. Kinsey is entitled to a certificate for the skill in workmanship, and the good taste displayed in the form and fashion of his articles."

Records of later Fairs were also found and these included notices of certificates and prizes awarded to E. Kinsey and E. & D. Kinsey for silverware entered in the Fair, the most interesting being a record of 1851, when the entry of E. & D. Kinsey was a silver speaking trumpet. One can't help but wonder what became of that silver trumpet.

One other interesting bit of information found in the old Fair records was an 1857 entry of crayon drawings by Miss Eugenia Kinsey (Edward's daughter) which were described as "very prettily penciled, for a maid of fourteen."

The panic of 1839 must have affected Kinsey as it did all men of the time, but his ad in the *Daily Gazette* of August 26, 1840 stated that "not withstanding the hard times he still continues the manufacture of silverware...."

The 1840 Cincinnati City Directory carried the ad on the following page.

EDWARD KINSEY,

SILVER WARE MANUFACTURER,

Corner of Sixth & Walnut streets,

CINCINNATI.

In March of 1843 Edward Kinsey sold his stock in trade to David Kinsey (see David Kinsey) for some unexplained reason. In July of the same year, the included notice that he had recommenced business appeared in the newspaper. Then in January of 1844, the notice of the formation of the E. & D. Kinsey Silver Ware Manufactory appeared in the newspaper. (See notice on the following page.) This partnership of the Kinsey brothers lasted until Edward's retirement in 1861.

Cincinnati Daily Gazette, July 8, 1843

A group of cups of varying sizes, all made by E. & D. Kinsey.

Private collection.

The two brothers produced a large quantity of holloware and flatware, and silver by E. & D. Kinsey continues to turn up frequently.

In 1840 Edward had married Temperance H., born in Indiana in 1821. In 1841 their daughter Eugenia was born. The Kinseys had two other children, Catherine and Edward, both of whom died at two years of age.

The 1850 Census listed as living in the same household, Edward and David Kinsey, their wives Temperance and Julia, as well as Thomas Kinsey, 77 years old, a silversmith from Wales, and Edward and Temperance's daughter Eugenia.

Edward Kinsey's will, written in 1855, made provisions for his aged father Thomas, then 83, and his daughter Eugenia. But Eugenia died in 1862, and Thomas Kinsey in July of 1865, so when Edward died in October of 1865, only his wife survived him.

Cincinnati Daily Gazette, January 24, 1844

A beautiful water pitcher by Edwd. Kinsey. This pitcher is nearly fourteen inches high and weighs 43 troy oz. *Private collection.*

Much beautiful silver remains made by the Kinseys. Marks found on silver by E. Kinsey are included below.

SCOVIL & KINSEY

Edward Kinsey

E. KINSEY

E & D. KINSEY

E & D. KINSEY

E. & D. KINSEY (incised)

KINSEY (incised)

Another mark of E. Kinsey is illustrated below. His marks sometimes include an eagle and the word Cincinnati.

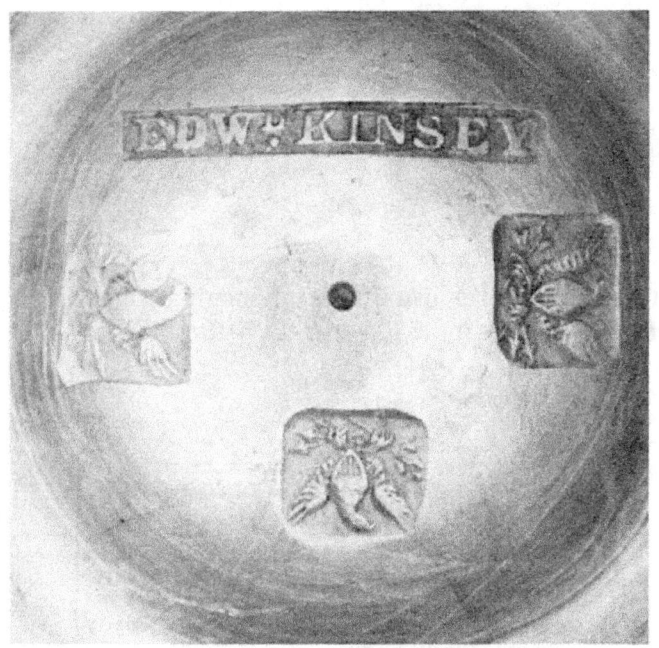

The mark which appears on the pitcher illustrated on the opposite page.

Illustrations of E. Kinsey's work can be found on the following pages: On page 122 two cups by Scovil & Kinsey; on page 18 a pair of early spectacles by Scovil & Kinsey; on page 85 a group of cups of varying sizes by E. & D. Kinsey; on page xiii a twist handled butter knife by E. & D. Kinsey; and on page 86 a beautiful early water pitcher by E. Kinsey.

E. & D. KINSEY .... *(1844-1861)*

LABOYTEAUX, ISAAC N. *(b. 1824, d. 1894)* .... (w. 1850-1857)

According to cemetery records, Isaac N. Laboyteaux was born in Cincinnati in 1824, the son of Peter and Phoebe Laboyteaux.

From 1850 until 1857 Laboyteaux was a partner of William Huntington in the jewelry business (see Huntington). In later years Laboyteaux worked for Herman Duhme, the jeweler, as a salesman. Laboyteaux died in Cincinnati in 1894 and is buried in Spring Grove Cemetery.

He left behind his mark on silver spoons, as private collections and the Ohio Historical Society Collection include spoons marked:

HUNTINGTON & LABOYTEAUX

LEVI, BARNIT .... (w. 1822-1825)

The name Barnit Levi was never listed in the Cincinnati Directory, but the included ad, which appeared in the newspaper in 1822, attests to the fact that he was working in Cincinnati, at least for a brief time.

> **To Watch Makers.**
> THE subscribers have for sale, a set of Watch Makers' Tools; also, a good assortment of Watch Materials, which they will sell low for cash, at their store, No. 116, Main-street, (nearly opposite the Post Office.)
> BARNIT LEVI & CO.
> March 12.   48-3t
> N. B. WATCHES repaired on reasonable terms and at the shortest notice.

Cincinnati Advertiser, March 12, 1822

The *Cincinnati Advertiser* in 1824 and 1825, carried a weekly directory of merchants and the following listing appeared:

> Levi, Barnet, Silversmith and
> Watchmaker, Main and Third.

By the end of 1825, however, Levi's name was no longer listed and no further mention of him was found.

LEVY, JONAS (w. 1825-1834)

Jonas Levy, from England, appeared in the 1825 Cincinnati Directory as a watchmaker and silversmith on Lower Market.

In 1829 he opened his own store and the newspaper carried the included large advertisement.

The 1831 Directory listed him as a jeweler and also as the owner of clothing stores, but in 1834 he was listed only as a jeweler. Currier lists a Jonas Levy working in New York from 1835 through 1838, and since the Cincinnati Directory does not carry his name, there is a possibility that Levy went to New York to work for a few years. But in 1838 a Cincinnati newspaper carried a notice of a new establishment, the auction and commission business of Mr. Jonas Levy (see below).

Cincinnati Daily Gazette, January 11, 1838

The Cincinnati Directory of 1840 listed Levy as an auction and commission merchant; this was the last directory listing of Levy in Cincinnati.

B. H. Caldwell, Jr. in his article on Tennessee silversmiths, appearing in *The Magazine Antiques* in December 1971, lists Jonas Levy as working in Memphis from 1855 to 1860.

Currier's book on the marks of early American silversmiths includes the following mark and states that it is probably the mark of Jonas Levy, Jeweler, New York, N.Y., (1836-1838).

National Republican, October 26, 1829

LONG, HARMON (HERMAN) *(b. ?, d. 1824)* .... (w. 1804-1806)

Harmon Long is included in this book because for a brief time he was a partner of Philip Price in the clock and watchmaking and jewelry business. The included ad for Long & Price appeared in the *Western Spy* in September of 1804. This partnership was dissolved on June 10, 1806. Harmon Long continued in the tinning business.

A Harmon Long was listed in the first Cincinnati City Directory in 1819 as a tailor. This could have been the same man.

From J. Deterly's diary we learn that Herman Long died October 24, 1824.

The subscribers

Respectfuly inform the public that they have commenced the Clock & Watchmaking business at the corner of main & front street where they have Clocks of all kinds for sale. Watches will be cleaned and repaired and other kinds of gold and silver work done on the most reasonable terms and on the shortest notice. They hope from their knowledge in the business and attention, they will be able to give the public general satisfaction.

Long & Price.

Cincinnati, Sept. 4, 1804.

N. B. The public is likewise informed, that Harman Long carries on the Tinning business, in all its various branches, where merchants and others may be supplied at the above mentioned place on reasonable terms by wholesale and retail. (tbctf.)

Western Spy, September 4, 1804

MARTIN, JAMES H. *(b. 1814, d. 1890)* .... (w. 1836-1853)

James H. Martin was born in Rhode Island in 1814. He worked as a watchmaker and jeweler in Cincinnati for about seventeen years. His first listing in the Cincinnati Directory occurred in 1836. In this same year he became the partner of William Eaves and the included ad appeared in the newspaper. We do not know when this partnership was dissolved, but the 1840 Cincinnati Directory did not list the firm. In 1841 Martin became a partner of John Owen and the included ad appeared in October of that year. But by the time of the publishing of the 1842 Directory, these two men were no longer listed as partners.

JEWELRY MANUFACTORY.

EAVES & MARTIN, on Walnut street between Pearl and Third streets, in the upper part of Coopers & Saulnier's Silver Smith Shop, have commenced the above business in all its branches. All orders executed in the best workmanship manner, and at the shortest notice.

N. B. Jewelry neatly repaired at the above place.

Cincinnati Daily Gazette, January 4, 1836

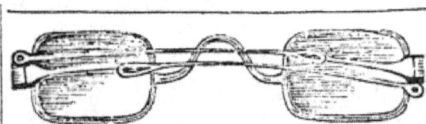

MARTIN & OWEN, Manufacturers of SPECTACLES and JEWELRY, on Third street 3 doors West of Walnut, where can be found at all times a complete assortment of SPECTACLES and JEWELRY, of the latest and most approved styles. From their long experience in business they feel confident of being able to give perfect satisfaction to those who may favor them with their custom.

N. B—GLASSES to suit all sights warranted for one year. oc 1 3m

Daily Times, October 20, 1841

Martin was listed in succeeding directories as a watchmaker or jeweler until 1853. In the years following 1853 a James Martin was listed with no occupation and in later directories as a real estate broker.

The 1850 Census included in the household of James H. Martin his wife Jane and two sons and a daughter. James H. and his wife both died in Decatur, Illinois, but are buried in Spring Grove Cemetery.

A private collection includes a sauce ladle marked:

J. H. MARTIN

MARTIN & OWEN .... *(1841)*

McCULLOUGH, C. B. .... (w. 1827-1828)

C. B. McCullough's name does not appear in any Cincinnati directory, but he did work in Cincinnati as a watch repairer, for a short time.

Deterly's diary entry for November 14, 1827, was the following: "C.B. McCullough set in to work at watch repairing", (at S. A. M. Shipp's). McCullough's name is also mentioned in the Shipp ad appearing on page 125.

McCullough eventually became a partner of G. L. White, from Cincinnati, in Madison Indiana. An ad for the two men appeared in the *Republican and Banner* newspaper on February 27, 1834.

McGREW, ALEXANDER *(b. ?, d. 1843)* .... (w. 1805-1836)

Alexander McGrew was born in Williamsport, Pa., date unknown. According to an article which appeared in *Kenny's Illustrated Cincinnati of 1875,* McGrew commenced his business in Cincinnati in 1805. But the first information about McGrew found in the Cincinnati newspapers dates from September 14, 1811, when the *Western Spy* carried a notice of the marriage of M. Aurelia Heywood to Alexander McGrew of Williamsport, Pa.

We can be certain that Alexander McGrew was a firm believer in the institution of marriage. Aurelia died in 1820 and by 1822 McGrew had married Alvira L. Fisher, from New Jersey, the daughter of Browlow and Elizabeth Fisher. When Alvira died in 1824, Alexander married again. This time his bride was Margaret Amelia, who died in 1834 at forty-one years of age. And when Alexander died in 1843, his wife was Carolina Carter, so he had taken a fourth wife!

McGrew's children mentioned in his will were Alexander M., William K., Robert I., Amelia M., and Caroline E.C.

ALEX. McGREW & JOS. JONAS,
Clock and Watch Makers
AND
Silversmiths and Jewellers,

[*Mr. Jonas being immediately from LONDON*]
TAKE this method to inform the citizens of Cincinnati and the public in general, that they have commenced business in the above branches at their shop on Main street, one door above the Post Office, where they hope by their strict attention to business to merit a share of public patronage.

JOSEPH JONAS, having studied the Watch finishing business in London, they feel confident in assuring the public, that Clocks, Watches and Timepieces of every description, entrusted to them, shall be carefully repaired and duly attended to.

Cincinnati, April 14.   54-tf

Western Spy, April 14, 1817

From 1817 until he retired in 1836, Alexander McGrew advertised more than any silversmith of the time. The first ad found in the newspapers appeared in 1817, when McGrew formed a partnership with Joseph Jonas, noting that Mr. Jonas was "immediately from London". (See ad on previous page.)

This partnership lasted only two years, and the included notice of dissolution of partnership appeared in the newspaper in May of 1819. McGrew remained at his old stand, as shops were then called.

Alexander McGrew was listed in the Cincinnati directories, from the first Directory in 1819 until his retirement in 1836, as a silversmith or watchmaker. The included ad, which appeared in 1829, is typical of the ads which he ran in the newspaper during his years in

Dissolution of Partnership.

THE partnership heretofore existing between Alexander M'Grew and Joseph Jonas, watch makers, this day ceases, and is dissolved by mutual consent. All debts owing by the firm will be paid as before, and all due to it, will be received by Alexander M'Grew, who is authorized to receive the same. Those who stand indebted to the above firm, are respectfully solicited to call and settle their accounts immediately. The business will be continued by Alexander M'Grew, at the old stand on Main street, next door to the Post Office.   ALEXANDER M'GREW,
JOSEPH JONAS.

May 17, 1819.   48 tf

Removal.

JOSEPH JONAS, begs leave to inform his friends and the public in general, that he has removed to No. 121, corner of Main and Third streets, where he hopes by a strict attention to the watch repairing business still to merit a share of their favours.

The Inquisitor & Cincinnati Advertiser, May 17, 1819

THE undersigned having disposed of his entire stock in trade in the Watch and Jewelry business to Wilson M'Grew, respectfully requests a settlement with all who have accounts with him. He embraces the occasion of his withdrawing from business, to return his acknowledgements for the liberal patronage bestowed upon him, and of respectfully recommending his successor, (who remains in the old stand) to the consideration and favors of his friends and the public.
Jan. 25. 51tf   ALEX'R. M'GREW.

Cincinnati Daily Gazette, January 25, 1836

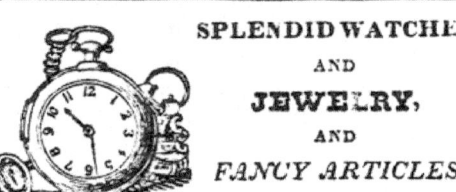

SPLENDID WATCHES
AND
JEWELRY,
AND
FANCY ARTICLES,

Now just opening nearly opposite the U. S. Bank, Main street, and between the Cincinnati Hotel and Sycamore on Front streets.

THE undersigned has just returned from N. York, and now offers goods in his line of a superior quality at the lowest prices; consisting in part of the following articles: Ladies and gentlemens gold lever, lapine, extra jeweled watches, silver lever lapine and vertical do., superior mantle and Chamber time pieces, the latter repeating hours and quarters, gold chains, seals, keys, hooks miniature frames, and medallions, coral, cameo, mosaic, topaz and filagree ear-rings, diamond, pearl, ruby, garnet and friendship finger-rings and breast pins, gold and silver mounted tortoise shell, pearl and ivory snuff boxes, open end silver thimbles, silver pens and ever pointed pencil cases, gold and silver double and single eyed spectacles, Brittania tea setts, new patterns, plated liquor stands, castors, candlesticks, bread, cake, and fruit baskets, gold and gilt bracelets and waist buckles, guard and cable chains, crosses and hearts, plated soup, table, tea, mustard and salt spoons, metallic bronze astral and mantle lamps newest pattern, suspending entry and glass lamps, percussion lock guns & pistols, swords, epaulets, tassel, lace, binding, plumes, eagles, belt spurs, ivory ballance handle setts knives and forks, brass shovel's and tongs, bellows, hearth brushes, brass stair rods and eyes, spy glasses, tellescopes and eye glasses, ladies' dress buttons, &c. together with a great variety of *Fancy Goods.* Ladies and gentlemen are respectfully invited to call and examine for themselves.

ALSO—A complete assortment of clock and watch makers' tools and materials, clock movements, dials, bells, and which he will sell to country watchmaker on reasonable terms.
ALEXANDER M'GREW.
N. B. *One splendid Silver Tea Sett.*
May 21.   91tf

Cincinnati Daily Gazette, May 21, 1829

A pair of early Cincinnati spoons made by Alexander McGrew and marked A. McGrew in a cartouche.

Private collection.

business. At the end of this ad McGrew mentions "One Splendid Silver Tea Sett". We cannot help but wonder if that "Splendid Tea Sett" is still in existence.

An editorial in the *Cincinnati Daily Gazette* of December, 1830, discussing a proposal McGrew had made for the construction of a railroad, describes him as a "talented and enterprising citizen of this place."

In 1836 the notice on the preceeding page appeared in the newspaper, announcing that Alexander was disposing of his entire stock in trade to Wilson McGrew, probably his younger brother. Alexander died seven years later, in 1843. The McGrew family continued in the jewelry and watchmaking business in Cincinnati for many years. (See Wilson and William Wilson McGrew.)

Flat silver made by Alexander McGrew is in private collections. The mark used was:

A.McGREW

An illustration of an early tablespoon bearing this mark appears on page 15. Another illustration of A. McGrew spoons appears above.

McGREW, WILSON *(b. 1800, d. 1859)* .... **(w. 1825-1859)**

Wilson McGrew was born in Pennsylvania in 1800. The first eleven years of his silversmithing career in Cincinnati (1825-1836) were spent at the shop of Alexander McGrew, who was most probably Wilson's older brother.

In January of 1836 Alexander McGrew retired from the business and disposed of his entire stock to Wilson. (See A. McGrew.) In the same year the *Cincinnati Daily Evening Post* of December 12 carried a notice of the death of Sarah McGrew, aged twenty-nine, wife of Wilson McGrew.

In September of 1840 McGrew ran the included ad. As we can see he was also advertising in Maysville and Lexington, Ky.

We cannot help but wonder for what reason Wilson McGrew published the in-

> **WATCHES, JEWELRY, AND SILVERWARE.**
> I HAVE lately returned from the eastern cities with a large and splendid assortment of Gold and Silver patent lever, lepine, common, English and French Watches; gold Chains, Seals, Keys, Breast-pins, Finger-rings; gold and silver Spectacles, Pencils, and Thimbles. Also, silver Tea setts, plated ware, consisting of Candlesticks and branches, Waiters, Baskets, &c; new and beautiful patterns Brittania ware; table Cutlery; Penknives and Scissors; mantel Clocks; dining-room Timepieces. With a general assortment of useful and ornamental goods in my line, which I will sell on the best terms.
> sep 15 84-1m   WILSON McGREW.
> Maysville Eagle and Lexington Observer and Reporter will publish weekly to amount of $2 each, and charge this office.

Daily Gazette, Sept. 15, 1840

cluded notice in 1841. Possibly he went to another city, as his name did not appear in the 1842 and 1843 Directories. But McGrew returned to work in Cincinnati as an ad appeared in the *Cincinnati Daily Gazette* in June of that year for Wilson McGrew and Joseph P. Beggs (McGrew & Beggs), and in 1844 Kimball's Mississippi Valley Directory carried this large ad for the partnership.

> **LAST NOTICE.**
> THE subscriber has left his books and accounts with Joseph P. Beggs, at the stand lately occupied by him and earnestly requests all indebted to him to call and settle without delay.
> J. P. Beggs continues the business in the same store and is authorized to make all settlements, and receipt for all monies due me.   WILSON McGREW.
> may 20   (Repub copy 1 week)

Daily Gazette, May 20, 1841

McGREW & BEGGS,

DEALERS IN

WATCHES, JEWELRY, SILVER WARE,

AND

FANCY GOODS,

No. 157, Main Street, between Third and Fourth.

N. B. All kinds of Watches, Clocks and Jewelry repaired and warranted.

McGrew & Beggs continued to advertise often during the years of their partnership, but by 1848 Beggs had become a partner of Harry Smith (Beggs & Smith) and Wilson McGrew was working alone.

The 1850 Census listed Wilson McGrew as a jeweler and included his children, William Wilson, 17, and Sallie, 16.

McGrew's shop was listed under his name until 1855, when the listing became W. McGrew & Son. Wilson McGrew died in 1859, leaving the business to his young son, William Wilson McGrew.

The marks found on silver are:

W. McGREW

McGREW & BEGGS

W. McGREW & SON

Flatware with the above marks is not uncommon. The Cincinnati Art Museum had some W. McGrew flat silver on display, and illustrated on page 117 is a sugar tongs marked W. McGrew. Other illustrations included are a butter knife on page xiii and a miniature spoon on page 42, both by McGrew & Beggs.

The front view of a Victorian engraved water pitcher bearing the mark W.W. McGrew, incised. *Private collection.*

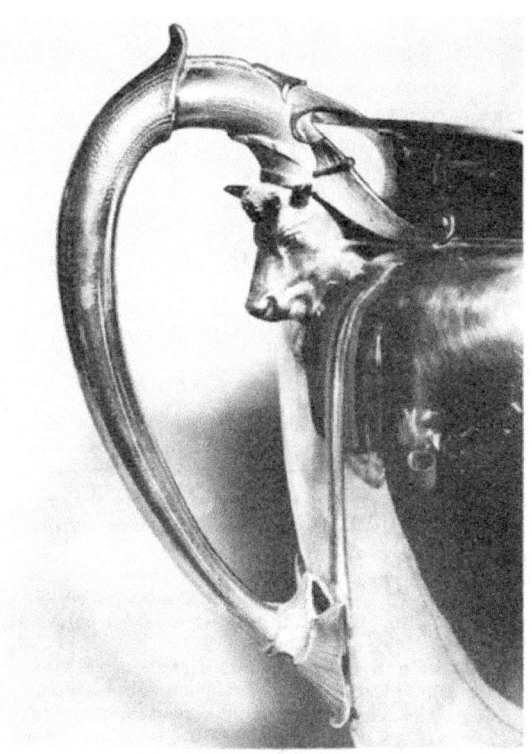

A detail of the handle of the water pitcher.

McGREW, WILLIAM WILSON (b. 1832, d. 1892) .... (w. 1856-1875)

William Wilson McGrew, born in Cincinnati in 1832, was the son of Wilson and Sarah McGrew. His obituary states that "he indicated a great aptitude for business at the early age of seventeen and left college and entered the store of his father, Wilson, then the leading jeweler of the city." When he was twenty four the firm became W. McGrew & Son, and when his father died three years later William Wilson took over the business.

The McGrew business in Cincinnati was started by Alexander McGrew in 1805 and continued until 1878. Although William Wilson McGrew started in the business after 1850, he is included in this book because of the long association of the McGrew name with Cincinnati silver, and also because quite a bit of silver marked W. W. McGrew or William W McGrew exists today.

Describing Mr. McGrew, his obituary states: "Conspicuous among the many leading traits of his character was his sterling integrity, his industry and his rare kindness to the poor, but most prominent of all was his gentle disposition and loyal devotion to his family."

Included on page 95 is an illustration of an interesting Victorian water pitcher and a detail of the handle. The pitcher is marked:

W. W. MCGREW (incised)

McGREW & BEGGS .... *(1843-1848)*

McGREW & JONAS .... *(1817-1819)*

W. McGREW & SON .... *(1855-1859)*

McHENRY, DENNIS .... **(w. 1832-1851)**

Conway & McHenry,
Jewellers, Watchmakers & Silversmiths,
NO. 159, MAIN STREET,
(*Opposite United States' Bank,*)
HAVE this day opened a splendid assortment of articles in their line, consisting of
Gold and Silver patent Levers and plain Watches; Ladies' and Gentlemens' gold Chains, Seals and Keys; coral, cameo, enamelled, topaz, and jet Ear Rings and Breast Pins, new patterns; Diamond, Enamelled, Ruby, Pearl and Jet Finger Rings; Ruby, Pearl, Jet and Enamelled Breast and Collar Buttons; Miniature Settings; Filagree, Jet and Enamelled Lockets; Gold and Silver Spectacles; Ever Pointed Pencils, elegant patterns; Silver Table, Tea, Desert and Cream Spoons and Sugar Tongs; Silver Thimbles; plated Table and Tea Spoons; Music Boxes; Snuff Boxes; Dirk Knives; Pen Knives; Scissors; Dirks; Pocket Books; &c. &c. &c.
PLATED STEEL HANDLED CASTORS (a new article,) & CANDLESTICKS of a superior quality.
BRITTANIA WARE in sets, and a general assortment of articles in the FANCY LINE selected by themselves in the cities of New York, Philadelphia and Baltimore.
A practical knowledge of the above branches will enable them to execute any article to order.
Diamonds and Pearls set. Filagree and Strung Pearl work neatly repaired and re-coloured. Watches and Clocks repaired,
Highest price for old Gold and Silver.
May 1   100-5

Cincinnati Daily Gazette, May 1, 1832

Pleasants and Sill, in their book on Maryland silversmiths, listed Dennis McHenry as working in Baltimore from 1827 until 1830. This book also mentions a record of the marriage of Dennis McHenry, Jr. and Sarah Macauley in 1827.

When McHenry left Baltimore in 1830 he may have come directly to Cincinnati, since a daily newspaper of 1832 carried the included ad for the firm of Conway & McHenry. (Thomas Conway had also come from Baltimore.)

This partnership lasted less than two years, as in February of 1834 a Cincinnati newspaper carried the following notice of the dissolution of the firm of Conway & McHenry.

McHenry continued to work at the old stand and the 1834 and 1836 City Directories listed him as a silversmith. The ad shown on the following page appeared in the newspaper in 1834.

> **DISSOLUTION OF PARTNERSHIP.**
>
> THE partnership heretofore existing under the firm of Conway & M'Henry, is dissolved by mutual consent. All persons having claims against the said firm, are requested to send the same for payment to D. McHenry who is authorised to settle the same, and all persons indebted, are requested to make immediate payment to him.
>
> T. A. CONWAY,
> D. McHENRY.
>
> feb 10

Cincinnati Whig, Feb. 10, 1834

> **D. McHENRY,**
>
> AT the old stand on Main street, opposite the United States Bank, still continues the Jewelry, Watch-making, & Silversmith Business, in all their branches, and solicits a continuance of the public patronage.
> feb 10

Cincinnati Whig, February 10, 1834

McHenry's shop must not have been very successful, as the 1840 Directory listed him as a silversmith at Palmer & Hanks.

Dennis McHenry continued to be listed in the directories as a silversmith or jeweler until 1851, but after that time nothing further is known of him.

McQUARTERS, HUGH .... (w. 1817-1819)

The household of Hugh McQuarters which appeared on the 1817 tax list included two adult males, two adult females and one male child under twelve. McQuarters did not own property.

The 1819 Cincinnati Directory listed McQuarters as a silversmith at 111 Main, his residence on 6th between Main and Walnut. McQuarters was not listed, however, in the 1820 Census, and nothing more is known of him.

MOORE, SAMUEL P. *(b. ?, d. 1832)* .... (w. 1832)

Samuel P. Moore was, for a brief time, a partner in the jewelry and watchmaking business of Thomas F. Rhodes. In May of 1832 a notice appeared in the newspaper of the establishment of the firm of Moore & Rhodes (see Thomas F. Rhodes). In June of 1832 the partnership was dissolved due to the death of Moore.

Whether this was the same Samuel Moore who was listed in the 1825 Cincinnati Directory as a merchant, we do not know. But since this book is concerned with silversmiths, jewelers, watch and clockmakers we include Samuel Moore because of his business association with Thomas F. Rhodes.

MOORE & RHODES .... *(1832)*

MORROW (MORO, MOREAU), FRANCIS .... (w. 1836-1844)

Francis Morrow was listed in the 1836 Cincinnati Directory as a clockmaker, located on 6th between John and Smith.

In 1839 the included ad appeared in a Cincinnati newspaper.

> **FRANCIS MORROW,**
> **CLOCK MAKER,**
> *Corner of Sixth and Elm streets.*
> ☞ Clocks, Watches, and Jewellery repaired at the shortest notice, on reasonable terms.

Cincinnati Advertiser & Journal, December 3, 1839

The last listing of Morrow occurred in 1844, when he was listed as a watchmaker, located on London between Carr and Horne.

MUSGROVE, SAMUEL *(b. 1800, d. ?)* .... (w. 1820-1840)

The Kovels, in their book on American silversmiths, list an S. Musgrove, location unknown. The following information should be helpful to students and collectors of coin silver.

According to correspondence received from Kentucky, Samuel Musgrove was born in Kentucky in 1800, the son of Cuthbert and Elizabeth Moore Musgrove.

Although Musgrove's name did not appear in a Cincinnati Directory until 1831, J. Deterly's diary gives us much additional information. On March 7, 1820, Deterly noted that Abner Sotcher and Samuel Musgrove had commenced business together. But this partnership lasted only a month as on April 7, 1820, Deterly remarked, "Messrs Sotcher and Musgrove dissolved their partnership concerns."

Deterly mentioned Musgrove again on May 14, 1827, when he stated, "James Phillips returned to set in again to work with Samuel Musgrove to learn the silversmithing business." Deterly also noted Samuel Musgrove's marriage on May 15, 1828.

Without a doubt the most unusual entry in Deterly's diary concerning Musgrove was the following, "Aug. 21, 1831. DETECTION. The silver breast plate which had been attached to David Kilgour's coffin when his body was interred, was a few days ago detect'd, it was offer'd for sale as old silver braised up: at S. Musgrove's shop."

Musgrove was listed as a silversmith in the Cincinnati Directories from 1831 until 1840. When Musgrove left Cincinnati, he returned to Larue County Kentucky, and the 1850 census for that county, listed him as a gold and silversmith.

B.H. Caldwell, Jr., in his article on Tennessee silversmiths, listed Musgrove as working in Nashville from 1850 until 1860.

Flat silver in private collection bears the following marks:

S.MUSGROVE

S.MUSGROVE

From the shape of the spoons we can conclude that the first mark is the earlier of the two.

NAGELE, VITAL .... (w. 1846-1875)

In 1846 Vital Nagele appeared in the Cincinnati Directory listed as a watchmaker. The 1848 Business Directory listed him under watch and clockmakers, and located him on the south side of 5th between Western Row and John. He continued to be listed as a watchmaker at varying addresses until 1875.

The 1850 Census listed him as a silversmith from Germany, and also listed his wife Mary, and his children Louis, Amala (?), and Elizabeth.

There seems to have been some confusion on the spelling of Nagele's name. Listed are some of the variations encountered: Vitle Nagale; Fedal Nagel; Videl Nageld; Vital Naegele; Fidele Nagele.

NASH, COLEMAN .... (w. 1825)

Coleman Nash, from Rhode Island, was listed in the 1825 Cincinnati Directory as working at 58 Main as a watchmaker and silversmith. 58 Main was the shop address of Enos Woodruff, watchmaker and silversmith, so it is doubtful that any silver will be found marked with Nash's name. By the time of the publishing of the next Directory in 1829, Nash was no longer listed.

NORTH, ALEXANDER H. .... (w. 1831-1834)

Alexander North, from Connecticut, was listed in the 1831 and 1834 Cincinnati Directories as a clockmaker. In the 1836 Directory he was listed as a finisher and by 1842 his name no longer appeared in the directories.

NUTTMAN, JOHN C.

The following ad is included because a Nutman was recorded in Lexington in 1818. The Hiatts' book on Kentucky silversmiths states: "The firm of January and Nutman, silver platers, were in business on Main Street in Lexington in 1818." The Nuttman in this ad might be the same man.

> **SEAL ENGRAVING.**
> SEALS for *LODGES, COURTS, RECORDERS, NOTARIES,* and *PUBLIC OFFICES;* Stamps for *POST-OFFICES;* Rolls, Flowers, and Letters for *BOOK-BINDERS,* &c. will be executed in the best manner, and on moderate terms, by the subscriber, at SEYMOUR & WILLISTON's, Silversmiths and Jewellers, No 95, Main street. Orders will receive prompt attention.
> JOHN C. NUTTMAN.
> Cincinnati, 8th July, 1820.   es40-tf

Liberty Hall, August 2, 1820

OSKAMP, CLEMENS *(b. 1822, d. 1887)* .... (w. 1852-1887)

According to his obituary, Clemens Oskamp "was born in Westphalia, Prussia in 1822, one of seven sons of Caspar and Theresa Oskamp. His father brought his family to America to avoid being forced into military service, under the Prussian rules, and especially as he was a sympathizer with France."

Clemens Oskamp learned the trade of brass finisher in the foundry of Harkness & Niles, and was employed on the first locomotive built in Cincinnati.

Theodore, Clemens' brother, had established a jewelry business at 62 Main in about 1848, and in 1852 he induced Clemens to join him in the business. Shortly before Theodore's death in 1854, Clemens became a partner, and when Theodore died he bequeathed the business to Clemens.

The business remained and prospered at 62 Main until 1868 when Clemens Oskamp erected a five story building at 175 Main. At that time this was between Fourth and Fifth, since the blocks were not numbered as they are today. The included picture of the building appeared in *Kenny's Illustrated Cincinnati of 1875*.

CLEMENS OSKAMP.

The above book also included a picture of Oskamp's manufactory, shown at left, and the following description of it:

THE MANUFACTORY.

"The manufactory contains the newest and most perfect machinery and devices by which the firm is enabled to turn our patterns of workmanship of the most exquisite and beautiful finish. In tableware the firm excel, their production being considered equal to the best made tableware manufactured in this country...."

The days of the hand made silver produced by individual craftsmen were gone, but fine silver was produced in Oskamp's manufactory, and much of it remains and is used and enjoyed today.

The *History of Cincinnati and Hamilton County*, written in 1894, included an article which states of Oskamp "...By his individual enterprise and strict business integrity he built up a trade which extends through all the adjoining states and as far away as Virginia, Iowa, Kansas, Illinois and Tennessee."

Oskamp died in 1887, leaving his widow Mary Fisher Oskamp and four sons and four daughters. Oskamp's son Alfred and his son-in-law John Daller continued his business. Another son, William, became a partner of Charles Nolting in 1881 and founded Oskamp, Nolting.

Flat silver by Oskamp is frequently seen. Possibly the earliest mark used was

C **O**

sometimes accompanied by an anchor. Other marks used were:

C.OSKAMP

C. O. (incised)

C. OSKAMP (incised)

Beautiful twist flatware was made by Oskamp, as well as by Duhme & Co., the Kinseys, and C. Hellebush. Examples of twist flatware are illustrated on page xiii.

OSKAMP, THEODORE *(b. ?, d. 1854)* .... **(w. 1848-1854)**

Theodore Oskamp was the first Oskamp in the jewelry, watchmaking and silversmithing business. We know that he had started the business by 1848, since Williams' Business Directory of that year carried the listing of Theodore Oskamp at 62 Main. After Theodore had the business established, he induced his brother Clemens to join him. When Theodore died in 1854, his will left the business to Clemens: "I give and bequeath to my brother Clemens the stock in trade and business of the firm of which he is a partner and the good will of the firm as the successor thereof, on condition of his paying the cost of said stock, giving him ten years for the payment thereof with interest payable annually at six percent per annum."

The inventory of his estate lists assets of about $59,000, which must have been a sizeable estate for a young man in those days. It was interesting to find in the inventory several familiar names. Both Luke Kent and H. Duhme had notes payable to the estate.

Theodore Oskamp was one of seven sons of Caspar and Theresa Oskamp and was born in Westphalia, Prussia. His father brought the family to America in 1835 and they came almost directly to Cincinnati. Oskamp's wife was Margaret Freye, daughter of Henry Freye.

Silver marked T. Oskamp has been seen. The spoons are of the unusual shape of exaggerated fiddle illustrated on page xii.

The mark used was:

T.OSKAMP

OWEN, CHARLES *(b. 1824, d. 1900)* .... **(w. 1846-1887)**

Charles Owen, a brother of William Owen, was born in West Dedham, Massachuestts, in 1824. In 1846 he was listed in the Cincinnati Directory as a watchmaker boarding at William Owen's. In later directories he was listed as a jeweler or watchmaker working at his brother's shop.

From 1861 until 1867 the shop was listed under Charles Owen. Then in 1868 it became William Owen & Co. Charles was a partner of his brother William until he retired in 1887.

Charles Owen's wife was Maria Louise Mariana. In 1854 they moved from Cincinnati to Newport, Ky., where Owen died in 1900.

OWEN, JOHN *(b. 1810, d. ?)* .... *(w. 1836-1853)*

John Owen was a silversmith and spectacle maker from Pennsylvania, where he was born in 1810. The first Cincinnati Directory listing of Owen was found in 1836, when he was listed as a silversmith boarding at Cyrus Coffin's. In October of 1837 a Cincinnati newspaper carried the included notice of removal.

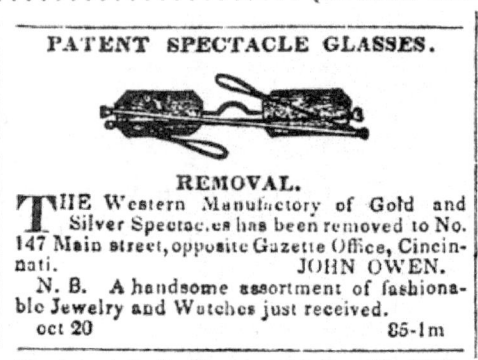

Cincinnati Daily Gazette, October 20, 1837.

Another Cincinnati newspaper carried the included ad, in which Owen stated that he carried spectacles, jewelry and silverware. For a brief time in 1841 Owen became a partner of James H. Martin (Martin & Owen) (see ad under Martin).

Cincinnati Advertiser & Journal, April 18, 1839

In the included notice of removal, which appeared in 1844, we note that Owen advertised silver spoons both on hand and made to order.

The listing of John Owen's Spectacle Manufactory appeared in the directories until 1853.

In 1839 Owen married Isabel Murray, born in Ireland. The 1850 Census listed six children born of this union, four sons and two daughters.

No information is available on John Owen after 1853.

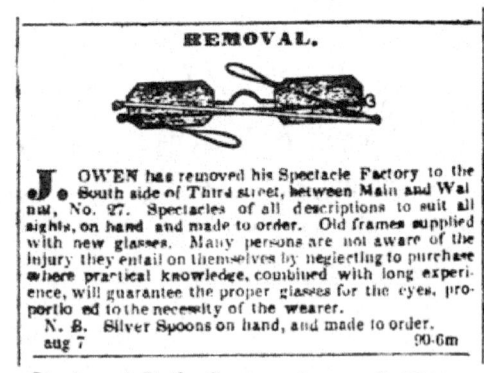

Cincinnati Daily Gazette, August 7, 1844

The Cincinnati Art Museum has an early salt spoon with the following mark:

J.OWEN

Silver spoons of the typical Cincinnati shape of the 1840's are in a private collection. The mark appearing on these spoons is:

An illustration of one of these spoons can be found on page xii.

OWEN, WILLIAM (b. 1810, d. 1888) .... (w. 1835-1885)

William Owen was born in Dedham, Mass. in 1810. According to his obituary, he learned and practiced the clock and watchmaking trade in Boston, where at one time E. Howard, who later became the well known watchmaker, was an apprentice of his.

In 1835 Owen came to Cincinnati, and the 1836 Directory listed him as a clockmaker on the east side of Walnut between Third and Fourth, a partner of Stanley (Stanley & Owen). In 1837 Owen married Kiziah Abigail Merry, and in the same year formed a partnership with James Read (Owen & Read). The included ad appeared in a Cincinnati newspaper in March of that year. The shop was then located at 127 Main.

By 1840 the shop of Owen and Read had moved to 155 Main, and the directory of that year carried the interesting ad which appears below.

The partnership of Owen & Read lasted until 1844, and the notice of the dissolution of the firm appeared in *Cincinnati Daily Gazette,* May 1st, 1844.

By 1846 Owen had associated himself in another partnership, this time with S.T. Carley (Owen & Carley). This was a short-lived partnership, as in the 1848 Williams' Business Directory, William Owen was listed alone.

Owen entered still another partnership in 1850, when he became associated with A. Palmer (Palmer & Owen). This partnership lasted until 1859, with the business located at 135 Main.

OWEN & READ
WATCH AND CLOCK MAKERS,
No. 127, Main street,
A little above Third, Cincinnati:

Have, and keep continually for sale, an assortment of

GOLD AND SILVER
WATCHES.

Among which are Gold and Silver Patent Levers, Quartier and English Silver WATCHES, Gold and Silver SPECTACLES. —JEWELLRY, consting of an elegant assortment of Ear Drops, Finger Rings, Breast Pins, Gold and Silver Pencil Cases, Thimbles—Ladies and Gentlemen's Gold Safety Chains, Seals and Keys—Table, Dessert, Tea, Mustard and Salt SPOONS on hand or manufactured to order—plated Tea and Table Spoons.

☞ SILVER WORK and JEWELLRY of all kinds, made and repaired at the *shortest notice.*

A Boy wanted, twelve or fourteen years old.
mar 27   tf

Daily Evening Post, March 27, 1837

In 1860 the business was again listed under the name William Owen, and Owen's younger brother Charles was working with him. From 1861 until 1867 the business was listed under the name Charles Owen, at the same address as formerly, 135 Main, but in 1868 the name of the business was again changed, this time to William Owen & Co. This listing continued until 1886.

William Owen died in 1888 and was survived by his second wife, Sara Permer, three daughters and four sons.

Examples of flat silver by Owen bear the following marks:

OWEN & CARLEY   Owen & Read

Illustrations of spoons bearing these marks appear on page xii.

PALMER & OWEN (Roman Capitals, incised)

WM. OWEN (Roman Capitals, incised)

W. OWEN & CO. (Roman Capitals, incised)

A beautiful engraved serving spoon by Palmer & Owen is illustrated on page xiii.

OWEN & READ .... *(1837-1844)*

OWEN & CARLEY .... *(1846-1848)*

WM. OWEN .... *(1860-1861)*

W. OWEN & CO. .... *(1868-1886)*

PALMER, ABRAHAM *(b. 1811, d. 1880)* .... **(w. 1834-1859)**

Abraham Palmer was born in Pennsylvania in 1811. He worked for many years as a silversmith and jeweler in Cincinnati. The first Cincinnati Directory listing of Palmer occurred in 1834, where he was listed as a silversmith. In 1835 he was advertising that he was manufacturing silverware and jewelry, and the included ad appeared in the newspaper in that year. The 1838 Ohio Mechanics Institute records of the Committee on Silverware show that A. Palmer entered "a set of castors" in the first Annual Fair to be given by the Institute.

By 1839 Palmer had become a partner of G. L. Hanks (Palmer & Hanks); they advertised instruments for engineers, as the following ad states.

Daily Evening Post, November 24, 1835

A lovely sugar bowl, 10¾ inches tall, marked A. Palmer, incised. *Private collection.*

By 1842 Hanks had become associated with a bell and brass foundry, and Palmer continued in the silversmithing and jewelry business alone. But he again took a partner in 1844, when he became associated in business with Harry R. Smith (Palmer & Smith). The interesting ad for this partnership shown below appeared in the newspaper in 1847.

The partnership of Palmer & Smith was of short duration, like so many partnerships of the time, and in 1848 Palmer was again working alone. The following ad appeared in the newspaper in 1849.

Daily Gazette, June 12, 1839

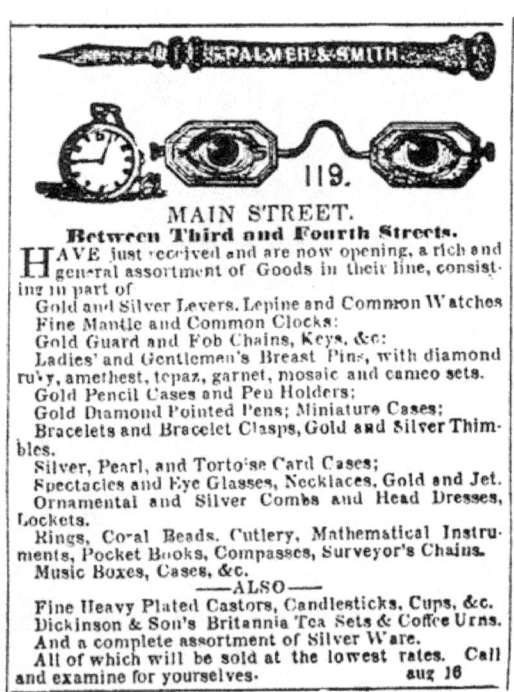

Daily Times, October 27, 1849

Cist's Daily Advertiser, August 16, 1847

By 1850 Palmer had a new partner, this time William Owen (Palmer & Owen). In Charles Cist's account of Cincinnati in 1851, Palmer & Owen were listed under Silver and Goldsmiths, with the following description: "Palmer and Owen, 135 Main, keep three hands engaged in the manufacture of silverware, on a product yearly of $12,000. Watches and jewelry also sold here." The ad shown on the following page for Palmer and Owen appeared in the newspaper in 1850. Palmer and Owen continued to work together until 1859. For a short time after that Palmer was the proprietor of the Western Museum; later he became a real estate agent.

Daily Times, April 21, 1850

Piecing together bits of information, we can surmise that Palmer brought his bride from the east in 1834. She was Julietta, born in Baltimore. She died in Cincinnati in 1836, possibly in childbirth, as a son, William S., was born in that year. There was one other child of this union, Eugene, born in 1833. The 1850 Census listed Eugene Palmer as a finisher; possibly he worked as a silver finisher in his father's shop.

Court House records show that in 1837 Abraham Palmer married Manor Trutebuss. Undoubtedly Palmer needed a mother for his two young sons. From Census records we can deduce that Manor and Abraham Palmer had a son and a daughter. Manor died sometime between 1841 and 1844, and Court House records show that in 1844 Abraham Palmer married Sarah Nehemiah. Abraham and Sarah had five children of whom record was found. In 1868 Abraham lost another wife, as Sarah died of consumption. Abraham Palmer died in 1880 in Cincinnati, and is buried in Spring Grove Cemetery.

Marks seen on silver by Palmer are as follows:

PALMER & SMITH

A. PALMER (incised)

PALMER & OWEN (incised)

A beautiful sugar bowl by Palmer is illustrated on page 105, and an elegantly engraved serving piece marked Palmer & Owen is illustrated on page xiii.

PALMER & HANKS .... *(1839-1840)*

PALMER & OWEN .... *(1850-1859)*

PALMER & SMITH .... *(1844-1847)*

PALMER, H.L. .... (w. 1809)

The included ad appeared in a Cincinnati newspaper in 1809, but H.L. Palmer does not appear to have been listed in any book on silversmiths, and no other information on him has been encountered.

The by-line of the ad is Washington, D.C. so whether this was a mistake, or he was working in Washington and advertising in Cincinnati, we do not know.

Liberty Hall,
Wednesday, November 29, 1809

PERRET, PHILIP H. *(b. ?, d. 1826)* .... (w. 1819-1826)

Although Philip Perret's name does not appear in the 1819 Cincinnati Directory, he undoubtedly arrived some time that year, as the included ad for Perret and Mathey appeared in September of 1819.

This partnership lasted only a little more than a year, as a notice of dissolution appeared in the newspaper in December of 1820. (See following page)

An entry in J. Deterly's diary for August 27, 1822, related the following: "P. H. Perret's girl scrape. This day he received intelligence that the girl he was going to marry in about a fornight from this time ran off with another sweetheart and got married, so

Western Spy, September 3, 1819

> **Dissolution of Partnership.**
>
> THE firm of PERRETT & MATHEY was dissolved on the 15th day of November last by mutual consent. Those indebted to to said concern are requested to call and pay their dues to PHILIP H. PERRETT, who still continues the business of *Watchmaking, Repairing, and Jewelling*, in all its various branches, at the old stand *No. 27, Main street*. He flatters himself that from his experience in the above branches, he will be able to give general satisfaction to those who may favor him with their custom. PHILIP H. PERRETT.
> Cincinnati, December 28, 1820. 43*5

Western Spy, December 28, 1820

Monsieur is left unmarried." Perret did find a bride as Deterly's entry for June 11, 1824: "Marriage. It is rumoured that Philip H. Perret was married last night." Poor Perret did not keep his bride for long, as Deterly recorded her death in October of 1825.

Deterly also recorded other problems encountered by Perret as his entry for October 18, 1822, was the following: "An attempt was made last night on P.H. Perret's shop Door, the lock was nearly forced off with an iron bar, the theiving villain would have got in had he not been disturbed by the approaching of one of neighbors." And then on May 26, 1823 a robbery did occur, as Deterly's entry was: "Robbery on Tuesday afternoon whilst P.H. Perret was out hunting some rogue enter'd his shop thro' the back window and took from thence: 1 gold musical, 1 gold repeater, 2 silver and 1 gilt watches — $100 Reward." Perret did find the culprits, as on July 21st of that year Deterly said that Perret had returned from Lexington, Kentucky, with the two men who had his watches, they are now in jail.

According to Deterly, Perret became a partner of S.A.M. Shipp (Perret & Shipp) in July of 1823, and the Cincinnati Directory listing of 1825 was Perret & Shipp, watchmakers, at 27 Main.

The national Republican of April 11, 1826 carried the included notice of the death of Philip Perret.

> DIED—On Thursday last, Mr. PHILIP H. PERRET, a native of Switzerland, but for several years past a respectable, citizen of this place. His remains were attended to the grave by the Cincinnati Guards and Hussars, of which companies he had been a member.

PERRET & MATHEY .... *(1819-1820)*

PERRET & SHIPP .... *(1823-1826)*

PICARD, J.C. .... **(w. 1840)**

J.C. Picard appeared only once in the Cincinnati Directories, in 1840, when he was listed as a watchmaker from France. His address was given as West 4th between Main and Walnut. He is included in this book because a J.C. Picard was working in Mowrytown, Highland County, Ohio, in the early 1850's. It may have been the same man.

PICKERING, GEORGE M. *(b. 1813, d. ?)* .... **(w. 1842-1862)**

George M. Pickering was born in 1813. He came to Cincinnati from Pennsylvania and his name first appeared in the 1836 Cincinnati Dirctory. The listing was as follows: Coffee house, north east corner of Seventh and Main. In the 1840 Directory no occupation was given, but the 1842 Directory carried the included ad. From this time until 1862 Pickering was listed as a clockmaker, clock repairer or clock manufacturer.

The 1850 Census, lists Pickering, his wife Maria and three children, George, Marcellus and Cornelia.

```
CLOCKS OF ALL KINDS,
EITHER
BRASS OR WOOD,
CAREFULLY CLEANED, REPAIRED,
AND
WARRANTED,
BY G. M. PICKERING,
CLOCK MAKER,
Seventh Street, between Main and Sycamore,
CINCINNATI.
```

PICKERING, JOHN .... (w. 1831-1840)

The Kovels list a John Pickering, working in Philadelphia 1823-1824. Possibly it was the John Pickering whose name first appeared in the Cincinnati Directory in 1829, when he was listed as a coachmaker. This could have been a typographical error, as Pickering was listed as a clockmaker or clock repairer, from 1831 until 1840. The included ad appeared in the 1839-1840 Directory. By the time of the publishing of the next directory John Pickering was listed as an actuary at the Mechanics Institute, and G. M. Pickering had taken over the clock making business.

```
CLOCKS
of all kinds,
EITHER OF BRASS OR WOOD,
CAREFULLY CLEANED,
CORRECTLY REPAIRED,
And Warranted by
JOHN PICKERING,
CLOCK MAKER,
At the Mechanics' Institute, 3d near Broadway,
CINCINNATI.
WHERE all orders in his line of business will be thankfully received
and promptly executed, either in the city or country.
```

PIGMAN, JOHN *(b. 1820, d. ?)* .... (w. 1840-1850)

John Pigman was born in Virginia in about 1820. His wife Nancy was born in Ohio.

Pigman was first listed in the Cincinnati Directory in 1840, when he appeared as a silversmith working at E. Kinsey's. The directories continued to list him as a silversmith at varying addresses until 1850. It is probable that he worked for E. Kinsey, and then for E. & D. Kinsey, while he was in Cincinnati. The Kinseys had a silverware manufactory, as it was called in those days, and had a number of silversmiths working for them.

Pigman was listed in the 1850 Census as a silversmith, but after 1850 his name disappeared from the directories.

PRATT, E.P. *(b. 1801, d. 1866)* .... (w. 1828-1829)

The Kovels list E.P. Pratt as a silversmith in the nineteenth century, location unknown; it is possible, however, to shed some light on Pratt's career.

Pratt came to Cincinnati from Chillicothe in 1828, and the included ad appeared in a Cincinnati newspaper in July of that year. Ads were found for E.P. Pratt in a Chillicothe newspaper in 1827, and in March of 1828 when he advertised the formation of his partnership with C.C. Beard (Pratt & Beard).

Whether they intended to operate shops in both towns, or Beard followed Pratt to Cincinnati, we can only surmise, but in August of 1828 the ad appearing on the following page was published in a Cincinnati newspaper.

Saturday Evening Chronicle, July 19, 1828

THE subscribers having entered into co-partnership, business will hereafter be conducted at *NO. 26, MAIN STREET*, under the firm of

PRATT, STRETCHER & BEARD;

Where they offer for sale Gold and Silver Levers and plain Watches, Pearl, Filagree, Jet, Paste, and Berlin Jewellery, Cable Chains, Watch Hooks, and Crosses, Miniature Settings and Medallions, Ladies and Gentlemen's Chains, Seals, and Keys; Gold, Plated and Silk Guards; Gold, Silver, and Steel Spectacles and Goggles; Ever pointed Pencils; Gilt, Jet and Mohair Bracelets and Belts; Silver Table and Tea Spoons, Soup and Cream Ladles and Sugar Tongs; Silver Plated Cake Baskets, Casters, Bottle Stands, Candlesticks, Snuffers and Trays; Brittania Tea Sets and Coffee Pots; Best Eight-day Brass Clocks and Willard's Patent Time Pieces; Fine Cutlery and Military Goods;

Together with a great variety of FANCY ARTICLES, now in fashionable use: All of which will be sold at reduced prices.

N. B. Clocks and Watches of every description (except wood) repaired and warranted. Cash paid for old Gold and Silver. Silver plate manufactered to order, at short notice.

E. P. PRATT,
J. E. STRETCHER,
C. C. BEARD.

Cincinnati, August, 1828.   1tf

The Western Tiller, September 12, 1828

The partnership of Pratt, Stretcher, and Beard lasted only until March of 1829, when the notice of dissolution appeared in the newspaper (see Stretcher). Pratt and Stretcher continued in business for a short time, and the Cincinnati Directory of 1829 listed them as watchmakers at 26 Main. The last ad found for this partnership appeared in *The Western Tiller* in May of 1829.

E.P. Pratt was again advertising in Chillicothe in July of 1829, when *The Scioto Gazette* carried a large ad for his shop. Pratt was still listed as a silversmith in Chillicothe, shortly before his death there in 1866.

E.P. Pratt was born in Massachusetts in 1801. His wife Catherine was born in 1806, and died in Chillicothe in the same year as her husband, 1866. They are both buried in Cincinnati, in Spring Grove Cemeterey.

In her booklet on Ohio silversmiths, Rhea Knittle listed an E.W. Pratt as a silversmith in Chillicothe, but we can presume that she was referring to E.P. Pratt, since no records of E.W. Pratt were found.

Early spoons marked

can be found in private collections, and later spoons marked

E.P. Pratt (Roman Capitals, incised)

have been seen.

PRATT, STRETCHER & BEARD .... *(1828-1829)*

PRATT & STRETCHER .... *(1829)*

PRICE, PHILIP P. .... (w. 1804-1812; also w. 1814-1816; also w. 1829-1836)

The early Cincinnati newspapers contained quite a bit of information about Philip Price. In 1804 the *Western Spy* announced that Philip Price and Harmon Long (Long & Price) had commenced the clock and watchmaking business. In March of 1805 *Liberty Hall* carried a notice of the death of Mary Price, wife of Philip Price. In June of the same year, the included ad appeared for Long & Price, mentioning "all other kinds of gold and silver work".

> **NOTICE.**
>
> THE subscribers respectfully informs the public, that they have commenced the CLOCK & WATCH making business, at the corner of Main and Columbia streets, at the house formerly occupied by John Humes, where they have clocks of all kinds for sale; watches will be cleaned and repaired, and all other kinds of gold and silver work done on the most reasonable terms and on the shortest notice. They hope from their knowledge in the business and attention they will be able to give the public general satisfaction.
>
> LONG & PRICE.
>
> Cincinnati, June 3, 1805.

Liberty Hall, June 3, 1805

In 1806 the included notice of dissolution appeared in the newspaper. Also in June of that year Price married again, as *Liberty Hall* of June 30 carried a notice of his marriage to Maria Malsbery.

The next newspaper notice appeared in 1810 when Price advertised in the *Western Spy* on September 15 that he had a handsome two-story brick house for sale, at the second door above the corner of Main and Market Streets. In December of the same year, Price became a partner of A. Simpson, and *Liberty Hall* carried an ad for the partners (see A. Simpson). This partnership was very shortlived, as in January of 1811 the notice appearing on the following page was carried by a Cincinnati newspaper.

> **DISSOLUTION OF PARTNERSHIP.**
>
> THE partnership of Long & Price, is this day by mutual consent dissolved, and all persons indebted to the above firm are notified to make payment to Philip Price, who is authorised to receive the same and those having accounts against said firm are requested to bring them forward for settlement.
>
> HARMAN LONG.
> PHILLIP PRICE.
>
> The Clock, Watchmaking, and Jewelry business are carried on by the subscriber as heretofore in the house of Thomas Williams, on Main street opposite to that occupied by Long & Price, where he will be happy to receive the commands of his friends and the public.
>
> An apprentice to the above business is wanted, about 13 or 14 years of age.
>
> PHILLIP PRICE.
> Cincinnati, June 10 h. 1806.

Western Spy, June 10, 1806

Price lost his second wife, Maria, in March of 1811, as the *Western Spy* of March 30 carried a notice of her death. Life could not have been easy for the women in those early times, if we judge by the number of men who lost their wives.

According to the *Western Spy* of June 11, 1812, Price was an enlistment officer in the army, of Middletown and Eaton, Preble County, Ohio. The included notice for a deserter appeared in the newspaper in 1813.

By December of 1814 Price was back in the silversmithing and watchmaking business and was advertising in the *Western Spy*. The included ad appeared in the newspaper in April of 1815.

> **TEN DOLLARS REWARD.**
> Deserted from the rendezvous at Cincinnati on the 7th an enlisted soldier named
> SAMUEL WILMOTH,
> born in England, aged 25 years five feet 10 inches high, of fair complexion profession a labourer. Whoever will deliver said deserter to the rendezvous in Cincinnati or any other in the United States shall receive the above reward.
> PHILIP P. PRICE, 2d Lieut.
> 14th Reg Infantry.
> Cincinnati August 14. 1813.   54 3w.

Western Spy, August 14, 1813

> **Clock & Watch-Making.**
> THE subscriber respectfully takes the liberty to inform his friends and the public generaly that he has commenced the
> **Clock & Watch-Making,**
> **Silversmith & Jewelry**
> **Business,**
> at the second door above the corner of Main and upper Market Streets, where he solicits the patronage of the public. He hopes from his attention and ability to be able to answer any commands with which he may be favored.   PHILIP P. PRICE

Spirit of the Times, April 8, 1815

> **Philip P. Price.**
> Watch and Clock Maker, Gold and Silver Smith, having dissolved his late partnership with Mr. Alexander Simpson, informs the public that he has returned to his former stand in Main Street, where he carries on the above branches of business with punctuality, neatness and despatch; he acknowledges past favours and solicits a share of the public patronage in future.
> Watches, repaired, will be insured for one year.
> ☞ Old Gold, Silver, Copper, and Brass will be received as heretofore, at the highest prices-

Western Spy, January 5, 1811

From this time on the career of Philip Price is a little more difficult to follow. He was not listed in the 1819 Cincinnati Directory, and in 1823 the *Western Star and Lebanon Gazette* (Lebanon, Ohio) carried an ad for Price in which he described himself as "late from Cincinnati". According to Warren Co. Ohio Records Philip P. Price married Nancy R. Rook in 1824.

By 1829 Price was again working in Cincinnati, as he was listed in the directory for that year. He continued to be listed until 1836.

The 1850 Ohio Census does list a Philip Price in Jackson Township, Jackson County, Ohio. Some future researcher may discover whether it was the same P.P. Price.

No silver marked P. Price has been seen, but the Cincinnati Art Museum has an early spoon marked:

P.P

Possibly this is the mark of Philip Price.

RADEMACHER, CHARLES .... (W. 1842-1850)

Williams' Cincinnati Business Directories of 1848 and 1850 carried the name G. Rademacher under watch and clockmaker's stores, locating the store on the west side of Race between 14th and 15th. The G. was probably a typographical error, since Charles Rademacher was listed as a watchmaker in the directories from 1842 until 1850, and last address given was the west side of Race between 14th and 15th, as above.

After 1850 Rademacher was no longer listed and nothing further is known of him.

READ, JAMES *(b. 1810, d. ?)* .... (W. 1830-1844)

On March 5th, 1830, J. Deterly commented in his diary "James Read just returned from England, set in to work for Shipp & Collins, Main St."

Read was listed in the 1831 Directory as a silversmith and engraver, located on Elm between Fourth and Fifth. The 1834 Directory listed him as a silversmith, the 1836 Directory as a jeweler. By 1837 Read and William Owen had become partners (Owen & Read). The 1840 Cincinnati Directory carried the following ad for their firm.

```
OWEN & READ,
CLOCK & WATCH MAKERS,
SILVERSMITHS AND JEWELLERS,
155, Main street, between Fifth & Sixth,
CINCINNATI:
Lamps & Castors, Tea-trays, Knives. Forks, &c.
11
```

The partnership of Owen & Read was dissolved in 1844 (see W. Owen).

In 1846 the Cincinnati Directory listed James Read as a printer, and in 1849 as a deputy marshall. The 1850 Census listed Read as a deputy marshall, and noted England as his place of birth. The 1850 Census also included his wife Margaret, born in Virginia, his son Francis, 17, listed as a watchmaker, and his daughters Sara and Margaret. Read's name no longer appeared in the directories after 1851.

No silver marked J. Read has been seen, but flat silver marked

Owen & Read

is in private collections. A spoon with the above mark is illustrated on page xii.

RHODES, JAMES F. .... (w. 1844-1856)

James F. Rhodes' first listing is the Cincinnati Directory occurred in 1844, when he was listed as a silversmith located on Main between 3rd and 4th. According to descendants of Mr. Rhodes, he came from Rhode Island as a young man and married Laura Lyon, of Cincinnati. They had three children, Howard, Clara and Linda.

Rhodes continued to be listed as a silversmith and jeweler at 103 Main until 1856. At that time he left Cincinnati for reasons of health, and went to Lancaster, Wisconsin. The climate of Lancaster must have agreed with him, since he lived there to the age of 76. He and his wife became outstanding citizens of Lancaster and are buried there.

There may have been some relationship between Thomas F. Rhodes and James Rhodes and John G. Anthony; Anthony's wife was Ann Rhodes, and she and her husband also came from Rhode Island. Anthony worked with Thomas Rhodes when he came to Cincinnati, and then James Rhodes boarded with the Anthonys when he came to the city.

While Rhodes was working in Cincinnati, the wonderful ad reproduced below appeared in the Cincinnati Business Directory.

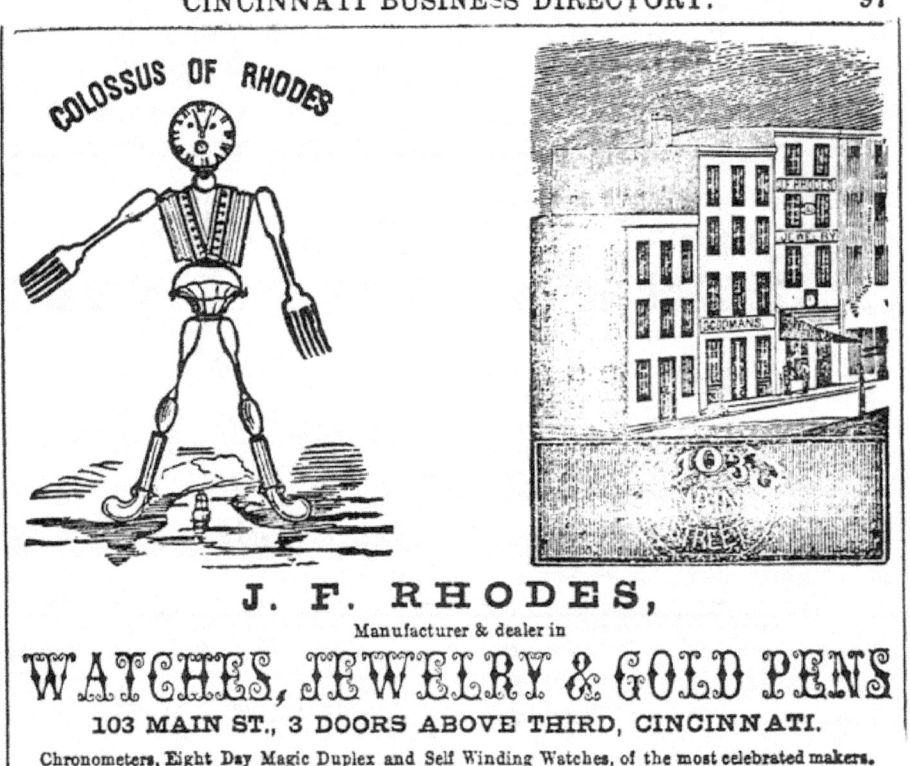

The Cincinnati Art Museum collection includes several spoons donated by descendants of the Rhodes family. The mark on the spoons is:

RHODES

Fiddle thread spoons have also been seen marked:

RHODES

RHODES, THOMAS F. .... (w. 1832-1836)

A CARD.

MOORE & RHODES have recently arrived in this city from the east, and purpose to establish themselves in the manufactory of JEWELRY of every description, and respectfully solicit orders from dealers, who may depend on getting their goods as low as they can be had in any of the eastern cities.

Their manufactory is on Lower Market street, No. 36.

March 3d,　　　　　　　　　　　　　　　270 3w

Cincinnati Chronicle, March 3, 1832

NOTICE.

IN consequence of the death of Samuel P. Moore, the firm of Moore & Rhodes is dissolved. The business of the firm will be settled by the subscriber.

Cin. June 16, 1832.　　　　THOS. F. RHODES.

N. B. The business will be continued at the old stand, No. 36. Lower Market-st. by the subscriber, where a general assortment of Jewelry and Watch materials will be kept constantly on hand, for sale at wholesale.

265-4w　　　　　　　　　　　　THOS. F. RHODES.

Cincinnati Chronicle, June 16, 1832

NEW PARTNERSHIP.

ALLEN & RHODES, having associated with them, Mr. John G. Anthony, the business, hereafter, will be continued under the firm of

ALLEN, RHODES & CO.

C. ALLEN,
T. F. RHODES,
J. G. ANTHONY,

aug 19　　　　　　　　　　　　　　　7-tf

Daily Gazette, September 6, 1834

SILVER PLATE.

THE subscribers are prepared to execute all orders for Silver Plate, Coffee and Tea setts,—Goblets, Mugs, Tumblers, Dessert Knives, Forks, Communion setts, &c. made to order.

ON HAND—A large supply of Table, Desserts, Tea, Cream, Salt, and Mustard spoons, Sugar Tongs, Soup Ladles, Tumblers, Butter and Dessert Knives, which they warrant equal to coin.

Country dealers constantly supplied.

ALLEN, RHODES & CO.

aug 30　　　　　　　　　　　　　　　16-tf

The first positive indication of Thomas Rhodes' arrival in Cincinnati, is the included notice which appeared in the newspaper in 1832, announcing that Moore & Rhodes had recently come to the city from the east.

Later that year the included notice of the death of Samuel Moore appeared in the newspaper. By June of 1833 Rhodes had become a partner of Caleb Allen (Allen & Rhodes) (See ad under C. Allen.) In August of 1834 Allen and Rhodes took John G. Anthony into the firm, as the included newspaper notice attests. By the end of the month Allen, Rhodes & Co. were advertising all types of silver plate, as the following ad shows.

Although the 1836 Directory lists Rhodes as a partner of Allen, at this time he was also advertising with John Anthony (see Anthony). As mentioned in the section on Anthony, it is possible that these two men were related by marriage.

In 1837 an ad for Rhodes, Anthony & Carley appeared in the Western Address Directory, and listed them as manufacturers of silverware & jewelery. Rhodes' name was not listed in the 1839 Directory, and no more is known of him.

Daily Gazette, August 30, 1834

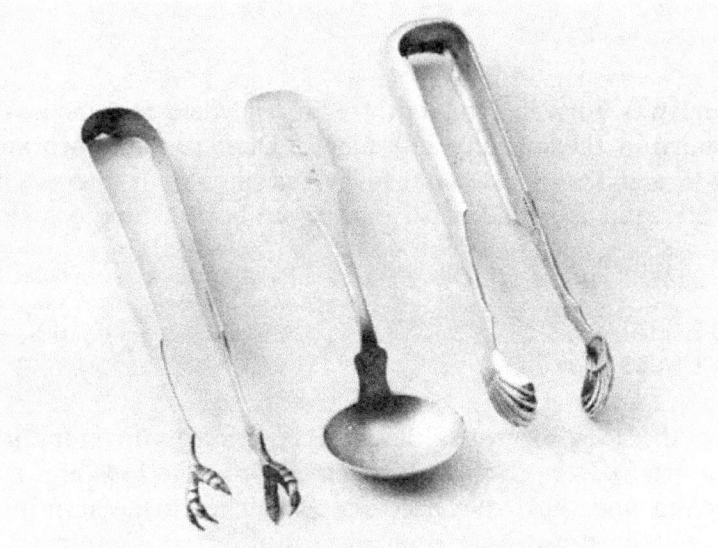

Three examples of Cincinnati serving pieces, on the left a claw end sugar tongs by Rhodes, Anthony & Co., in the center a gravy ladle by Allen & Rhodes, and on the right shell end sugar tongs by W. McGrew.　　　　　　　　　　　　*Private collections.*

Flat silver marked Allen & Rhodes, and Allen, Rhodes & Co. is fairly often seen, so we can assume that during the years these two men were working together, quite a bit of silver was produced.

The marks used were:

Allen & Rhodes

ALLEN, RHODES & Co

(This mark is also found with a serrated edge cartouche.)

Rhodes & Anthony

Rhodes, Anthony & Co

Illustrated on page 29 is a tablespoon by Allen, Rhodes & Co., on page 117 a gravy ladle by Allen & Rhodes, and a sugar tongs by Rhodes, Anthony & Co.

RHODES & ANTHONY .... *(1836)*

RHODES, ANTHONY & CO. .... *(1837)*

RHODES, ANOTHONY & CARLEY .... *(1837)*

RYLAND, JAMES .... **(W. 1843-1844)**

James Ryland was born in England in 1777 and died in Cincinnati in 1855. He had a son James W., born in England in 1820. One of these two men worked as a silversmith in Cincinnati in 1843 and 1844. The younger Ryland later went into the hardware business in Cincinnati, but the name is included because of the brief listing as a silversmith.

RYLAND, WILLIAM T. *(b. 1821, d. ?)* .... **(w. 1844-1849)**

According to the 1850 Census William Ryland was a silversmith born in England in 1821. He worked briefly as a silversmith in Cincinnati. The 1844 and 1846 Directories listed him as a silversmith and the 1849 Directory listed the partnership of Dunlevy & Ryland, silversmiths. Ryland must not have been successful in the silversmithing business, as later directories listed him as a bartender and saloon-keeper.

It is possible, looking at the dates, that there was some relationship between the James Rylands and William T. Ryland, but no proof of this was found.

SALMON, ALFRED .... (w. 1825-1844)

In 1825 Alfred Salmon, from England, was listed in the Cincinnati Directory as a silversmith, his address Fourth between Main and Walnut. From 1829 until 1844 he was listed as a watchmaker at various addresses, the last being Elm between Ninth and Court.

In 1849, however, Alfred Salmon, at the above address, was listed as a music teacher. This listing continued until 1853, the last listing in which Salmon appeared.

The only other information found was an 1866 cemetery record of the death of Mary Frances Salmon, the daughter of Elizabeth and Alfred Salmon.

SAYRE, A. .... (w. 1810-1811)

This interesting ad appeared in *Liberty Hall* in 1810. In it Sayre advertised that he had lately removed his shop, so at least we know that he had been working in Cincinnati for some time prior to June of 1810.

Sayre was still working in Cincinnati in 1811, as the notice for a runaway apprentice, shown below, indicates. He was not listed in either the 1817 tax lists or the 1819 Directory, so what happened to him after 1811 remains a question.

Liberty Hall, June 13, 1810

Western Spy, November 16, 1811

SAYRE, LEONARD

Leonard Sayre's name is included in this book as he may be the L. Sayre who was mentioned in the Hiatts' book on Kentucky silversmiths. According to the information in that book, silver marked L. Sayre is in existence.

The included ad appeared in the newspaper in 1808. Leonard Sayre had arrived in Cincinnati, it tells us, and opened a shop; it also mentions jewelry work done at the same place.

Sayre became a prominent merchant in Cincinnati, where he died in 1864.

Liberty Hall & Cincinnati Mercury, June 16, 1808

Store Department.

Fresh Goods

THE SUBSCRIBER,
Respectfully informs the public that he has just opened
A LARGE ASSORTMENT OF
Ladies' Bonnets & Hats,
DRY GOODS,
China ware, Tin ware,
Jewelry,
Coffee, Tea, Sugar &c.
At Capt. Gordon's store in Main street, near Front street, formerly occupied by Mr. Smith, where he will sell at the lowest prices.
Jewelry work done at the same place.
LEONARD SAYRE.

☞ Bees wax and country linen, taken for goods.
Cincinnati, June 16, 1808.

SCHNEIDER, CHRISTOPHER .... (w. 1848-1850)

The 1848 and 1850 Williams' Business Directories listed the name of Christopher Schneider, on Main between Hunt and Abigail, under clock and watchmakers' stores. The 1850 Census also listed Christopher Schneider, thirty years old, a watchmaker born in Germany, but no other information about this man was found.

SCHOOLFIELD, JOHN Q.A. *(b. 1821, d. 1892)* .... (w. 1836-1855)

John Q.A. (Quincy Adams?) Schoolfield was born in Baltimore, Maryland in 1821. The first appearance of Schoolfield's name in Cincinnati records occurred in 1836. The directory of that year listed him as a silversmith, boarding at William Borland's. By 1842 he was boarding at A. Palmer's, and possibly working for him.

The *Cincinnati Daily Gazette* of December 24, 1845 carried a notice of the marriage of John Q.A. Schoolfield to Miss Honora Simms. The 1850 Census listed one child of this marriage, a daughter, Ella, born in 1846. Schoolfield's wife died in 1853. He was last listed in the Cincinnati Directory in 1855.

The following mark appears in Currier's book on the marks of American silversmiths:

SCHOOLFIELD
1855

Whether this was John Q.A. Schoolfield is unknown.

A cup marked Schoolfield is in a private collection in St. Louis, and it has been said that a silversmith named Schoolfield worked in Columbia, Missouri. Some further research may determine whether the Missouri Schoolfield was actually John Q.A.

At some time John Q.A. returned to Cincinnati, as he died in an old men's home there in 1892. He and his wife Honora were buried in Spring Grove Cemetery.

SCOVIL, PULASKI (Polaski) .... (W. 1833-1837)

According to Scovil family genealogy records compiled by Homer W. Brainard, Pulaski Scovil was the son of Roswell and Anna Ames Scovil. Very little else is known of Pulaski Scovil, but silver marked with his name is frequently seen.

We do know that P. Scovil was in Cincinnati in 1833, as the included notice appeared in the newspaper in that year.

By 1836 Scovil had become a partner of Bushnell Willey and the partnership was listed in the Cincinnati Directory of that year (Scovil & Willey).

A quantity of silver exists marked Scovil & Kinsey, and since Kinsey had his own silverware manufactory by 1836, we must assume that silver made by these two men was made prior to 1836. From the design of the silver we can also conclude that it was made in the 1830's.

> NOTICE—P. SCOVIL, having transferred his copartnership interest to Mr. T. F. Rhodes, the copartnership heretofore existing under the firm of C. ALLEN & CO., is this day, by mutual consent dissolved.
>
> C. ALLEN, JR.,
> POLASKI SCOVIL.
> june 17   47tf.

Cincinnati Daily Gazette, June 17, 1833

By the time of the publishing of the next Cincinnati Directory in 1840, neither P. Scovil nor B. Willey were listed.

Early spoons marked P. Scovil are in private collections, and one is illustrated on page 15. Whether these spoons were made in Cincinnati or in some other locale has not been conclusively proven.

Illustrated on page 18 is a pair of spectacles by Scovil & Kinsey, and on page 147 a cup by Scovil & Willey and on page 122 cups by Scovil & Co. and Scovil & Kinsey, and on page 32 a soup ladle by Scovil & Co. Later spoons, late 1840's in design, have also been seen with the mark of Scovil & Co. Future research may determine if Scovil worked in a locale other than Cincinnati in the 1840's.

The following are reproductions of the marks found on silver:

P. SCOVIL

SCOVIL & KINSEY

SCOVIL, WILLEY & CO

Scovil & Co.

SCOVIL, WILLEY & CO. *(1836-1837)*

A trio of Cincinnati cups from the 1830's. The cup on the left bearing the mark which is illustrated below, the cup in the center by Scovil & Co., and the cup on the right by Scovil & Kinsey.

Private collections.

An enlargement of the mark appearing on the cup on the left in the illustration above.

SEYMOUR, JEFFREY (b. 1793, d. 1865) .... (w. 1816-1820)

According to the 1850 Census Jeffrey Seymour was born in Connecticut in 1793. He first advertised in Cincinnati in 1816, when the included ad appeared in the newspaper. Seymour's partner was Othniel Williston (Seymour & Williston).

The following notice of Seymour's marriage appeared in the *Western Spy* on October 10, 1818:

> MARRIED—At West-Springfield, Mass. on the 21st Sept. by the Rev. Dr. Lathrop, Mr. JEFFERY SEYMOUR, of this city, to Miss CLARISSA BAGG, of the former place.

By 1819 Seymour & Williston had a new partner, G.L. Benson (Seymour, Williston & Benson), and they were advertising "all kinds of gold and silverware manufactured on the shortest notice." (See ad below.)

On December 24th 1819, J. Deterly notes in his diary: "Jeffrey Seymour return'd from the West on Monday evening 22nd inst. Met with a poor market, — brought back the greater part of the goods he had, — it appears the St. Louis merchants can be better accomodated from the South — however on better terms."

> **SEYMOUR & WILLISTON,**
> *(From Newark N. J.)*
>
> Inform the citizens of this and the adjoining states that they have commenced the Manufacturing of Jewelry in this place, where they will make and supply the retailers of jewelry with all the various kinds of work in their line, of the newest patterns, and of superior workmanship, (of this however they are willing the buyer should be the judge,) having had experience with some of the best workmen in the U. S. and having also all the appurtenances necessary for doing business with neatness and despatch, they flatter themselves they can furnish as cheap and as good work as can be obtained from N. Y. or Philadelphia, which will save the trouble and loss in exchange and the impolicy of sending money out of the country. All orders punctually attended to and thankfully received at their situation on Front, two doors from Vine street.
> Cincinnati, May 2d   94 5w
> N. B. Wanted immediately two smart active lads, about 15 years of age, as apprentices to the above business; none need apply without the best recommendations.

Western Spy, May 2, 1816

The 1819 Directory listed Seymour as a jeweler residing at 80 W. Front. Then in 1820 Seymour & Williston were mentioned in an ad (see John Nuttman). Seymour's name did not appear in the 1825 Directory, although cemetery records show a son, Charles, born in Cincinnati that year.

Later directories listed Seymour at a variety of trades, including printing press maker, engine builder, city fire engineer, and finally as a hose and belt manufacturer.

Seymour died in 1865 and was buried in Spring Grove Cemetery.

The Cincinnati Art Museum has an early spoon marked **S&W** which could very possibly have been the mark used by Seymour & Williston.

> **Seymour, Williston, & Benson,**
> **Watchmakers,**
> **SILVERSMITHS & JEWELLERS,**
> NO. 95, Main street, four doors below the U. States' Branch Bank, Cincinnati, have taken the stand and stock lately occupied by Robert Best, where they offer for sale a general assortment of
> **JEWELLERY, &c.**
> Consisting in part of elegant and common Gold and Silver Watches, Fine and Jewellers' Gold Watch Chains, Seals and Keys, elegant Gold Ear and Finger Rings, Breast Pins, Necklaces, Bracelets, Gold, Cornelian, and Gilt Vest Buttons
> *Gilt and Silver Wares.*
> Ladies' elegant Reticule Clasps, Chrystalized Purses, Amulet Beads, Bracelets, and Ear Rings—a general assortment of Gilt Watch Chains, Seals, and Keys, Silver and Plated Table and Tea Spoons, &c. &c.
> ☞ All kinds of Gold and Silver Ware manufactured on the shortest notice. Watches of every description repaired and warranted. Orders punctually attended to.
> ⁂ Hair work of every description handsomely braided and mounted. Cash given for human hair from 20 to 30 inches in length.
> June 22.   64 tf

The Inquisitor and Cincinnati Advertiser, June 22, 1819

SEYMOUR & WILLISTON .... *(1816-1820)*

SEYMOUR, WILLISTON & BENSON .... *(1819)*

SHEPHERD (SHEPARD), EPHRAIM E. .... **(w. 1836-1840)**

Ephraim Shepherd, from New York, is listed as a silversmith boarding at A. Rugg's, in the Newport, Kentucky section of the Cincinnati Directory of 1834. In 1836 the Cincinnati Directory lists Shepherd as a silversmith boarding at William Borland's. The last Cincinnati listing of Ephraim Shepherd occurred in 1840, when he was listed as a silversmith working at E. Kinsey's.

The Cincinnati Historical Society collection includes a tablespoon marked:

> E. E. SHEPARD

A letter accompanying the spoon, written by Miss Virginia Rugg in 1912, states that her father ran the first steam ferry across the Ohio River, from Newport to Cincinnati, and her mother boarded the hands. It also states that these men paid her mother in silver which she used to have a few table and tea spoons made. The aforementioned spoon is one of these spoons, and is dated 1831. It is interesting to note that in 1834, E. Shepherd is listed as boarding at A. Rugg's.

SHIPP, SAMUEL A. M. *(b. ?, d. 1843)* .... **(w. 1819-1835)**

S. A. M. Shipp, from Virginia, had arrived in Cincinnati by December of 1819, as Jacob Deterly notes in his diary on December the 25th, 1819, that he was very sick and "was waited on by the good self of S. A. M. Shipp." Deterly and Shipp must have been good friends as Deterly's diary contains many references to Shipp.

Shipp was employed at some time by the firm of Woodruff & Deterly (1817-1821) as Deterly mentioned on Thursday, March 24, 1924, that he paid Shipp $25 for services rendered at Woodruff and Deterly's shop. He then added, "This E. Woodruff should have paid — refused to do it according to the meaning of the dissolution."

The first directory listing of Shipp occured in 1825. He was listed that year as a partner of Philip Perret (Perret & Shipp), watchmakers at 27 Main. This partnership was terminated in 1826 by the death of Perret.

On December 22, 1826, Deterly notes: "MONEY, advanced Mr. S. A. M. Shipp five hundred dollars, a part of stock for a connection in business." Three days later his diary included the following notes: "Mr. Shipp left this morning for New York to purchase Jewellery, Military goods & so forth."

In 1826 Deterly stated that Shipp took a lease on the house at 44 Main Street for $400 a year. From the included ad which appeared in the newspaper in March of 1828, we see that Shipp was well established at 44 Main and Deterly was still working with him as a watch repairer.

Gold and Silver Lever, and Plain English Watches, Superb Jewellery, Fine Cutlery, Military Goods, &c.

S. A. M. SHIPP,

NO. 44, Main street, Cincinnati, has the satisfaction of informing his friends and the public that he has just returned from New-York and Philadelphia, with the best assortment of the above articles ever offered in this city.

They consist in part as follows—

Gold Lever Watches, full jewelled, expansion curbs and chronometer balances,
" " with 2, 3, 4, and 5 pr. extra jewels, do.
Silver " full jewelled, - do.
" " without, all of which are detached escapements.

Gold and Silver English and French vertical and horizontal Watches, superb setts of Pearl, Pearl do. and Garnet, do. and Topaz, Ear rings and pins in setts, Amethyst, Topaz, Fillagree, Coral, Jet, Cameo and Paste ear rings and pins in setts, Diamond, Pearl, do. & Garnet, do. & Topaz, Paste, Fillagree, and Hair finger rings and breast pins, (a very large and well selected assortment;) Ladies' and Gentlemen's Gold Chains, Seals and Keys, Miniature settings and Medallions, all sizes: New fashion Gold Guard Chains, Cable Chains, Gold Crosses, Gilt, Hair, and Steel Bracelets and Belts, Clasps for the same. Music Boxes, (plays three tunes and changes itself,) Coral Beads, Glass and Wax do. Plated Candlesticks, Castors, Butter Knives, Snuffers and Trays. Swords, Epauletts, Pistols, Plumes, Belts, Belt Mountings, Sword Chains, Pompoons, Sword Knots, Tassells, Laces, Stars, Eagles, Cap Plates, Swivels. Rogers' fine silver steel Razors and Pen Knives, Flutes, gold and silver Spectacles, Scotch Pebble Glasses for do. ever point Pencils silver Thimbles, steel Chains, Seals and Keys, gilt do. Watch Ribbons, plated Table and Tea Spoons.— Watch Glasses and Watch Materials, Tools, &c. &c. He manufactures and keeps on hand a good supply of silver Spoons of all kinds. Masonic Jewels made to order, and of the best workmanship.

Having permanently engaged Mr. Jacob Deterly, who is well known as a first rate workman, and Mr. C. B. M'Cullough to attend entirely to the repairing of Watches, he confidently hopes to give general satisfaction in that branch of his business.

For past favors, the public and his friends will re-receive his sincere acknowledgments, and the assurance that his exertions will be unremitted to insure a farther continuance of them.

Cincinnati, March 15, 1828.

Saturday Evening Chronicle, March 15, 1828

From the ad appearing above, we can also see that Shipp had recently made another trip to the east and returned with a variety of articles! The ad also mentions that he "manufactures and keeps on hand a good supply of silver spoons of all kinds."

By 1828 Shipp had become a partner of Peleg Collins (Shipp & Collins) and the included ad appeared in the directory of that year.

In 1832 during the cholera epidemic in Cincinnati, Deterly's entry for October 22nd was as follows: "Cholera deaths 23 — Showery and warm — S. A. M. Shipp lying sick in his shop." But Shipp did not die and he continued to work with Collins until 1834 when the partnership was dissolved.

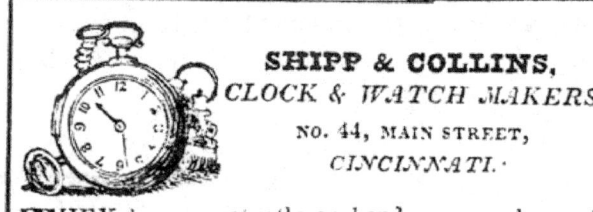

HAVING sold my entire stock in trade and store, to my former partner, Mr. P. Collins, would beg leave to present my sincere thanks to friends and customers, for the patronage afforded me while in business, and would ask the continuance of that patronage to my successor; who, I confidently assure my friends, is amply qualified, and will do all in his power to give equal and general satisfaction.

The principal cause of my retiring from business is known to the public, a more urgent request to those indebted to call and settle their accounts is deemed unnecessary. I can be found at all times, at my old stand, where I hope the promptitude of friends, will lighten by ready payment, my recent loss by robbery!
S. A. M. SHIPP.

P. COLLINS, No. 53, Main street, Cincinnati, the old stand of Shipp & Collins, and recently by S. A. M. Shipp, where I offer to my friends, and those of the former concerns, a handsome assortment of Watches, (all descriptions,) Jewelry, fancy goods, Plated and Brittania Ware, Clocks, Silver Ware, &c. &c. Watches and Clocks repaired in the best manner, and warranted.
P. COLLINS.
jan 17   33-2m

Cincinnati Daily Gazette, January 17, 1835

In November of 1834 Shipp's shop was robbed, and Deterly who was then in Marietta, Ohio, noted on December 13th: "Robbery. Received a handbill from S. A. M. Shipp, who was robbed of all his watches, jewelry and silverware on the 28th of November. $500 reward." After the robbery Shipp sold his remaining stock to his former partner Peleg Collins, as the included notice relates.

Shipp did work again as a silversmith, as Mrs. Roach, in her book on St. Louis silversmiths, notes that Shipp was a partner of Horace Woodbridge in St. Louis in 1842. Illustrated in her book is a silver spoon by Shipp and Woodbridge. According to Deterly's diary Woodbridge had worked for Shipp & Collins in Cincinnati in 1832.

When Shipp died in St. Louis in 1843 he left a most interesting will. Included in his bequests was a gold watch left to George Carlisle of Cincinnati. Much searching has been done by the descendants of Carlisle in Cincinnati to locate this watch, but at this writing the search has been unsuccessful. There were many other bequests in the will, which is reproduced on the opposite page, and anyone taking the time to read it should find it interesting.

In his book on American silversmiths and their marks, Currier includes the following mark:

SHIPP & COLLINS .... *(1829-1834)*

I, Samuel A. M. Shipp, of the City of St Louis State of Missouri, do make and publish this my last will and testament. First. I direct that my funeral expenses and all my just debts be paid. Second. I devise and bequeath to my Sister Frances C Shipp who resides with Thomas G Tupman of the State of Kentucky and to my nephew Christopher Blackburn of Boone County Kentucky a house and lot which I own in the City of St Louis, acquired of Joseph G. Shands. To have and to hold the same to them & their heirs and assigns forever. — Third. I devise and bequeath to Samuel Tupman son of the aforesaid Thomas G. Tupman, Lots number two and three of the North East quarter of Section five in township Thirty three north of Range five east, for which there is a patent among my papers from the United States. — Fourth — The remainder of my real estate wherever situated I devise & bequeath to my said sister & my said nephew. To have and to hold the same unto them & their heirs and assigns forever. — Fifth — I bequeath to my friend Doctor William C Morris, from my store a handsome set of Brittania Ware, a set of silver table spoons worth Twenty dollars, & my silver rimmed spectacles. Sixth. I bequeath to my friend George Carlisle, of the City of Cincinnati, a Gold Lever watch with repeating movement, now in the Show case in my Store, and marked as made in Liverpool & London by John E Hyde & Son for S. A. M. Shipp St Louis, Missouri, with the chain & key attached to it. — Seventh. I bequeath to my friend John Ford of the City of St Louis, a gold watch out of my Store worth at cost One hundred and thirty or one hundred and forty dollars, to be chosen by him. — Eighth — I bequeath to my partner Horace P Woodbridge all my interest in the horses & carriages & harness owned by us in partnership, and also the sum of Five hundred dollars, and I further direct that he be released & discharged from the payment of any interest on the one thousand dollars of capital which I put into our partnership concerns over the amount which he put in, and further I bequeath to him the diamond breast pin he wears & which belongs to the firm. — Ninth — I bequeath to Albert M Cohen who is employed in our Store a breast pin worth from Fifteen to Twenty dollars. — Tenth. I bequeath to Joseph G Shands a gold pencil worth from Fifteen to eighteen dollars — Eleventh — I bequeath to Mrs Bissell wife of Capt. Lewis Bissell a gold thimble, and to him and to each of his children a silver pencil worth from one dollar and a half to two dollars and a half. — Twelfth. I bequeath to Doctor Joseph J Clark a diamond ring worth from Fifteen to eighteen dollars. — Thirteenth. I bequeath to Mrs Wade with whom I formerly boarded and to her daughter Mary each a half dozen silver tea spoons — Fourteenth. I bequeath to Charles Morris Son of Dr William C Morris a Silver lever watch worth twenty eight or thirty dollars. — Fifteenth. I bequeath to Mrs Morris wife of Dr William C Morris a Gold thimble, and a gold pencil to be selected by her. — Sixteenth. I bequeath to Mrs Tupman wife of the aforesaid Thomas G Tupman a good heavy set of tea spoons to cost not less than seven dollars. — Seventeenth — I bequeath to Mrs Carlisle wife of the aforesaid George Carlisle a gold thimble — Eighteenth — I bequeath to Charles D Drake a half dozen silver table spoons worth from twenty one to twenty five dollars & a half dozen tea spoons worth seven dollars, two salt spoons and one mustard spoon & a pair of sugar tongs. The remainder of my personal estate I bequeath to my said sister & nephew to be divided equally between them. — I appoint Lewis Bissell & John Ford executors of this will

S. A. M. Shipp

Will of S.A.M. Shipp, probated April 6, 1843.

SHOURDS, SAMUEL .... (w. 1840-1844)

The name of Samuel Shourds, from New Jersey, appeared in the Cincinnati Directories in 1840, 1843 and 1844. He was listed as a silversmith, his residence on Longworth between Smith and Mound.

It is doubtful that any silver marked S. Shourds will be found, but his name is included in this book in the hope that some future researcher may find this listing helpful. Shourds may have worked as a silversmith in some other locality before or after his years in Cincinnati.

SIMPSON, ALEXANDER .... (w. 1809-1814)

> AT the Supreme court, which sole on Saturday last, a divorce was decreed between Alexander Simpson and Rebecca his wife, without allowing her any of his property, he having proven that she was caught at two different times in bed with two different men, who were brothers, by the names of Reuben Doty and John Doty
> ALEXANDER SIMPSON.
> September 19, 1804.

Western Spy, September 19, 1804

> **A. SIMPSON,**
> *CLOCK, WATCH and MATHEMATICAL IN-STRUMENT-MAKER,*
> Respectfully informs the public that he has commenced business at the corner of Market and Sycamore-street, where he is ready to serve in his profession, with punctuality.
> He has on hand an elegant tellescopic minute instrument, calculated to shew the variation by a moving index, to determine the altitude of hills to a certainty.
> Clocks and watches repaired on the shortest notice and warranted to perform with accuracy.
> Any metalic Ore will be analyzed gratis—and the specific qualities given.
> Artificial TEETH made and set in an elegant manner.
> Cincinnati, May 18, 1809.
>
> CERTIFICATE.
> WE the subscribers have carefully examined an Instrument made by A. Simpson, and do not hesitate to say, that it is better calculated to make a true survey than any other we have ever seen.
> (Signed by)   JOHN St. CLAIR,
>   Professor of the Languages, Natural Philosophy, Mathematics, &c. Union town Academy, Pennsylvania.
>   Rev. ROBERT AYRES,
>   JOHN SHELDON,
>   JOHN M'CLURE HESLEP,
>   THOMAS STOKELEY.
> Brownsville, (Penn.) June 24, 1806.   34 4t.

Liberty Hall, May 18, 1809

The above notice appeared in a Cincinnati newspaper in 1804, showing that even the early frontier town of Cincinnati had its scandals!

Very possibly the notice was placed by Alexander Simpson the clock and watchmaker, but there is some confusion about dates. Pleasants and Sill, in their book on Maryland silversmiths, listed Alexander Simpson as having worked in Hagerstown, Md. from 1799 until 1805. The first ad found for Simpson in Cincinnati newspapers did not appear until 1809.

By December of 1810 Alexander Simpson had moved and formed a partnership with Philip Price (Simpson & Price). An announcement of the formation of the firm appears on the following page.

The partnership of Simpson & Price was of very short duration, as by January 5, 1811 it had been dissolved (see notice under Philip Price).

Alexander Simpson continued to advertise until 1814. After 1814 no more information was found. His name appeared neither in the 1817 tax lists nor in the 1819 Directory. A Lebanon, Ohio record was found, listing the marriage of Alexander Simpson to Hannah Rogers in 1824, so possibly Simpson moved to Lebanon.

Simpson definitely states that he was a silversmith, the removal notice that appeared in 1809 stating "...he carries on the business of silversmith, clock, watch and mathematical instrument maker." But no silver marked with his name has been seen.

> **ALEXANDER SIMPSON** INFORMS the public, that he has removed his CLOCK, WATCH & MATHEMATICAL SHOP, from Herman Long's to the house of James C. Morris in Main-street, near the Columbian Inn, and opposite to A. Dunseth's Tin Manufactory, where the business in future will be carried on under the firm of
> SIMPSON & PRICE,
> and where the public may be served with the following articles, viz. MUSICAL & CHIME CLOCKS, to move either by weight or spring; Time pieces, on a new construction; Surveying Instruments, made on the Rittenhouse plan, and warranted equal to them; Protractors, Scales, &c. &c.
> Watch work executed in the neatest manner, and warranted to perform for one year.
> All kinds of gold and silver work made on the shortest notice and finished with elegance.
> The highest price, in Cash, will be given for old Gold, Silver, Copper & Brass.
> ☞ A Journeyman, who understands his business, will meet with constant employ.
> S. & P.
> Cincinnati, December 5, 1810. 1596

Liberty Hall, December 5, 1810

SIMPSON & PRICE .... *(1810-1811)*

SMITH, CONRAD .... (w. 1829; also w. 1842-1850)

Conrad Smith, from Pennsylvania, first appeared in the Cincinnati Directory in 1829, listed as a silversmith boarding at Mrs. Thomson's. He is not listed in the 1831 and 1836 Directories, but he appeared again in 1840, this time listed as a silversmith and jeweler boarding at 4 N. Sycamore.

From 1842 to 1844 the directory listing was silversmith, boarding at Mrs. Floyd's. In the 1846 and 1849 Directories, the east side of Bank Alley was the address given, which was also the address of George A. Stinger, silversmith.

The 1850 Census listed Smith as a silversmith, his age fifty-three. The elusive Mr. Smith was not listed again until 1856, when a Conrad Smith appeared as a shoemaker, but after that time the name disappeared from the Cincinnati directories.

It is doubtful that Smith ever had his own shop, or that any silver marked C. Smith was made.

SMITH, HARRY R. *(b. 1821, d. 1903)* .... (w. 1842-1900)

Harry Smith worked for years as a jeweler in Cincinnati, but it is the earlier years of his career with which this book is mainly concerned.

Smith was born in Columbus, Ohio in 1821, the son of Ruth and John Smith. He was first listed in Cincinnati in 1842, the directory of that year listing him as a watchmaker boarding at P. Collins'. By 1844 Smith had become a partner of Abraham Palmer, and Kimball and James' Mississippi Valley Business Directory of that year carried the following ad.

> **PALMER & SMITH,**
> MANUFACTURERS OF
> **SILVER WARE & JEWELRY,**
> AND DEALERS IN
> **WATCHES, FANCY GOODS, CUTLERY, &c.**
> *No. 143, Main Street.*

Cincinnati Daily Times, October 1, 1850

By 1848 Smith had changed partners, becoming associated with J.P. Beggs (Beggs & Smith). The included ad for this partnership appeared in the newspaper in 1850. This ad mentions silverware "much of which is manufactured by themselves." Smith's partnership with Beggs lasted until 1861, when Beggs retired from business. In 1862 and 1863 Charles Boerner was a partner of Smith's (Smith & Boerner), but this partnership was shortlived, as in 1864 the company was listed under the name Harry R. Smith. From 1869 until 1900 the listing was Harry R. Smith & Co.

Joblin & Co.'s *Cincinnati Past and Present,* published in 1872, carried a descriptive chapter on Smith, as well as his picture. The following is information taken from this source:

Smith's family came from Rhode Island in about 1815. When he was about five his father decided to invest in land and located a village where he thought prospects were favorable to rapid growth and the increase in value of property. The place selected was Hebron, in Licking County, Ohio, equidistant from Newark and Granville and at the junction of the Ohio Canal and the National Road. . . .

The associations of young Smith's childhood were a large hewed log house which his father build, the native forests of immense trees, the shooting of wild ducks and pigeons. . . . His father became a local proprietor, started a country store, and was the postmaster and a leading citizen. . . .

Mr. Smith was married in Dayton in 1851 to Anna McNaughton. They had three children, two boys and one girl. . . .

While Mr. Smith has been unremitting in his attention to business, and quick to perceive the wants of the public, he has always maintained a quiet demeanor and an affable carriage. His private character is exemplary and in point of business integrity the record of none stands higher than that of Harry R. Smith. . . .

Smith died in Cincinnati in 1903 and was buried in Spring Grove Cemetery.

Private collections include flat silver marked:

PALMER & SMITH

BEGGS & SMITH (incised)

Illustrated on page 10 is a handsome tea set marked Beggs & Smith, and on the same page the mark appearing on the tea set. Silver from the later years marked Smith & Boerner, Harry R. Smith and Harry R. Smith & Co. is often seen.

SMITH, JOHN .... (w. 1802)

On August 7, 1802, a John Smith advertised in the *Western Spy* that he had "commenced the goldsmith and watchmaking business in the house opposite Mr. Daniel Ruders' store on Main St." This was the only ad found for John Smith and no other information on him has come to light.

SMITH, THADDEUS .... (w. 1849-1856)

In 1849, the Cincinnati Directory carried the name Thaddeus Smith, listing him as a clock manufacturer at 12 E. Fifth, his house on the north side of Sixth between Race and Elm.

The ad shown on the following page appeared in Reilly's Ohio State Business Directory of 1853-54, and gives a wonderful illustration of the types of clocks sold at the time.

The ad also includes the names of many clock manufacturers, which should be helpful to those interested in horology.

Smith's name was no longer listed in the directories after 1856, and nothing more is known of him.

T. SMITH,

Dealer in

Eight Day and Thirty Hour Brass

CLOCKS,

AND CLOCK TRIMMINGS,

12 E. FIFTH ST. OPP. DENNISON HOUSE, CIN'TI,

And No. 88 Main St. Saint Louis, Mo.

My assortment consists of every style and variety of Clocks, manufactured by Chauncey Jerome, Seth Thomas, Smith & Goodrich, Wm. L. Gilbert, J. C. Brown, Birge, Peck & Co., Litchfield Manufacturing Co., and others, comprising in all an assortment of some 150 different styles and kinds. Orders from Dealers at a distance filled at prices that will give satisfaction.

No. 1 Octagon 8 day Clocks and Time Pieces.
Height 22 inches.

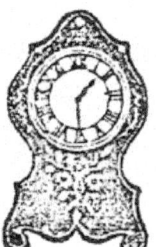

Paris 8 and 1 day Pearl inlaid.
Height 17 in.

Extra column; 30 hours. Weight and Spring.
He't 25 1-4 & 18 1-4 in.

Octagon 8 day No. 2 Clocks & Time pieces.
Height 24 in.

Kossuth 8 day and 1 day. Pearl inlaid.
Height 19 in.

Victoria 8 day and 30 hour Spring.
Height 15 1-4 in.

Jerome's Union 1 day Spring.
Height 13 1-2 in.

Round top Gothic No. 1 & 2 & with alarm.
He't 19 in.

Round Gilt 8 day time pieces.
3 sizes.

Cottage Time Piece, and with Alarm.
Height 12 inches.

Union 8 and 1 day. Pearl inlaid.
Height 13 in.

Octagon Level Time pieces, 8 day & 30 hour. 6, 8 & 10 in. Dial.

SOTCHER, ABNER (b. ?, d. 1826) .... (w. 1817-1826)

Abner Sotcher had arrived in Cincinnati from London by 1817, as his name appeared on the 1817 tax lists. The 1819 Cincinnati Directory listed Sotcher as a silversmith at 58 Main; this was the place of business of Woodruff & Deterly.

J. Deterly's diary entry for March 2, 1820 carried the following interesting notation about Sotcher. "Not a Yanky trick, A. Sotcher sold his thimble apparatus to Messrs. Seymour & Williston who have not yet obtain'd everything they feel inclined to think they are entitled to, have equivocated concerning said sale, and hesitate making any payment to said Sotcher."

Additional information obtained from Deterly's diary was the formation of the partnership of Abner Sotcher and Samuel Musgrove on March 7, 1820. The partnership lasted only a month as Deterly related on April 7, 1820, "Sotcher and Musgrove have dissolved their partnership concerns."

Estate of Abner Sotcher.

NOTICE is hereby given to all persons having just and legal claims against the estate of *Abner Sotcher*, late of Hamilton county, Cincinnati township, and state of Ohio, deceased, that they exhibit their claims, legally proven, for adjustment, within one year from the date hereof: And all those indebted to said estate, are requested to make immediate payment to SARAH SOTCHER,
Adm'r. of Abner Sotcher, dec'd.
September 7th, 1826.   87t4-

National Republican & Ohio Political Register, September 7, 1826

Sotcher undoubtedly continued to work in Cincinnati until his death in 1826, although his name did not appear in the 1825 Directory. The included notice of his estate appeared in the newspaper in September of 1826. Sarah Sotcher who appears as administrator of his estate was most probably his wife.

Rhea Knittle lists an Abner Solcher in her booklet on Ohio silversmiths. We can conclude this was a typographical error.

SPILLER, JOHN (b. 1796, d. ?) .... (w. 1842-1849)

John Spiller was born in England in 1796. His name first appeared in a Cincinnati Directory in 1842, when he was listed as a clockmaker and bell hanger. He continued to be listed as a clockmaker or bell hanger or both until 1849.

STALL, GEORGE W. .... (w. 1811-1817?)

We know that G.W. Stall was in Cincinnati in 1799, as the following appeared in the Smith & Findlay Account Book in April of that year:

Torrence Manuscripts, Box 57, Folder 4

Nothing more was found about Stall until July of 1811, when the included interesting ad appeared in the newspaper.

Stall was still in Cincinnati in 1817, as his name appeared on the 1817 tax lists, but the 1819 Directory did not include his name.

Early spoons in private collections of Cincinnati families include spoons marked:

This could have been the mark either of George Stall or of George Sullivan.

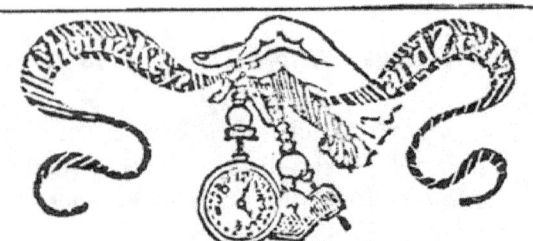

STANLEY, I.M. .... (w. 1836)

In the 1836 Cincinnati Directory I.M. Stanley was listed as a partner of William Owen (Stanley & Owen), in the clockmaking business. By 1837 W. Owen had become a partner of James Read (Owen & Read) and we do not know what became of Stanley, as his name did not appear in any later directories.

STANLEY & OWEN .... *(1836)*

STINGER, GEORGE A. *(b. 1812, d. ?)* .... (w. 1836-1883)

George A. Stinger, from Washington, D.C., worked for years as a silversmith in Cincinnati, but very little of his work has been found.

Stinger was first listed in the 1836 Cincinnati Directory and was listed in all succeeding directories as a silversmith or silver manufacturer, until 1883. In 1846 his address was the east side of Bank Alley, where he worked until 1860. In later years the address given was Fourth and Main.

The 1850 Census listed Stinger, his wife Elizabeth, three sons and two daughters.

From early records of Annual Fairs given by the Ohio Mechanics' Institute we find that in 1851 Stinger entered a silver fireman's trumpet in the competition. So we do know that he made silver other than flatware.

The mark found on silver spoons in a private collection is:

G.A. STINGER (incised)

STRETCHER, JOHN E. .... (w. 1828-1829)

John E. Stretcher worked briefly in Cincinnati, first in the partnership of Pratt, Beard & Stretcher, and then in the partnership of Pratt & Stretcher. The first partnership advertised in August of 1828 (see Pratt); the second is clearly explained in the included ad. The last ad found for Pratt & Stretcher appeared in *The Western Tiller* in May of 1829. These two men were listed in the 1829 Cincinnati Directory as watchmakers at 26 Main. This was the only directory listing found. Perhaps Stretcher went to Hillsboro, Ohio from Cincinnati. An undated watch paper in a private collection bears the following inscription: "J.E. Stretcher, Clock and Watchmaker, Hillsboro, Ohio."

Dissolution of partnership.

NOTICE is hereby given that the partnership heretofore existing between E. P. Pratt, John E. Stretcher and Charles C. Beard, under the name of Pratt, Stretcher and Beard, is dissolved by mutual consent, this 11th day of March, 1829.

E. P. PRATT,
J. E. STRETCHER,
C. C. BEARD.

All persons having accounts against the above concern, are requested to bring them forward for settlement. And all those indebted to it, are requested to call and pay their accounts to E. P. Pratt and John E. Stretcher.

E. P. PRATT & JOHN E. STRETCHER,

HAVING entered into partnership, business will be hereafter conducted under the firm of

PRATT & STRETCHER,

At *NO. 26, MAIN STREET*, where they have on hand a large and splendid assortment of clocks, watches, and jewelry and military and fancy articles in their line. They hope by an unremitted attention to business, to merit and receive a share of public patronage. Clocks and Watches of every description carefully repaired and warranted.

E. P. PRATT,
J. E. STRETCHER.

Cin. March 11, 1829.   29-tf

The Western Tiller, March 11, 1829

STUTTELBERG, ARNOLD .... (w. 1842-1844)

The 1839 marriage records of Hamilton County, Ohio include the marriage of Arnold Stuttelberg to Caroline Wessler. Stuttelberg was listed in the 1842 Cincinnati Directory as a silversmith; in 1843 and 1844 he appeared as a goldsmith. These were the only listings of Stuttelberg found in the Cincinnati Directories.

SULLIVAN, GEORGE .... (w. 1811)

> **GEORGE SULLIVAN**
> HAS COMMENCED THE
> **Silver-Plating Business,**
> NEXT door to Mr. Hafer's bake-house and nearly opposite the Columbian Inn, where he intends to carry on the above business in all its various branches, viz:— such as plating Stirrup-Irons, Bridle-bits, Buckles, Bosses, Heads & Cantels, and all kinds of *Coach & Gig Mountings*. He will keep on hand an assortment of SILVER WORK, such as *Table & Tea-spoons, Soup, Cream and Mustard Ladles, Sugar-tongs, Salt-shovels, Heads & Cantels*, &c. all of which will be sold on the most reasonable terms.
> Stirrup-Irons and bridle-bits *replated*.
> N. B. He will allow the full value for *cut silver* in any of the above articles, and will give the highest price for old Silver, Pewter, Brass and Copper.
> **Mrs. SULLIVAN**
> Has now on hand, and will continue to keep an assortment of the most fashionable BONNETS, ARTIFICIAL FLOWERS & BANDBOXES; all of which she will sell on very reasonable terms.
> Cincinnati, May 31, 1811.

In his book on Virginia silversmiths, Cutten listed a George Sullivan as a silversmith in Lynchburg from 1802 until 1806. From correspondence with Mrs. Noble Hiatt we have the information that George Sullivan advertised on May 23, 1809 in the *Kentucky Gazette,* Lexington, Kentucky.

In 1811 the included ad for George Sullivan appeared in a Cincinnati newspaper, but no further information about him was found in Cincinnati records.

Silver in private Cincinnati collections includes flat silver marked:

GS

GS

One of these may have been the mark of George Sullivan.

Western Spy, May 31, 1811

SWIFT, WILLIAM C. *(b. 1815, d. ?)* .... (w. 1836-1865)

Swift, with no first name given, appeared in the 1836 Cincinnati Directory as a silversmith. Later directories listed William Swift as a watchmaker and jeweler. The 1850 Census listed William Swift as a jeweler from Connecticut, his wife Elinore, from Kentucky, and a son and daughter.

Swift's name continued to be listed in the directories until 1865, and although for many of those years he worked in the shop of other jewelers, silver spoons in a private collection bear the following mark.

WM SWIFT

SYMMES, CELADON *(b. 1770, d. 1837)* .... (w. 1798?)

Celadon Symmes was born in 1770, the son of Timothy Symmes and Abigail Tuthill, and a nephew of John Cleves Symmes. It is believed that he came to Cincinnati with his father in 1789.

He served in the militia, and Greve's *Centennial History of Cincinnati* contains three references to him. The first reference mentions that in January of 1793 he was appointed an ensign; the second reference is to his promotion to lieutenant in November of 1794; the third reference is to an incident of a killing by the Indians in the village of North Bend, it being reported that Symmes and a party of twenty-seven men pursued the Indians but were unable to catch them.

The account books of Smith & Findlay, Merchants, carried quite a few listings of Celadon Symmes' accounts. Included below is a reproduction of an entry for purchases made in December of 1792. Other listings in these account books were found up until February of 1800.

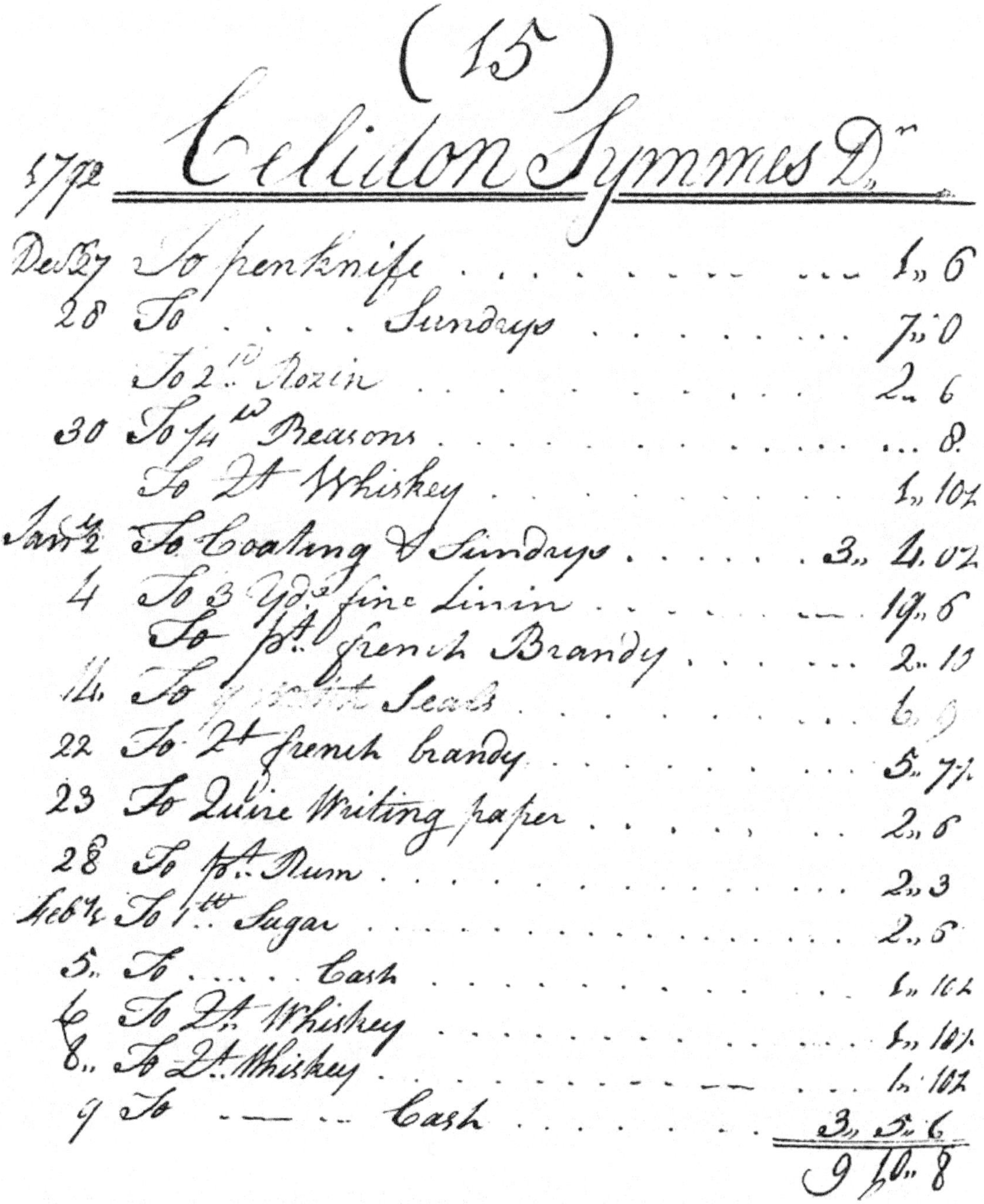

(handwritten ledger entry)

(15)

1792 Celidon Symmes Dr

Dec 27	To penknife	1,, 6
28	To ..... Sundrys	7,, 0
	To 2 lb Rozin	2,, 6
30	To ¼ lb Reasons	... 8
	To 2 t Whiskey	1,, 10½
Jan 2	To Coating & Sundrys	3,, 4,, 0½
4	To 3 Yds fine Linin	19,, 6
	To pt french Brandy	2,, 10
14	To ..... Seals	6
22	To 2 t french brandy	5,, 7½
23	To Quire Writing paper	2,, 6
28	To pt Rum	2,, 3
Feb 4	To 1 lb Sugar	2,, 6
5,,	To ..... Cash	1,, 10½
6	To 2 t Whiskey	1,, 10½
8,,	To 2 t Whiskey	1,, 10½
9	To ..... Cash	3,, 5,, 6
		9,, 10,, 8

Torrence Papers, Smith & Findlay Account Books, Box 56, Folder 4.

No information was found on Celadon Symmes working as a silversmith, with the exception of a spoon mold in the Cincinnati Historical Society, the identifying placard stating: "Silver spoon mold, Used by Celadon Symmes, the first silversmith in Cincinnati, presented by his grandson, William Symmes, of Hamilton, Ohio, May 1899." The back of the placard states: "Celadon Symmes was a nephew of John Cleves Symmes and the first silversmith in Cincinnati, 1798."

Rhea Knittle related that Symmes worked as a silversmith in Cincinnati in 1789. Since no bibliography was included in her booklet on Ohio silversmiths, her source for this date could not be verified. But it hardly seems likely that the date 1789 could be correct. From research done on the city of Cincinnati at that period, a man would have been lucky to have had a cabin to live in, or tools to build such a cabin. Refinements such as silver spoons had not yet arrived in the city.

The earliest record found of a silversmith in Cincinnati was an account found in 1793 (see J. Whitesides). Whitesides is listed as a silversmith, but whether he was actually carrying on his trade we do not know.

From James McBride's *Pioneer Biographies* we learned that Celadon Symmes moved from Cincinnati to Butler County, Ohio, where he owned a section of land about three miles south of Hamilton on the Turnpike Road from Cincinnati to Hamilton, and he lived there for the rest of his life. The village of Symmes Corners, at the southwest corner of the section, derives its name from him.

Celadon Symmes was elected a justice of the peace of Butler County in 1803, and in 1806 he was chosen by the State Legislature to serve as an Associate Judge of the Court of Common Pleas of Butler County, which position he held for seven years. Symmes died in July of 1837.

Illustrated on page 3 is a spoon recently made from the spoon mold, referred to above, in the Cincinnati Historical Society Collection. As can be seen, the spoon is rather primitive in design.

THORNTON, JOSEPH .... (w. 1825)

A memorial bronze plaque at Fourth and Sycamore commemorates the landing of the first boatload of Cincinnati pioneers at Yeatman's Cove on December 28, 1788. Included on the plaque are the names of the men who landed there, among them that of Joseph Thornton. Thornton's name also appeared on the 1817 tax list, and the 1819 Directory listed him with no occupation given.

In 1825 Thornton was listed as a watchmaker and silversmith at 58 Main. This was the address of the shop of Woodruff & White, so Thornton was apparently working for them. This was the only listing of Thornton as a silversmith. Other directories listed him with no occupation, as a commission merchant, or in other occupations.

Thornton's name is included in this book because it appears in both Knittle's and the Kovels' books. We must conclude from the above information, however, that it is very doubtful that any silver was made marked with Joseph Thornton's name.

THORPE, FRANKLIN *(b. 1812, d. ?)* .... (w. 1842-1850)

Franklin Thorpe advertised in the 1842 Directory, that year being the first in which the Cincinnati directory carried his name. He continued to advertise for the next two years and the included ad appeared in the 1844 Directory.

> **FRANKLIN THORPE,**
> **CLOCK AND WATCH MAKER, AND JEWELER.**
> SIXTH STREET, SOUTH SIDE, NEAR PLUM,
> **CINCINNATI,**
> Respectfully informs the public that he is prepared to repair Clocks Watches of every description, in a manner that will give satisfaction.
> Jewelry made and repaired. Door Plates engraved. Prices moderate. work warranted.

Then, in 1846, the included ad, with the beautiful little engraving of the shop front, appeared in a Cincinnati newspaper. This ad mentions that Thorpe also carried silverware in his shop.

In 1847 a notice of removal appeared in the newspaper. Thorpe remained on the south side of Sixth Street, but this time three doors east of Elm. In 1849 the Directory did not include Thorpe's name, but the following ad, which appeared in the newspaper in that year, mentions that he had returned to the city.

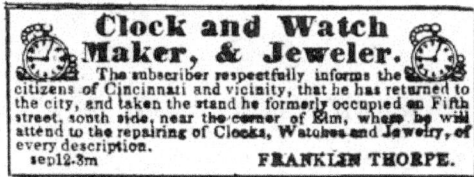

Cincinnati Daily Commercial, September 12, 1849

Cincinnati Weekly Advertiser, August 31, 1846

The 1850 Census included the following listing: Franklin Thorpe, age thirty-eight, trade watchmaker, place of birth, Washington, D.C. It also listed his wife Ann, age thirty-eight, birthplace, Kentucky.

The 1850 Directory listing was the last found for Thorpe. What became of him after 1850 is unknown.

TROTTER, JEREMIAH (w. 1836-1868)

Jeremiah Trotter was listed in the Cincinnati Directories as a watchmaker and jeweler from 1836 until 1868. His shop was located first on Main, then on Sycamore, and finally on Central Avenue.

The only Trotter newspaper ad which has been found, appeared in 1839 and is included here.

It is very doubtful that Trotter ever worked as a silversmith, since he is never listed as such, and no silver marked with his name has been seen.

> **Trotter,**
> WATCH MAKER,
> Main st., between Sixth and Seventh.
> ap 10

Cincinnati Advertiser, April 10, 1839

VAN NUYS, ISAAC *(b. 1765, d. 1848?)* (w. 1805-1807)

We know that Isaac Van Nuys was working as a clock and watchmaker in Cincinnati in 1805, as the included ad for an apprentice appeared in the newspaper in that year.

Also in 1805, the *Western Spy* carried a notice including the information that Van Nuys was administrator of the estate of Isaac Gildersleeve. What wonderful names we find in the early newspapers!

> **Wanted,**
> AS apprentices to the CLOCK & WATCH MAKING & TINNING business, two apprentices from 14 to 16 years of age—boys from the country will be preferred—boys who can come well recommended will meet with advantageous terms, by applying to
> *Isaac Van Nuys.*
> Cincinnati, June 12th, 1805.

Western Spy, June 12, 1805

In 1806 Van Nuys became a partner of Thomas Best in the clock, watchmaking, silversmithing and jewelry business (see T. Best). This partnership was dissolved in 1807, and no later ads were found. Possibly Van Nuys moved to Rossville, Ohio, as a record was found of a William Van Nuys, son of Isaac, born in Rossville in 1810.

VERDIN FRANCIS *(b. 1806, d. 1884)* (w. 1841-1863)

VERDIN, MICHAEL *(b. 1805, d. ?)* (w. 1841-1862)

The Verdin brothers are being included together as they came from France, apparently at the same time, and were the founders of the business which is still flourishing today. According to Dearborn County, Indiana records, the Verdins had arrived in America by 1837.

From Ohio Mechanics Institute records, we know the Verdins were in Cincinnati in 1841, as they were awarded a certificate for a town clock exhibited in the Fourth Annual Fair sponsored by the Institute. It is interesting to note that the judges for the clocks entered in the Fair were E.H. Hill and John Pickering, both of whom are included in this book.

The first Cincinnati Directory listing of the Verdin brothers occurred in 1842, when they are listed as clockmakers. They continued to be listed in succeeding directories, and by 1849

Photo courtesy of The I.T. Verdin Co.

One of the first Verdin clocks manufactured. Still in perfect timekeeping operation. Square bearings were used in this clock.

were listed as Town Clock Makers in Cincinnati business directories. At that time, town clocks were hand wound and it was Francis who developed a mechanical winder. This eventually led to the design of a similar mechanism for bell ringing, which was to set the pattern for the future of the company.

I.T. Verdin, after whom the present Company is named, was the grandson of Francis Verdin. The I.T. Verdin Co., located on Eastern Ave. in Cincinnati, still makes town or tower clocks and all types of bells, even carillons. They are known as "The Bell Ringers of America".

Included on the preceeding page is a picture of an early town clock mechanism, marked Verdin, Cincinnati, Ohio.

WARNER, WARREN *(b. 1812, d. ?)* .... (w. 1831-1843)

The 1831 Cincinnati Directory listed three Warners, Warren, James and Thomas, as clockmakers. All three were listed as boarding at David P. Williams, who was a cabinet maker. Possibly he was making clock cases, and the Warners were working for him. The only Warner who continued to be listed as a clockmaker, was Warren, who was listed as such until 1843. In later directories Warren was listed as an edge tool finisher or as a finisher. The 1850 Census also listed Warren as a finisher.

WATSON, LUMAN *(b. 1790, d. 1834)* .... (w. 1809-1834)

Much has been written about Luman Watson, who was undoubtedly Cincinnati's most prolific clockmaker. This article will not attempt to embellish on the articles written, but will merely relate the essential facts of Watson's life.

Luman Watson was born in Harwinton, Connecticut in 1790. By the time he was 19 he had moved to Cincinnati and was working with the Read brothers in the firm of Read & Watson. This firm was dissolved in 1815, and Watson commenced his own clock manufacturing business. In 1819 when the first Cincinnati Directory was published, Watson was listed as a wood and ivory clockmaker, with his business located on Seventh between Main and Sycamore. In succeeding directories up until his death in 1834 he was listed as a clockmaker and organ builder, a clockmaker and a clock manufacturer. The included ad appeared in the 1829 Directory.

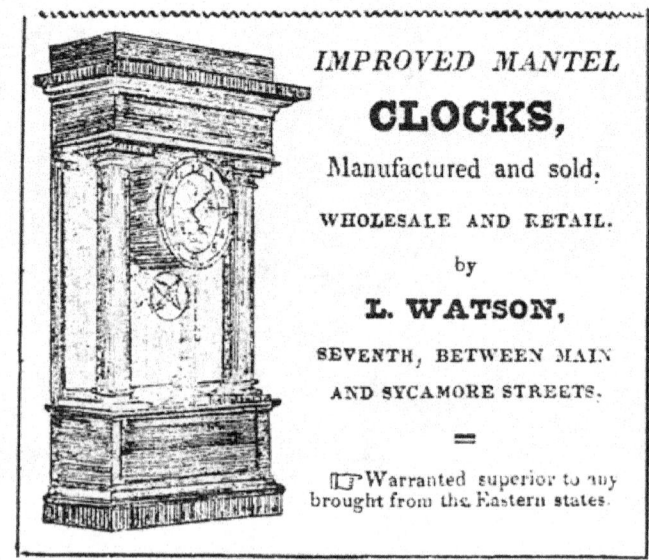

Watson was active in civic affairs, serving as a director of the U.S. Branch Bank, and was one of the founders of the Ohio Mechanics Institute. He was also active in numerous other societies.

Quite a number of Watson clocks have survived the years, and are treasured possessions of those who own them.

For further information on Luman Watson the reader is referred to the article by John A. Diehl which appeared in *The Magazine Antiques* in June of 1968.

Illustrated below is a clock made by Luman Watson.

Thirty-hour wood movement hollow column clock made by Luman Watson, Cincinnati c-1829

WENNING, WILLIAM *(b. 1822, d. ?)* .... **(w. 1848-1860)**

William Wenning was born in Germany in 1822. The exact year of his arrival in Cincinnati is unknown, but his name and that of his brother Henry appeared in the Williams Business Directory of 1848, as dealers in watches, jewelry and silverware at 340 Main.

Henry Wenning did not continue in the business and in 1850 William was listed alone as a jeweler. The included ad appeared in the newspaper in that year.

The 1850 Census listed William Wenning as a watchmaker and also listed his wife, Elizabeth.

From information available we know that William Wenning worked as a jeweler at various addresses on Main Street until 1860.

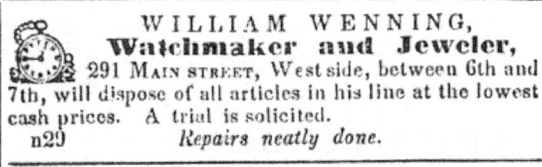

Catholic Telegraph, September 7, 1850

WHITE, EDWARD T. .... (w. 1842-1843)

Edward T. White's name appeared only twice in the Cincinnati Directories. In 1842 he was listed as a silversmith boarding at Mrs. W. Wright's, and in 1843 he appeared as a watchmaker boarding at Marshall House. No other information about him was found in Cincinnati records.

WHITE, GEORGE L. .... (w. 1827-1834)

The first definite evidence of George White's appearance in Cincinnati was an ad which appeared in the *Saturday Evening Chronicle* of November, 1827, in which Enos Woodruff and George White advertised their shop at 58 Main.

Woodruff and White were listed in the 1829 Cincinnati Directory as silversmiths at 58 Main. The 1831 Directory carried the included ad for the two men.

The last listing of Woodruff and White appeared in the 1834 Directory.

MILITARY STORE.
WOODRUFF & WHITE,
NO. 58, MAIN STREET,
CINCINNATI,
Have constantly on hand a general assortment of
MILITARY GOODS.

ALSO—Watches and Jewelry, Ladies and Gentlemen's Gold Patent Lever, Silver Lever, English capped, jeweled and plain Watches; chains, seals, keys, ear-rings, finger-rings, &c. of all descriptions. Silver Ware, &c.

From Cincinnati White went to Madison, Indiana. The *Republican and Banner* newspaper of that city carried an ad on February 27, 1834, stating that White had become the partner of C.B. McCullough.

The Cincinnati Art Museum has in its collection a silver spoon marked:

WHITESIDES, JOHN .... (w. 1793)

The Torrence Manuscripts in the Cincinnati Historical Society include account books of Smith & Findlay, Merchants. In the account book for 1793 the following listing of John Whitesides, Silversmith, appeared:

Torrence Papers, Box 56, Folder 3, p. 134

If Whitesides was working at his trade of silversmithing at that time, he was most probably Cincinnati's earliest silversmith. If any further information is available about Whitesides, perhaps this book will help bring it to light.

WHITESIDES, SAMUEL *(b. ?, d. 1851)* .... **(w. 1813-1819)**

Cutten's book on Virginia silversmiths includes the following information: "Samuel Whitesides announced that he had commenced business in Staunton on August 4, 1802. He took the shop recently occupied by Charles Page near the Court House, and as a clockmaker and jeweler solicted the patronage of his friends and the public. . . ."

The first information about Whitesides found in Cincinnati records, was the included ad, which appeared in the newspaper in 1813.

In October of the same year, the notice of removal shown on the following page appeared in the newspaper.

The 1817 tax lists included Whitesides' name, and the 1819 Cincinnati Di-

> SAMUEL. H. WHITESIDES.
> **WATCH & CLOCK MAKER,**
> SILVER-SMITH & JEWELLER,
> CINCINNATI,
> RESPECTFULLY informs the citizens of Cincinnati and its vicinity, that he has commenced business in the shop formerly occupied by PHILIP P. PRICE, in the above business, in Main-street, one door above Messrs. *Barr & Key's Store*, where he carries on the above business in all its various branches, in the most accurate manner and on the shortest notice.
> May 18.   45-m6

Liberty Hall, June 22, 1813.

> **REMOVAL.**
> **SAMUEL H. WHITESIDE,**
> **Watch & Clock-Maker, Silversmith & Jeweller,**
> Informs the citizens of Cincinnati and the vicinity, that he has removed to the shop lately occupied by ANDREW SIMON, in Main-Street, three doors from Columbia street—where he carries on the above business in all its various branches, in the neatest manner, and on the shortest notice. Oct. 1813. 67-tf
>
> *Liberty Hall*, December 21, 1813

rectory listed him as a silversmith at 52 Main, his house between Fourth and Fifth. Undoubtedly Whitesides moved out of the city before 1825, as he is not listed in the 1825 or 1829 Directories.

Whitesides died in Hamilton County, Ohio in 1851. In his will, found in the Court House records, he left everything to his wife, Anne S. He asked that she pay the tuition of his grandson, Amandus Silsby, at Farmers College in Hamilton County, if his father so desires. Whitesides' son, Addison H., was also mentioned in the will.

If silver made by Samuel Whitesides exists, none has yet been found.

WILLEY, BUSHNELL *(b. 1806, d. 1855)* .... (w. 1834?-1837)

According to Willey family records, Bushnell Willey was the son of Asa and Phebe Waters Willey. Bushnell's aunt, Sara Willey, married a Captain Bushnell, and this was undoubtedly how he got his name.

The only documented proof of Willey's presence in Cincinnati, is the 1836 Cincinnati Directory listing, in which he was listed as a partner of P. Scovil. Quite a bit of silver made by these two men exists today.

Cups marked Willey & Blaksley, Cincinnati, are in private collections, so we can assume that Willey worked with Blaksley in Cincinnati as well (see H. Blaksley).

Willey family descendants state that records show that Bushnell Willey went to Kentucky in the late 1830's and died there around 1855. Where he went in Kentucky and whether he worked as a silversmith there have never been determined. Possibly some future research will clear up this mystery.

Marks found on silver in private collections include:

WILLEY & BLAKSLEY

SCOVIL, WILLEY & CO

WILLEY & CO

(This mark was found on a spoon circa 1850.)

B. WILLEY

An illustration of cups marked Scovil, Willey & Co., Willey & Blaksley, and Willey & Co. appear on the following page and spoons marked Scovil & Willey are illustrated on page 29.

Three very similar cups, all bearing Willey's name. The cup on left is marked Willey & Blaksley as per enlargement below, the cup in the center is marked Willey & Co., the cup on the right is marked Scovil, Willey & Co.
Private collection.

An enlargement of the mark appearing on the cup on the left in the photo above.

WILLISTON, OTHNIEL .... (w. 1816-1820)

In 1816 Othniel Williston came from New Jersey to Cincinnati, where he opened a jewelry shop with Jeffrey Seymour (see J. Seymour). In June of that year the included ad appeared in the newspaper. In December of the same year, the *Western Spy* carried a Help Wanted notice for apprentices to the jewelry and goldsmithing business of Seymour & Williston.

By 1819 G.L. Benson had become a member of the firm and the included ad appeared in the newspaper in that year.

Williston's name appeared on the 1817 tax list, and the 1819 Cincinnati Directory listed him as a jewelry manufacturer at 78 W. Front. This was the last listing found of Williston in Cincinnati.

An early salt spoon in the Cincinnati Art Museum bears the mark:

S&W

This could possibly have been the mark used by Seymour & Williston.

HUMAN HAIR.

THE SUBSCRIBERS WILL PAY CASH FOR

Human Hair,

From 20 to 32 inches in length, dark brown and black will be prefered.
SEYMOUR & WILLISTON.
Front-street, two doors
below Vine-street.
N. B. A premium given for SPECIE.
Cincinnati, June 28.   O2 3w

Western Spy, June 28, 1816

Seymour, Williston, & Benson,
WATCHMAKERS,
Silversmiths and Jewellers,
No. 95, MAIN-STREET,
Four doors below the U. States' Branch Bank,
CINCINNATI,

HAVE taken the stand and stock lately occupied by ROBERT BEST, where they offer for sale a general assortment of
JEWELLERY, &c.

Consisting in part of elegant and common Gold and Silver Watches, Fine and Jewellers' Gold Watch Chains, Seals and Keys, elegant Gold Ear and Finger Rings, Breast Pins, Necklaces, Bracelets, Gold, Cornelian and Gilt Vest Buttons.

Gilt and Silver Wares.

Ladies' elegant Reticule Clasps, Chrystalized Purses, Amulet Beads, Bracelets and Ear Rings —a general assortment of Gilt Watch Chains, Seals and Keys, Silver and Plated Table and Tea Spoons, a great variety of steel Watch Chains, Seals, and Keys, &c. &c.
☞ All kinds of Gold and Silver Ware manufactured on the shortest notice. Watches of every description repaired and warranted. Orders punctually attended to.
∗⁎∗ Hair work of every description handsomely braided and mounted. Cash given for HUMAN HAIR from 20 to 30 inches in length.
September 4, 1819.   74 tf

Western Spy, September 4, 1819

WOODRUFF, ENOS (w. 1813-1834)

> **WOODRUFF & DETERLY,**
> EAST SIDE OF MAIN STREET,
> Opposite Samuel Lowry's Store,
> HAVE JUST RECEIVED,
> Directly from England,
> A QUANTITY OF
> **Gold and Silver Watches,**
> Of a very superior quality,
> Which they offer for sale on reasonable terms.
> *Among them are the following,*
> Gold *Patent Levers,* detached scapement,
> do. common do.
> do. LADIES' do do.
> The above watches are
> *Cased in a Very Superb Style,*
> SILVER PATENT LEVERS,
> do. common scapement capp'd and jewell'd;
> And a variety of low priced ones, making a much better assortment than can be found elsewhere in this place—all of which they warrant to perform well.
> They continue the WATCH REPAIRING as usual. This branch is conducted by one of the firm, who, although he cannot boast of "having learnt the Watch *Finishing* business in London," nor even "having learnt his business in Europe," yet he can boast of having repaired [*not botched*] more watches in this town, within the last six years, than any other person—the humiliating fact of his having learnt the business in the back-woods to the contrary notwithstanding.
> They have always for sale almost every article of
> **SILVER WARE**
> Used in this country, not inferior in quality or workmanship to any made here or brought from the Eastward. They have likewise a large assortment of
> **JEWELLERY.**
> Also, a large quantity of *PLATED BRIDLE BITS, STIRRUP IRONS, &c. &c.* which they offer unusually low.
> Cincinnati, Nov. 24, 1817. 88tf

Liberty Hall,
November 24, 1817

In 1813, Enos Woodruff, from New Jersey, purchased the interest of J. Deterly in the firm of Best & Deterly, and the firm of Best & Woodruff was formed. In 1815 this firm became R. Best & Co., in which Best, Woodruff and Deterly were partners. This combination of partners lasted only two years, and in 1817 Enos Woodruff and Jacob Deterly became partners (Woodruff & Deterly). From the included ad, which appeared in the newspaper in 1817, we get a very good idea of the articles handled in their shop.

Woodruff and Deterly also had an interest in a shop in Louisville, as on March 2, 1820 Deterly's diary contained the following entry, "Enos Woodruff left here for Louisville in the Steam Boat 'Genl Pike' on business concerning the Establishment there, to take Inventory & etc." A few days later Deterly noted, "Enos Woodruff returned from Louisville in company with Elias Ayers." Woodruff & Deterly must not have been happy with their business in Louisville, as on March 16, 1820, Deterly stated, "This day the firm of Elias Ayers & Co. is considered dissolved and Woodruff & Deterly's divident sold to Elias Ayers for $2500." This information should be of interest to Kentucky silver collectors, as the only listing the Hiatts gave of E. Ayers & Co. was 1816.

The 1819 Cincinnati Directory listed Woodruff & Deterly as silversmiths at 58 Main Street. This partnership continued until 1821, when it was dissolved (see J. Deterly for notice of dissolution).

Deterly did not have much respect for Woodruff, if we are to judge by the many entries in his diary referring to old debts of the firm. For example an entry which appeared for June 22, 1825 stated, "An Account, Settled with Danl T. Evens $2.84 which is another act of Enos Woodruff's honourable mode of adjusting accounts!!"

Enos Woodruff continued to carry on his business at 58 Main, and in April of 1826, the ad shown on the following page, appeared in the newspaper.

By 1827 Woodruff had a new partner, George L. White. The ad on the following page for Woodruff & White appeared in the newspaper in November of that year.

The 1829 Cincinnati Directory listed Woodruff & White as silversmiths at 58 Main. Also, in the 1829 Directory, Enos Woodruff was listed as an associate judge of the Court of Common Pleas.

```
                MILITARY GOODS.
E. WOODRUFF, No. 58 Main street, Cincinnati, has
   just received a general assortment of MILITARY
GOODS, which he will dispose of at very reduced prices.
The following are a few of the articles:
    Silver plated and gilt mounted sabres; plated, gilt and
steel mounted cut and thrusts; gold, silver, gilt and plated
epauletts and wings; gold and silver lace; hat tassels and
stars; waist belts, plates and swivels; plumes of all kinds;
silk and worsted sashes; hat plates; worsted wings; abridg-
ment of Scott's Military Discipline, &c. &c.
    P.S.   E. Woodruff has constantly on hand, a large assort-
ment of Silver ware and Jewelry. Watches of every descrip-
tion repaired and warranted.
    April 21.                                    68-6t*
```
Cincinnati Commercial Register, April 21, 1826

```
          NEW JEWELLERY
        AND WATCHES.
           NO. 58, MAIN STREET.
WOODRUFF & WHITE, beg leave to
    inform the Ladies and Gentlemen of
Cincinnati, that they have just received from
New-York and Philadelphia, an elegant as-
sortment of fashionable JEWELLERY,
WATCHES, &c. which they offer for sale
at reduced prices.
    The following articles constitute part of
their assortment:
    Gold Patent Lever WATCHES,
    Silver    do.         do.
    English, Swiss, and French do.
    Ladies' and Gentlemen's Gold Watch
        Chains, Seals and Keys,
    Gold Cable Neck Chains,
    Diamond, Pearl and Topaz, Amethyst
        Coral, Jet and Paste Ear Rings,
    Finger Rings and Breast Pins,
    Bracelets, Clasps, and Coral Beads,
    Medallions and Miniature Settings,
    Silver Spectacles, Dirks,
    Ever-point Pencils,
    Silver Table, Tea, Sugar & Soup Spoons,
    Steel Chains, Seals and Keys,
    Gilt    do.    do.    do.
Cincinnati, Nov. 24.              43 6t
```
Saturday Evening Chronicle, November 24, 1827

```
        WOODRUFF & WHITE,
      WATCH & CLOCK MAKERS,
              JEWELERS,
           And Silversmiths,
             NO. 58, MAIN STREET,
KEEP constantly a general assortment of all arti-
    cles in their line, consisting of Gold and Silver
patent and plain Watches, Jewellery, Silver Ware,
Military Equipments, &c. &c.
```
(H.W. Fagin, Publisher)

Woodruff & White continued to advertise and in 1829 the ad shown above appeared in the Cincinnati Directory. The last listing of Woodruff & White appeared in the 1834 Directory where they were listed as silversmiths on Main Street. Woodruff was listed in several later directories with no occupation given; perhaps he retired at that time.

In the section on Jacob Deterly the following mark is shown:

As stated in that section, it was undoubtedly the mark of Woodruff & Deterly.

Illustrated below is a spoon in the Winterthur Museum bearing the following mark:

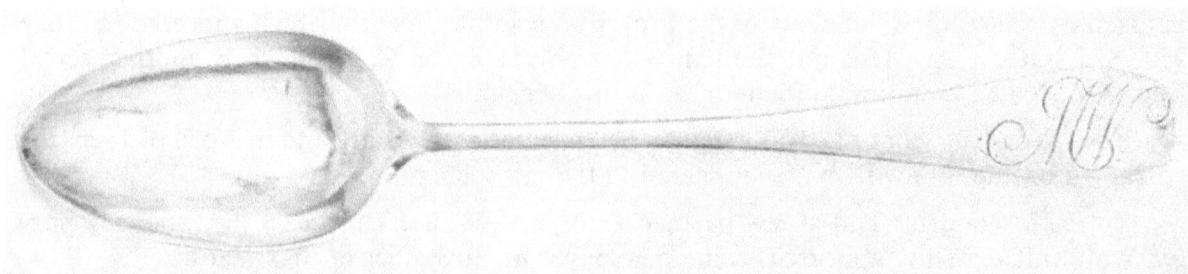

Coffin end spoon, marked E. Woodruff in script as shown above.
Photo, courtesy The Henry Francis du Pont Winterthur Museum. Gift of Mr. and Mrs. Alfred E. Bissell.

A spoon in the Cincinnati Art Museum bears the following mark:

WOODRUFF & WHITE

Illustrations of silver bearing the mark W & D appear on page 42.

WOODRUFF & DETERLY .... *(1817-1821)*

WOODRUFF & WHITE .... *(1827-1834)*

WRAY, HENRY .... **(w. 1849-1870)**

The 1849 Cincinnati Directory carried the following listing: "Henry Wray, (Carley & Wray), boards at S.T. Carley's." The 1850 and 1851 Directories listed him as working at S.T. Carley & Co.

By 1853 Henry Wray was listed as a manufacturing jeweler, with his own business at 141 Main. This listing continued until 1870, when Wray's name disappeared from the directories.

Although he was listed as a jewelry manufacturer, it would not be surprising if Wray carried silverware as well.

The included ad for Wray appeared in the Cincinnati Business Directory of 1853.

HENRY C. WRAY,
MANUFACTURING JEWELER,
NO. 141 MAIN STREET,
DERBY'S BUILDING, SECOND STORY,
Entrance, First Door South of Smead's Banking House.
CINCINNATI.
Diamonds set in the Newest Style, every variety of Jewelry made to order, and promptly executed.

ADDENDA

1819-1850
Silversmiths, Jewelers, Watch & Clockmakers Listed Only Once in the Directories.

Bromley, George (1842) Watchmaker; Sixth between Plum and Western Row.

Budd, Joseph (1836) Watchmaker; east side of Main between Seventh and Eighth.

Choat, R.W. (1840) Silversmith.

Coward, Samuel (1936) Silversmith; boards at C. Coffin's.

Crowell, William (1836) Watchmaker; E. Front.

Dalton, John (1840) Silversmith; residence Race between Green and Columbia. From England.

Fix, Ferdinand (1843) Clockmaker; boards V. Dufner.

Gedney, Charles (1936) Watchmaker; northeast corner Front and Vine.

Gerstecker, Frederick (1840), Silver finisher at J. Draper's; From Germany.

Goodfellow, Robin (1842) Jeweler; boards at Front Street House.

Guild, Jeremiah (1831) Clockmaker; Sycamore between 6th and 7th.

Harris, Henry (1836) Watchmaker; 117 Main.

Heil, John (1844) Jeweler; boards at S.T. Carley's.

Hogeland, Ralph (1834) Clockmaker; Walnut between 12th and 13th.

Jennings, David (1831) Clockmaker; Elm near Northern Row.

Johnston, Thomas (1840) Silversmith at E. Kinsey's. From Maryland.

Jones, William A. (1840) Jeweler; boards at Patrick Morris'. From Kentucky.

Lang, Christopher (1848) Listed in the Business Directory under Jewelry, Silverware and Watches; southwest corner Thirteenth and Clay.

Lary, William (1831) Silversmith.

Loton, George (1840) Silversmith; boards at Mrs. Martin's. From New Jersey.

Mayle, Ebenezer (1840) Silversmith at E. Kinsey's. From England.

McDonald, Alexander (1840) Silversmith.

McMurphy, Albert (1840) Boards at A. Palmer's. From Delaware.

McMurphy, Theodore B. (1840) Silversmith and watchmaker. From Delaware.

Milbis, Nathan (1831) Silversmith.

Miller, Lewis (1831) Jeweler; boards at W. Fleming's;

Naurd, Peter (1842) Watchmaker; Eighth between Main and Sycamore.

Nengas, Henry (1836) Jeweler; Front between Sycamore and Broadway.

Niles, James N. (1836) Jeweler; boards at J.S. Niles'. From Virginia.

Phillips, — (1829) Silversmith; boards at David Ross'.

Phluck, Joseph (1840) Watchmaker; boards at Green Tree House. From Germany.

Rafil, Joseph (1840) Jeweler and silversmith; E. Main between Columbia and Front. From Germany.

Reis, Edward J. (1840) Silversmith at J. Draper's. From Maryland.

Samuels S. (1842) Watchmaker; Sycamore between Front and Yeatman.

Sanford, R. (1834) Silversmith; Main between Canal and Abigail.

Shumard, Samuel (1834) Silversmith; Fifth, east of Broadway.

Slow, Clark (1840) Watchmaker at McGrew's; residence corner Fifth and Sycamore. From Nova Scotia.

Solman, Edward (1836) Silversmith; 4th between Plum and Western Row.

Suofield, H. (1834) Watchmaker; Main between Seventh and Eighth.

Swift, John D. (1846) Jeweler; boards at Henrie House.

Symonds, Philip (1843) Watchmaker; boards at S. Symonds'.

Todd, Tracy (1840) Silversmith; residence south side of Seventh between Plum and Western Row.

Traies, William (1836) Watchmaker; Fulton between Eighth and Ninth.

Trousdale, John L. (1831) Clockmaker; boards at W. Coopers.

Tucker, Albert (1842) Silversmith; boards at Mrs. Gilliand's;

Wachman, Abraham D. (1840) Watchmaker. From Germany.

Worrell, John (1842) Watchmaker; boards at G. Bromley's.

Yost, Henry (1842) Watchmaker and silversmith.

1850-1900
SILVERSMITHS — JEWELERS — WATCH AND CLOCKMAKERS

Listed below are some of the more prominent names of men and companies in the silver, jewelry and watch and clockmaking business between 1850 and 1900. Some of these companies are still in business today, but the last date given is 1900, which was the cutoff date for the research done.

*ANDREWS, LORING AND CO.	(1896-1900)
DORLAND, GARRET T.	(1861-1882)
*ELIAS, HENRY P.	(1855-1868)
EYSTER, ANDREW A.	(1855-1870)
FRANKENSTEIN, H.W.	(1873-1900)
FUERSTE, W. M. (Silversmith)	(1883-1900)
GRUEN WATCH CO.	(1874-1900)
*HERSCHEDE, FRANK	(1879-1900)
HUMMEL, LOUIS	(1887-1900)
*ISBELL, E.E.	(1874-1895)
KECK, HERMAN	(1861-1894)
KOCH, MARCUS	(1856-1892)
*KORF, HENRY	(1856-1900)
LANGE, J. & BROS.	(1860-1881)
*LANGE, LOUIS	(1882-1886)
*LANGE, HERMAN	(1887-1900)
MAUTHE, CHIRST, SR.	(1870-1890)
MAUTHE, CHRIST, JR.	(1872-1900)
MEHMERT, JOSEPH	(1878-1900)
*MICHIE, WM. & J.C.	(1868-1874)
*MICHIE (Kent & Michie)	(1874-1878)
MICHIE JEWELRY	(1879-1883)
*MICHIE BROS.	(1884-1900)
*MORRIS, JOHN B.	(1863-1878)
OSKAMP & CO.	(1853-1861)
OSKAMP A.	(1862-1867)
OSKAMP NOLTING CO.	(1889-1900)
*PARKS, GEO. D.	(1855-1866)
*PLAUT, BERNARD	(1887-1898)
*PLAUT, A & J	(1879-1900)
*SCHNEIDER, BEN	(1869-1900)
SCHNEIDER, J.B.	(1859-1889)
SCHWAB, A.G. & BROS.	(1879-1900)
SMITH, A. D. & CO.	(1864-1885)
STRUEVE, HERMAN R.	(1853-1900)
VOSS, JULIUS	(1853-1887)
VOSS, J. S.	(1853-1875)
VOSS, J. S. & SON	(1885-1895)
WILMS, J. C.	(1856-1891)
WILMS, J.C. & SON	(1891-1900)
WINSLOW, HARMON S. (Silversmith)	(1882-1886)

*The names starred indicate the existence of silver, so marked, found in research.

BIBLIOGRAPHY

Newspapers

Cincinnati*

Centinel [sic] *of the North-west Territory*, 1793-1796
Cincinnati Advertiser & Journal, 1818-1841
Cincinnati American, 1830-1832
Cincinnati Catholic Telegraph, 1849-1850
Cincinnati Chronicle, October 1837-September 1839
Cincinnati Chronicle & Literary Gazette, 1826-1835
Cincinnati Commercial Register, 1825-1826
Cincinnati Daily Gazette, 1827-1850
Cincinnati Daily Times, 1841-1850
Cincinnati Daily Whig, 1834-1839
Cincinnati Emporium, 1824-1825
Cincinnati Enquirer, December 11, 1884 (J.P. Beggs' obituary)
_____ March 10, 1901, "Ancient Tombs"
_____ October 28, 1923, "Conteur" (pseud. Edwin Henderson), "Manufacture and Sale of Jewelry in Cincinnati During Preceding Century."
Cincinnati Journal & Western Luminary, 1836-1837
Cincinnati Standard, 1831-1833
Cincinnati Times Star, Centennial Edition, April 25, 1940, "Manufacture of Timepieces Has Had Important Part in Industry."
Cincinnati Weekly Advertiser, 1846-1850
Cincinnati Western Tiller, 1826-1830
Cist's Daily Advertiser, 1847-1848
Cist's Weekly Advertiser, 1844-1850
Clermont Courier, 1844-1846
The Daily Chronicle, 1839-1846
Daily Cincinnati Commercial, 1849-1850
Daily Cincinnati Republican, 1823-1840
Daily Evening Post, 1835-1839
Freeman's Journal, 1796-1799
Inquisitor & Cincinnati Advertiser, June 1818-July 1822
Liberty Hall & Cincinnati Gazette, 1811-1850
Liberty Hall & Cincinnati Mercury, 1804-1811
National Republican & Ohio Political Register, 1823-1830
Philanthropist, 1837-1841
Saturday Evening Chronicle, 1826-1829
Spirit of the Times, 1840
Western Christian Advocate, 1834-1840
Western Spy & Hamilton Gazette, May 1799-December 1822

Other Cities

Republican & Banner, Madison, Indiana, February 27, 1834
Scioto Gazette, Chillicothe, Ohio, 1824-1841 (Ohio Historical Society)
West Union Village Register, West Union, Ohio, 1825

Western Star & Lebanon Gazette, Lebanon, Ohio, (1816-1825) (Lebanon, Ohio Historical Society)

*Unless otherwise noted, these newspapers are in the collection of the Cincinnati Historical Society.

Bibliography: Books

Allen, Carrie E. *Van Nuys Genealogy.* Privately Printed, 1916

Bond, Beverley W., Jr., editor. *The Intimate Letters of John Cleves Symmes and His Family.* Cincinnati: Historical and Philosophical Society of Ohio, 1956.

Brainard, Homer Worthington. *A Survey of the Scovils or Scovills in England and America; Seven Hundred Years of History and Genealogy.* Hartford: Privately Printed, 1915.

Brix, Maurice. *List of Philadelphia Silversmiths and Allied Artificers, 1692-1850.* Philadelphia: Privately Printed, 1920.

Buhler, Kathryn C. and Hood, Graham. *American Silver: Garvan and other Collections in the Yale University Art Gallery;* Volume One: *New England;* Volume Two: *Middle Colonies and the South.* New Haven & London: Yale University Press, 1970.

Burton, E. Milby. *South Carolina Silversmiths.* Charleston, S.C.: The Charleston Museum, 1942.

Cist, Charles. *Sketches and Statistics of Cincinnati in 1851.* Cincinnati: William H. Moore & Co., 1851.

Currier, Earnest M. *Marks of Early American Silversmiths.* (1938) Reprinted, Harrison, N.Y.: Robert Alan Green, Publisher, 1970.

Cutten, George Barton. *Silversmiths of Virginia.* The Dietz Press, 1952.

_____ *The Silversmiths, Watchmakers and Jewelers of the State of New York Outside New York City.* Hamilton, N.Y.: Privately Printed, 1939.

Deterly, Jacob. *Remarks of Jacob Deterly.* Transcribed indexed by Madge Hubbard and Opal Saffell. Seattle: Northwest Lineage Researcher, 1972.

Fales, Martha Gandy. *Early American Silver for the Cautious Collector.* New York: Funk & Wagnalls, 1970.

Greve, Charles Theodore. *Centennial History of Cincinnati and Representative Citizens.* Chicago: Biographical Publishing Company, 1904.

Harrington, Jessie. *Silversmiths of Delaware, 1700-1850.* Delaware National Society of Colonial Dames of America, 1939.

Hiatt, Noble W. and Lucy F. *The Silversmiths of Kentucky.* Louisville, Ky.: The Standard Printing Co., 1954.

Hood, Graham. *American Silver: A History of Style, 1650-1900.* (American Decorative Arts Series) New York: Praeger Publishers, 1971.

Jones, A.E. *Extracts from the History of Cincinnati and the Territory of Ohio.* Cincinnati: Cohen & Co., 1888.

Kenney, D.J. *Illustrated Cincinnati*. Cincinnati: Robert Clarke & Co., 1875.

_____ *Illustrated Cincinnati and Suburbs*. Cincinnati: Robert Clarke & Co., 1879.

Knittle, Rhea Mansfield. *Early Ohio Silversmiths and Pewterers, 1787-1847*. (Ohio Frontier Series) Cleveland, Ohio: Calvert-Hatch Co., 1943.

Kovel, Ralph M. and Terry H. *American Silver, Pewter and Silver Plate*. New York: Crown Publishers, Inc., 1961.

McBride, James. *Pioneer Biography*. (Manuscript; published as Ohio Valley Historical Series No. 4.) Cincinnati Historical Society, Cincinnati, Ohio.

McClinton, Katherine Morrison. *Collecting American Nineteenth Century Silver*. New York: Charles Scribner's Sons, 1968.

Palmer, Brooks. *A Treasury of American Clocks*. New York: Macmillan, 1967.

_____ *The Book of American Clocks*. New York: Macmillan, 1950.

Pleasants, J. Hall, and Sill, Howard. *Maryland Silversmiths, 1715-1830*. Reprinted: Harrison, N.Y.: Robert Alan Green, 1972 (1930).

Rainwater, Dorothy T. *American Silver Manufactures, Their Marks, Trademarks & History*. Hanover, Pa.: Everybody's Press, 1966.

Roach, Ruth Hunter. *St. Louis Silversmiths*. St. Louis, Mo.: Eden Publishing House, 1967.

Slade, Laura H., Scrapbook, Volume 2. Cincinnati Historical Society, Cincinnati, Ohio.

Torrence, Aaron. *Torrence Papers, Chiefly private letters and Papers relating to the early history of Cincinnati*. Arranged by E.F. Bliss. Historical and Philosophical Society of Ohio (Cincinnati Historical Society, Cincinnati, Ohio.).

Turner, Noel D. *American Silver Flatware*. South Brunswick and New York; A.S. Barnes & Co., 1972.

Williams, Carl Mark. *Silversmiths of New Jersey, 1700-1825*. Philadelphia: G.S. MacManus Co., 1949.

Wright, Smithson E., compiler. *Obituaries of Cincinnatians*. Cincinnati Historical Society, Cincinnati, Ohio.

N.a. *The Centennial Review of Cincinnati*. Cincinnati, Ohio: J.M. Esltner & Co., 1888.

N.a. *Cincinnati Graphic News*, 1884.

N.a. *Cincinnati in Bronze*. Published by William P. Randal, 1959.

N.a. *Cincinnati Past & Present: or, Its Industrial History, as Exhibited in the Life-Labors of Its Leading Men*. Cincinnati: M. Joblin & Co., 1872.

N.a. *History of Cincinnati and Hamilton County, Ohio*. Cincinnati: S.B. Nelson & Co., 1894.

N.a. *The Industries of Cincinnati*. The Metropolitian Publishing Co., 1886.

N.a. Ohio Mechanics Institute Collection (Unprocessed) Special Collections Department, University of Cincinnati.

N.a. *Ohio, The Future Great State*. Comley Bros. Manufacturing and Publishing Co., 1875.

N.a. *Proceedings of the Memorial Association, Eulogies at Music Hall and Biographical Sketches of Many Distinguished Citizens of Cincinnati*, Volume One. Cincinnati: A.E. Jones, 1881.

Directories

Cincinnati Directory, 1819

Cincinnati Directory, 1825

Cincinnati Directory, 1829

Cincinnati Directory, 1831

Cincinnati Directory, 1834

Cincinnati Directory, 1836-1837

Cincinnati Directory, 1839-1840

Cincinnati Directory, 1842

Cincinnati Directory, 1843

Cincinnati Directory, 1844

Cincinnati Directory, 1846

Cincinnati Directory, 1849-1850

Cincinnati Directories, 1851-1900

Cincinnati Wholesale Business Directory, for 1853. Cincinnati: W.H. Fagan, Publisher, 1853.

Gray & Co.'s Cincinnati Business Mirror and City Advertiser, for 1851-1852. Cincinnati: A. Gray & Co., 1851.

Kimball & James' Business Directory for the Mississippi Valley, 1844. Cincinnati: Printed by Kendall & Barnard, 1844.

J.F. Kimball & Co.'s Eastern, Western & Southern Business Directory. Cincinnati and New York: J.F. Kimball & Co., 1846.

The Ohio State Gazeteer, Shipper's Guide and Classified Business Directory, for 1864-1865. Indianapolis: Hawes & Redford, Publishers, 1864.

W.W. Reilly & Co.'s Ohio State Business Directory...for 1853-1854. Cincinnati: Morgan & Overend, 1853.

Western Address Directory. by W.G. Lyford. Baltimore: Printed by J. Robinson, 1837.

Williams' Cincinnati Guide and General Business Directory for 1848-1849. cincinnati: C.S. Williams, Publisher, 1848.

Periodical Articles

Caldwell, Benjamin H., Jr., "Tennessee Silversmiths Prior to 1860: a check list." *The Magazine Antiques,* December 1971.

Crouch, Tom D., "Up, Up, and — Sometimes — Away." *The Cincinnati Historical Society Bulletin,* XXVIII, No.2, (Summer, 1970), pp. 108-132.

Diehl, John A., "Luman Watson, Cincinnati Clockmaker." *The Magazine Antiques,* June, 1968.

Green, Robert Alan, "Ohio Silver." *The Magazine Silver,* January-February 1975, pp. 6-9.

Maurer, Maurer, "Richard Clayton — Aeronaut." *Historical and Philosophical Society of Ohio Bulletin,* XIII, No. 2, (April, 1955), pp. 143-150.

Sikes, Jane, "The Best Family of Silversmiths." Unpublished Ms., appeared in *The Magazine Antiques,* July, 1974.

Snow, Julia D. Sophronia, "The 'Clayton Ascent' Bandbox." *The Magazine Antiques,* September, 1928, pp. 240-241.

N.a. "Aerial Navigation." *The Western Monthly Magazine* (Cincinnati), III, June, 1835, pp. 354-363.

N.a. "Mr. Clayton." *The Western Monthly Magazine,* James Hall, editor, IV, October, 1835, pp. 231-238.

Records

Cincinnati 1817 Tax Lists

Hamilton County, Ohio Census Records: 1820; 1830; 1840; 1850.

Hamilton County, Ohio Records: Pioneers, marriages, deaths. Robert D. Craig, compiler, [n.p.] [n.d.]

Hamilton County, Ohio Court and other Records. 3 Volumes. Virginia Raymond Cummins, compiler. Cincinnati: General Printing Co., 1966-1969.

Hamilton County, Ohio Courthouse Records: Marriage Books; Will Books; Probate Court Estate Records.

Methodist Episcopal Church, Cincinnati Ohio: Isaac Covall's List of Cemetery Records, in Orders for Interments, Vault and Sale of Lots, 1828-1848.

Ohio State Census Records: 1820; 1830; 1840; 1850.

Spring Grove Cemetery Records.

Warren County, Ohio, Marriage Records.

INDEX

The italicized page numbers indicate the pages on which illustrations appear.

Adair, Robert, 24
Allen & Rhodes, 1,3,4,117,118,*117*
Allen, C. & Co., 1,2,3,4,*3*
Allen, C. & W.H., 2,4,24
Allen, Rhodes & Co., 1,2,3,4,6,117,118,*29*
Allen,
    Caleb Jr., 1-3,4,6,117
    Caleb Sr., 1,4
    Caroline Hastings, 3
    Hannah, 1,4
    Martha, 78
    William H., 2,4,24
Anderson, D.B., 43
Andrews, David B., 5
Andrews, Loring & Co., 155
Ange,
    Eliza, 5
    Evaline Mennet, 5
    Maria B. Damiael, 5
    Solomon, 5
    Theodore, 5
    William Henry, 5
Anthony,
    Ann Rhodes, 6,116
    John G., 1,6,116,117
    Thomas Rhodes, 6
Aspinwall & Eyster, 6
Aspinwall & Griffing, 6
Aspinwall, C. B. & Co., 7
Aspinwall,
    Chauncey B., 6,7
    Edward, 7
    Mary, 7
    Sara, 7
    Theodore, 7
    William Henry, 7
Atkinson,
    Clarence, 7
    Emma, 7
    George, 7
    Jeanette, 7
    John, 7
    John V., 7
Ayers, Elias, 149
Ayers, Elias & Co., 149
Bailey, Gamaliel, 7
Bailey, Gamaliel Jr., 7
Bangs, John, 7,8
Beard, C. C., 111,135
Beggs & Smith, 8,9,10,11,94,130,*10*
Beggs, J. P. & Co., 8,11,*15*
Beggs, Joseph P., 8-11,24,94,130
Benson,
    Abigail Mills, 12
    Gabriel L., 12,123,148
Benson, G. L. & Co., 12

Bertling,
    Ernst, 11,12
    Johanna, 11,12
Best & Deterly, 12,13,15,20,44,149
Best & Woodruff, 12,13,20,149
Best, R. & Co., 13,14,15,20,41
Best, S. & R., 18,20
Best,
    Ann, 19
    Eunice Winkler, 16,17
    Henry, 20
    Margaret, 20
    Mary Crouch, 17
    Mary Green, 17
    Robert, 12-15,16,17,41,*15*
    Samuel, 12,14,16-18,19,*18*
    Sara Greenham, 12,16,19
    Thomas, 19,20,140
    Thomas Sr., 12,16,19
Bisbee, Isiah, 21
Blakeslee,
    Edward, 21,22,39
    Garret S., 22
    Lyman W., 22
Blaksley, Harper, 22,146
Blanchard, Joshua, 23
Bliss,
    H. Jeanette, 23
    Henry, 23
Boerner, Charles, 23,130
Borland, William, 37
Boyd, Joseph B., 24
Brainard, Homer, 122
Brandt, Felix, 24
Brix, Maurice, 7
Brockman,
    Anna, 25
    Christian F., 25
    Dorothea, 25
    Ernst, 25
    F., 25
    Margaretha Meuthe, 25
Bromley, George, 153
Budd, Joseph, 153
Bush,
    Elizabeth, 25
    Henry, 25
    Mary, 25
Bushnell,
    Capt., 146
    Sara Willey, 146
Caldwell, B. H. Jr., 58,80,89,98
Callahan, John B., 83
Carey & Anthony, 27
Carley & Anthony, 27
Carley & Co., 26,261

Carley & Wray, 26,27,151
Carley,
    Eliza, 26
    Fay, 26
    Oliver, 26
    Samuel T., 6,26,27,57,103,151,153,29
    Sara Gano, 26
    Susan, 26
    William, 26
Carlisle, George, 125,126
Cazelles,
    Clarissa Mennesier, 27
    Peter, 27,28
Choat, R. W., 153
Choate, Stephem, 28
Cist, Charles, 21,63,106
Clark,
    Francis, 28,29
    James, 28
    Martha, 28
    Mary J., 28
Clayton,
    Charlotte, 34
    Jane Jenkins, 34
    Mary Ann Jenkins, 34
    Richard, 30-34,44,3,32
Coates, William, 34,35
Cobb,
    Charles, 35
    Nancy, 35
    Zachariah B., 35
Coffin, Cyrus, 28,102,153
Collins,
    Charles Edwin, 36
    Edwin, 36
    Mary, 36
    Nancy, 35,36
    Peleg, 35,36,125,130,15
Conway & McHenry, 37,96
Conway,
    Catherine, 37
    James, 37
    Laura, 37
    Margot, 37
    Mason, 37
    Sara Light, 37
    Thomas, 37
    Thomas A., 37,96
    Wilton, 37
Cooper & Saulnier, 37,39
Cooper, W. & A., 37,38,39
Cooper,
    Archibald, 37,38,39
    William, 37,38
Covall, Isaac, 58
Coward, Samuel, 153
Cox,
    Catherine, 40
    Eugene, 40
    Jesse, 40
    Kate, 40
    Lucy B., 40
    Marion, 40
    Rudolpho, 40
Crowell, William, 153
Cummins, 27
Currier, Earnest, 36,89,120,126
Cutten, George B., 6,34,64
Daller,
    John, 40,100
    Joseph, 40
    Mary, 40
    Theresa, 40
Dalton, John, 153
Daumont, Peter, 40,58
Deterly,
    Jacob, 12,13,14,28,40-44,58,60,71,90,98,108,
        123,124,125,133,149
    Johann Ludwig, 40
    Mary Elizabeth Keither, 40
De Young,
    Ralph, 44
    Raphael, 44
    Richard, 44
Diehl, John A., 143
Disney, Mary, 78
Doll,
    Francis, 44
    William, 44,45
Doran, John, 45
Dorland, Garret T., 155
Dornseifer,
    Charles, 45
    Henry, 45
Dover & Best, 20
Dover,
    James, 19
    Thomas, 14
Draper,
    Anne, 48
    George, 48
    Harrisonia, 48
    John, 48
    Joseph, 24,28,45-47,56,153,154,XII,3,15,78
    Louise, 48
    Martha, 48
    Martha Inskip, 48
Droz,
    Frederick, 48,49,15
    John, 48
Dueber, John C., 48,49
Dueber Watch Case Co., XI,48,49
Duffner,
    Anna, 49
    John, 49
    Vincent, 49,153
Duhme & Co., XI,XII,XIV,44,51,52,53,54,55,56,
        XIII,XIV,52,53
Duhme,
    Albert, 54
    Frank, 54

       Herman, 50-54,56,101
       Herman H., 52,56
       John, H., 56
       Lottie, 54
       Margaret, 52,56
       Mary Ann McNichol, 54
       Mary C. Galbraith, 54
Dunlevy & Ryland, 56,118
Dunlevy, William D., 56
Eaves & Herbel, 57
Eaves & Martin, 57,90
Eaves, William T., 57,90
Elias, Henry P., 155
Embree, Davis, 41
Ernst,
       Andrew, 80
       Elizabeth, 80
Evans,
       William M., 57
       William R., 57
Evens, Daniel T., 149
Eyster, Andrew A., 155
Falize, Alexander, 57
Feltmann,
       Mary Schmidt, 58
       William H., 58
Fisher, Ebenezer, 59
Fix, Ferdinand, 153
Fleming, W., 153
Foos,
       Griffith, 52
       Mrs., 52
Frankenstein, H. W., 153
Freye, Henry, 101
Fuerste, W. M., 155
Garner, John, 58
Gedney, Charles, 153
Gerstecker, Frederick, 153
Gildersleeve, Isaac, 140
Gilmore, Robert, 58,59
Goldsmith, David, 59
Goodfellow, Robin, 153
Gordon,
       Charles, 59
       Eliza, 59
       Henry, 59
       Jane Harsha, 59
       Jonathan, 59
       L., 60
       Margaret, 59
Gould, J., 60,61
Grandbeck,
       Charlotte Schenke, 61
       Daniel, 61
       Isabelle, 61
       Oscar, 61
Graves,
       Thomas, 61
       S., 61
Greve, Charles, 41,136

Gruen Watch Co., 155
Guild, Jeremiah, 153
Guinand,
       Edward (F. Edward), 61,62
       Frances, Duon, 62
Hanks,
       Alpheus, 62
       George L., 62,104,106
       Julia Bunce, 62
       Zeniah, 62
Harrington, Jessie, 45
Harris,
       Caleb K., 62
       Henry, 153
       William, 63
Hatch, Samuel, 71
Haynes,
       John R., 63
       Mary E., 63
Hazen & Collins, 36,65,66
Hazen,
       Hannah Jeanette, 23,65
       John F., 65
       Nathan L., 23,36,37,58,64-66,*XII,15,42,66,78*
       Nathan Lord, 65
       Phoebe, 64
Heil, John, 153
Hellebush,
       Clemens, XII,66,67,101,*XIII*
       Elizabeth Specker, 67
Herschede, Frank, 155
Hiatt, Lucy and Noble, 23,28,39,40,57,70,99,136
Hill,
       Edward, 67
       Edward H., 67,68,140,67
       Elizabeth, 67
       John, 67
       Samuel, 67
Hogeland, Ralph, 153
Holland, John, 68
Hollen, Stephen, 68,69
Horton,
       Henry V., 69,70
       Sophia Mathilda, 70
Howard, E., 103
Hummel, Louis, 155
Huntington & Laboyteaux, 70,71,88
Huntington, William C., 70,71,88
Isbell, E. E., 155
Jackson, Andrew, 41,42
Jamison, Jacob, 71
January & Nutman, 99
Jenkins & Hatch, 71
Jenkins, H. & Co., 71
Jenkins,
       Clara, 71
       Fanny, 34
       Henry, 71
       Lucinda, 71
       Martha, 34

Jennings, David, 153
Johnson,
    Thomas, 153
    William, 72
Jonas,
    Abraham, 74
    Joseph, 72-74,92
    Lucia, 74
    Rachel, 74
Jones, William, A., 153
Joseph, Joseph G., 67,74-76,75
Kautz, D., 7,45
Keck,
    Herman, 54,155
    Oscar, 54
Keller, Charles, 77
Kelly,
    Charles, 77
    Lydia, 77
Kent & Michie, 79,80
Kent, Luke & Co., 79
Kent, Luke & Son, 79
Kent,
    Adeline Ernst, 80
    Amelia, 80
    Asbury, 78
    Eliza Douglas, 78,79
    Herbert Townsend, 80
    Luke Jr., 78,79,80,101
    Luke Sr., 77-79,78
    Luke III, 80
    Thomas, 78,80
    Walter, 80
    William, 78
Kerdolff,
    Mrs. J., 80
    William, 80
Kilgour, David, 98
Kinkead,
    Elizabeth, 81
    George L., 80,81
Kinsey, D. & Co., 83
Kinsey, E. & D., XII,XIV,81,83,84,85,111,*XII,XV,85*
Kinsey,
    Ann, 81,84
    Charles S., 83
    David, 63,81-83,84,85,86,*XIII,82,83*
    Edward, 63,81,83,84-87,111,153,*86,87*
    Edward W., 83
    Eugenia, 84,86
    Julia A. Peacock, 83,86
    Louis A., 83
    Temperance H., 86
    Thomas, 81,84,86
Kirkby, Thomas, 30
Knittle, Rhea, 26,48,68,112,133,138
Koch, Marcus, 155
Korf, Henry, 155
Kovel, Ralph and Terry, 98,110,111,138

Laboyteaux, Isaac N., 70,88
Lafayette, General, 41
Lang, Christopher, 153
Lange,
    Herman, 155
    J. & Bros., 155
    Louis, 155
Lary, William, 153
Lawson, Fenton, 10
Lawton, Joshua, 19
Levi, Barnit, 88
Levy, Jonas, 89
Long & Price, 90,113
Long Harmon, 90,113
Loton, George, 153
Luck, William, 56
Lyon, Elizabeth, 78
Martin & Owen, 90,91,102
Martin,
    Elizabeth, 48
    James H., 57,90,91,102
    Jane, 90
    Mrs., 153
Mauthe,
    Christ Jr., 155
    Christ Sr., 155
Mayle, Ebenezer, 153
McBride, James, 138
McCullough, C. B., 91,144
McDonald, Alexander, 153
McGrew & Beggs, 8,11,42,94,95,96,*XII,42*
McGrew & Jonas, 72,74,91,96
McGrew, W. & Son, 95,96
McGrew,
    Alexander, 72,91-93,94,95,*15,93*
    Alexander M., 91
    Alvira L. Fisher, 91
    Amelia M., 91
    Aurelia, 91
    Carolina Carter, 91
    Caroline E.C., 91
    Margaret Amelia, 91
    Robert I., 91
    Sallie, 95
    Sarah, 94,95
    William K., 91
    William Wilson, 93,95,*XII,95*
    Wilson, XIV,8,93-95,96,*XII,117*
McHenry,
    Dennis, 37,96,97
    Sarah Macauley, 96
McMurphy,
    Albert, 153
    Theodore B., 153
McNichol, Peter, 54
McQuarters, Hugh, 97
Mehmert, Joseph, 155
Michie Bros., 155
Michie Jewelry, 155
Michie, Wm. & J. C., 155

Milbis, Nathan, 153
Miller,
    Amos, 43
    Lewis, 153
    Louise Deterly, 43
Moore & Rhodes, 97,117
Moore, Samuel P., 97,117
Morris,
    John B., 155
    Patrick, 153
Morrow, Francis, 97
Musgrove,
    Cuthbert, 98
    Elizabeth Moore, 98
    Samule, 98,133
Nagele,
    Amala, 98
    Elizabeth, 98
    Louis, 98
    Mary, 98
    Vital, 98
Nash, Coleman, 99
Naurd, Peter, 153
Nengas, Henry, 153
Niles,
    James N., 153
    J. S., 153
Nolting, Charles, 100
North, Alexander H., 99
Nuttman, John C., 99,125
Oskamp & Co., 155
Oskamp Nolting Co., 100,155
Oskamp,
    A., 155
    Alfred, 100
    Caspar, 99,101
    Clemens, XI,XII,66,99,100,*XIII*
    Margaret Freye, 101
    Mary Fisher, 100
    Theodore, 99,100,101,*XII*
    Theresa, 99,101
    William, 100
Owen & Carley, 26,27,103,104,*XII*
Owen & Read, 59,103,104,115,134,*XII*
Owen, W., & Co., 102,104
Owen,
    Charles, 101,102
    Isabel Murray, 102
    John, 67,90,102,XII
    Maria Louise Mariana, 102
    Sara Permer, 104
    William, 26,101,103,104,115,134
Palmer & Hanks, 62,97,104,107
Palmer & Owen, 23,103,104,106,107,*XIII*
Palmer & Smith, 107,130,131
Palmer,
    Abraham, 62,104-107,130,153,*15,105*
    Brooks, 22
    Eugene, 107
    H. L., 108

    Julietta, 107
    Manor Trutebuss, 107
    Sarah Nehemiah, 191
    William S., 107
Parks, George D., 155
Perret & Mathey, 61,108,109
Perret & Shipp, 109,124
Perret, Philip H., 108,109,124
Phillips,
    James, 98
    ---, 154
Phluck, Joseph, 154
Picard, J. C., 109
Pickering,
    Cornelia, 110
    George, 110
    John, 110
    Marcellus, 110
    Maria, 110
Pigman,
    John, 111
    Nancy, 111
Plaut,
    A & J, 155
    Bernard, 155
Pleasants & Sill, 27,37,61,62,96
Poncet, Louis, 27
Pratt & Bangs, 8
Pratt & Beard, 111
Pratt & Stretcher, 112,135
Pratt, Stretcher & Beard, 112,135
Pratt,
    Catherine, 112
    E. P., 8,111,112,135
    E. W., 112
Prell, John, 19
Price,
    Maria Malsbury, 113
    Mary, 113
    Nancy R. H., 114
    Philip, 90,113,114,128
Pyne, William, 44
Rademacher,
    Charles, 115
    G., 115
Rafil, Joseph, 154
Read & Watson, 142
Read Bros., 142
Read,
    Francis, 115
    James, 103,115,134
    Margaret, 115
    Sara, 115
Reis, Edward J., 154
Rhodes & Anthony, 6,118
Rhodes, Anthony & Co., 6,118,*117*
Rhodes, Anthony & Carley, 6,26,117,118
Rhodes,
    Clara, 116
    Howard, 116

Laura Lyon, 116
Linda, 116
James F., 29,116
Thomas F., 1,6,97,116,117
Roach, Ruth Hunter, 57,125
Ross, David, 154
Rugg,
A., 124
Virginia, 124
Ryland,
James, 118
William, 56,118
Salmon,
Alfred, 119
Elizabeth, 119
Mary Frances, 119
Samuels, S., 154
Sanford, R., 154
Saulnier, W. H., 38
Sayre,
A., 119
Leonard, 120
Schneider,
Ben, 155
Christopher, 120
A & J, 155
Schoolfield,
Ella, 120
Honora Simms, 120,121
John Q.A., 120,121
Schwab, A G, & Bros., 155
Scovil & Co., 121,122,*32,122*
Scovil & Kinsey, 18,84,87,121,122,*18,122*
Scovil, Willey & Co., 22,121,122,146,147,*29,147*
Scovil,
Anna Ames, 121
Pulaski, 1,22,84,121,122,146,*15*
Roswell, 121
Seymour & Williston, 123,124,133,148
Seymour, Williston & Benson, 11,123,124,148
Seymour,
Charles, 123
Clarissa Bagg, 123
Jeffrey, 11,123,148
Shepard, Ephraim E., 124
Shipp & Collins, 35,36,43,71,125,126
Shipp & Woodbridge, 125
Shipp, Samuel A. M., 35,41,43,71,109,124,125
Shourds, Samuel P., 128
Shumard, Samuel, 154
Sikes, Jane, 18,19
Simpson & Price, 113,128,129
Simpson,
Alexander, 113,128,129
Nancy Rogers, 128
Slow, Clark, 154
Smith, A. D., & Co., 155
Smith & Boerner, 24,130,131
Smith, Harry R., & Co., 131

Smith,
Anna McNaughton, 131
Conrad, 129
Harry R., 8,24,94,130,131
John, 130,131
Ruth, 130
Thaddeus, 131,132
Solman, Edward, 154
Sotcher,
Abner, 98,133
Sarah, 133
Spiller, John, 133
Stall, George W., 133,134
Stanley & Owen, 103,134
Stanley I.M., 134
Stinger,
Elizabeth, 134
George A., 129,134
Stretcher, John E., 112,135
Strueve, Herman R., 155
Stuttelberg, Arnold, 135
Sullivan, George, 134,136
Suofield, H., 154
Sutherland, John, 27
Swift,
Elinore, 136
John D., 154
William C., 136
Symmes,
Abigail Tuthill, 136
Celadon, 136-138,*3*
John Cleves, 136,138
Timothy, 136
William, 138
Symonds,
Philip, 154
S., 154
Thane,
Samuel, 26
Sarah J., 26
Thornton, Joseph, 138
Thorpe,
Ann, 139
Franklin, 139
Todd, Tracy, 154
Trais, William, 154
Trotter, Jeremiah, 140
Trousdale, John L., 154
Tucker, Albert, 154
Twitchell,
Hannah, 23
John, 23
Van Nuys & Best, 19,140
Van Nuys,
Isaac, 10,140
William, 140
Verdin,
Francis, 140-142,*141*
Michael, 140-142,*141*
I.T. Verdin, 141,142

Voss,
    J. S., 155
    J. S. & Son, 155
Wachman, Abraham D., 154
Wallace & Beggs, 8
Warner,
    James, 142
    Thomas, 142
    Warren, 142
Watson, Luman, XV,142,143,*143*
Wenning,
    Elizabeth, 143
    Henry, 143
    William, 143
Wesley, John, 18
White,
    Edward T., 144
    George L., 144,149
Whitesides,
    Addison H., 146
    Anne S., 146
    John, 138,144,145
    Samuel, 145,146

Willey & Blaksley, 22,146,147,*147*
Willey & Co., 146,147,*147*
Willey,
    Asa, 146
    Bushnell, 22,121,146,147
    Phebe Waters, 146
Williams,
    Carl M., 18
    David P., 142
Williston, Othniel, 11,123,148
Wilms,
    J. C., 155
    J.C., & Son, 155
Winslow, Harmon S., 155
Woodbridge, Horace, 71,125
Woodruff & Deterly, 41,42,44,124,133,149,151,*42*
Woodruff & White, 138,144,149,150,151
Woodruff, Enos, 13,41,42,43,99,124,144,149,150,*150*
Worrell, John, 154
Wray, Henry, 25,151
Wright, Mrs. W., 144
Yost, Henry, 154

Photographs
by C.W. Bostain
and McHale Studios Inc.

Type set by D.O.V. Graphics

Printed in the United States of America
by Litho-Color

Appendix

OHIO SILVERSMITHS AND RELATED TRADES WORKING OUTSIDE OF CINCINNATI

Based on research by Elizabeth D. Beckman,
compiled by Maurice R. Meslans, and edited by Wm. Erik Voss

Name
City, County, Years Active
Profession
Notes

Abbey, Henry S.
Akron, Summit Co., 1853-72
goldsmith, watchmaker, jeweler
nothing found to indicate he was anything besides a clockmaker, though he retailed goods

Ackley, Charles C.
Warren, Trumbull Co., 1875-90,
silversmith, jeweler
son of Joel

Ackley, Joel Woodworth
Fowler, Trumbull Co., 1835-50
jeweler
Bloomfield, Trumbull Co., 1850-80
jeweler

Ackley, Lott W.
Painesville, Lake Co., 1853-64
jeweler
birth: abt 1810 in New York; death: 21 JAN 1885 in Painesville, Lake, Ohio

Ackley, Thaddeus D.
Warren, Trumbull Co., 1860-90
silversmith, jeweler
son of Joel

Ackley, William Douglas
Warren, Trumbull Co., 1890-1920
silversmith, jeweler
son of Thaddeus

Adams, John
Steubenville, Jefferson Co., 1808
watchmaker

Adams, Thomas J.
Woodsfield, Monroe Co., 1853

Aiken, Charles G.
Cleveland, Cuyahoga Co., 1856

Aiken, (Charles) & Coon, (Jeremiah)
Cleveland, Cuyahoga Co., 1856
jewelers

Albertson, Joseph R.
Cleveland, Cuyahoga Co., 1849-58
jeweler

Allen, B.
Morristown, Belmont Co., 1850-53

Allen, Benjamin A.
Springfield, Clark Co., 1856-80
jeweler
born 1816 in VA; listed in the 1880 Springfield census as a jeweler

Amsden, (Austin O.) & Dickinson, (George W.)
Ashtabula, Ashtabula Co., 1859-72
jewelers, clockmakers, watchmakers
the partners were related by marriage; Amsden sold out to his partner for a short time, moving to California for his health. He returned in 1877 and took up the trade again with his sons Arther and Lewis.

Anderson, David Bush
Marietta, Washington Co., 1817-54
silversmith, jeweler

Anderson, David Bush, Jr. & Brothers
Marietta, Washington Co., 1854-72
silversmiths, jewelers, watchmakers
with brothers Henry and Joseph

Anthiaume, Jean B.
Gallipolis, Gallia Co., 1790

Amstrong, Joel
Marysville, Union Co., 1853-68

Ashley, Baxter
Milan, Erie Co., 1850-56

Albert, Charles
Dayton, Montgomery Co., 1853

Aubert, C. N.
Dayton, Montgomery Co., 1856
jeweler

Axman, Charles
Germantown, Montgomery Co., 1853-72
jeweler, clockmaker, watchmaker

Babcock, J. A.
Painesville, Lake Co., 1850-3

Backus, Alexander
Columbus, Franklin Co., 1841-50
jeweler, clockmaker, watchmaker, silversmith
Defiance, Defiance Co., 1853
jeweler, clockmaker, watchmaker, silversmith

Baird, Robert A.
Ravenna, Portage Co., 1850-61
jeweler

Baird, (Robert) & Waite
Ravenna, Portage Co., 1859-64

Baker, Joseph
Wilmington, Clinton Co., 1850-53

Baldwin, E. J.
Columbus, Franklin Co., 1851
jeweler
listed in 1850 city directory at the shop of Blynn (William) and Baldwin (Thomas) Jewelers

Baldwin, C. E.
Columbus, Franklin Co., 1870-1880
jeweler
listed in the 1880 census as a dealer in jewelry

Baldwin J. C.
Columbus, Franklin Co., 1870-1880
jeweler
listed in the 1880 census as a dealer in jewelry; living with C. E Baldwin in the house of Henry Dietz

Baldwin, Thomas S.
Columbus, Franklin Co., 1851
watchmaker
listed in 1850 city directory at the shop of Blynn (William) and Baldwin Jewelers

Bangs, J. J.
Maumee, Lucas Co., 1830-1840
jeweler, watchmaker
listed in the 1837 city directory

Bangs, John
Chillicothe, Ross Co., ca 1839-68
jeweler, watchmaker

Bapst, C. H.
Middletown, Butler Co., 1856
jeweler

Barkdull, Levi C.
Chillicothe, Ross Co., 1838-68
jeweler, silversmith, watchmaker
Sidney, Shelby Co.

Barkdull, (Levi) & Clark, (A. J.)
Chillicothe, Ross Co., 1838

Barrett, George B.
Cadiz, Harrison Co., 1856-64
jeweler, clockmaker, watchmaker

Bartholomew, H. M.
Chagrin Falls, Cuyahoga Co., 1853 -

Baxter, William H.
Urbana, Champaign Co., 1850-72
silversmith

Baxter, (William) & Benjamin
Urbana, Champaign Co., 1853

Bean, R. A. or R. S.
Dayton, Montgomery Co., 1853-56
jeweler

Becker, Charles
Cleveland, Cuyahoga Co., 1836-37
watchmaker

Benner, J. F.
New Lisbon, Columbiana Co., 1853-61
jeweler

Benton, Lucius A.
Cleveland, Cuyahoga Co., 1850-80
jeweler, watchmaker, silversmith
Worked in the 1840's for Crittenden, Benton & Maihivet; listed in the 1880 census as a jeweler

Best, Edward
Dayton, Montgomery Co., 1860-80
jeweler
son of Henry; listed in the 1880 census as a jeweler

Best, Henry
Dayton, Montgomery Co., 1850-72
jeweler, clockmaker, watchmaker
born 21 November 1804 in Cincinnati, died 26 January 1873 in Dayton

Best, Thomas
Lebanon, Warren Co., 1822-36
jeweler, clockmaker, watchmaker, silversmith

Biesenthal, Soloman Ralph
Hamilton, Butler Co., ca 1850-1855
jeweler, watchmaker
born in Prussia; went on to work in Lexington KY until 1899

Binninger, Wolfgang
Lancaster, Fairfield Co., 1853-80
jeweler, watchmaker
born in Germany; listed in the 1880 census as a jeweler in his son's household

Binninger, Philemon
Lancaster, Fairfield Co., 1860-1880
jeweler
born in Lancaster c 1844, son of Wolfgang; listed as a jeweler in the 1880 census; Harry Boyer, a nephew, is also listed as a jeweler

Bisbee, C. A.
Chardon, Geauga Co., 1850-68

Bixby, Edwin
Ironton, Lawrence Co., 1850-72
jeweler, clockmaker, watchmaker, silversmith
listed in the 1880 census as a keeper of clocks and watches

Blackner, John L.
Cleveland, Cuyahoga Co., 1836-37
watchmaker

Blanchard, J.
Ripley, Brown Co., 1830-53

Bliss, John
Zanesville, Muskingum Co., 1815

Bliss, Jonathan
Cleveland, Cuyahoga Co., 1815
silversmith
brother of William; only stayed a short time before returning to NY

Bliss, William
Cleveland, Cuyahoga Co., 1815-28
silversmith

Blynn, William
Columbus, Franklin Co., 1848-64
jeweler

Blynn, (William) & Baldwin, (Thomas S.)
Columbus, Franklin Co., 1850-59

Boisell, Oliver
Cumberland, Guernsey Co., 1853

Borton, Bethel
Washington, Guernsey Co., 1816
clockcmaker, watchmaker, silversmith

Borton, Bethel
Washington, Guernsey Co., 1856
jeweler, watchmaker
Winchester Guernsey 1880 j listed in the 1880 census as a jeweler

Bouvier, Daniel
Zanesville, Muskingum Co., 1815
clockmaker, watchmaker, silversmith

Bowman, George
Columbus, Franklin Co., 1843-68
clockmaker

Bratin, A. R.
Greenfield, Highland Co., 1856
jeweler

Briggs, (T. C.) & Co.
Cleveland, Cuyahoga Co., 1856
jeweler

Brown, George
St. Clairsville, Belmont Co., 1820-72
jeweler, clockmaker, watchmaker

Brown, J. B.
St. Clairsville, Belmont Co., 1826
jeweler, clockmaker, watchmaker

Brown, J. H.
Columbus, Franklin Co., 1848
silversmith

Brown, (J. H.) & Bach
Columbus, Franklin Co., 1851

Brown, W. B.
Mt. Vernon, Knox Co., 1859-72

Brunner, T. K.
Circleville, Pickaway Co., 1859-72
jeweler, clockmaker, watchmaker

Buffler, Frank
Darrtown, Butler Co., 1859-72
jeweler, clockmaker, watchmaker

Burger, J. & G.
Winesburg, Holmes Co., 1853

Burkhart, William H.
Bucyrus, Crawford Co., 1856-64
jeweler, watchmaker

Burkhart, (William H.) & Lake (Charles)
1864-66

Burr, Raymond
Deleware, Deleware Co., 1850-64
jeweler, watchmaker

Burrell, (John W.) & Co.
Elyria, Lorain Co., 1850-53

Bush, M.
Sidney, Shelby Co., 1850-53

Butch, L. C.
Lancaster, Fairfield Co., 1856-70
silversmith

Butler, Morgan
New Philadelphia, Tuscarawas Co., 1853-64

Cahill, R. F.
Findlay, Hancock Co., 1853

Cambell, James
Steubenville, Jefferson Co., 1808
jeweler, clockmaker, watchmaker, silversmith

Cambell, R. E.
Ravenna, Portage Co., 1849-53
jeweler, clockmaker, watchmaker

Canneff, J. W.
Toledo, Lucas Co., 1853-72

Cantrovitz & Shrier
Cleveland, Cuyahoga Co., 1853

Carey, Manson
Lexington, Richland Co., 1853-72
jeweler
born 4 Oct 1820 in Wyoming PA; listed in the 1880 Lexington census as a jeweler

Carter, O. G.
Norwalk, Huron Co., 1850-72

Cary, H.
Crestline, Crawford Co., 1859-62
jeweler, watchmaker

Cellars, John
Chillicothe, Ross Co., 1806

Chambers, Jacob
Eaton, Preble Co., 1853-72
silversmith, jeweler
listed in the 1880 Eaton census as a jeweler

Chapman, Harvey
Kenton, Hardin Co., 1853-80
jeweler
listed in the 1880 Kenton census as a jeweler

Chapman, (Harvey) & Rogers
Kenton, Hardin Co, 1853

Charter, (David M. & George)
Xenia, Greene Co., 1853-66
jeweler

Clugsten, John
Portsmouth, Scioto Co., 1853-64
jeweler

Clackner, J. F.
Ravenna, Portage Co., 1849
watchmaker, clockmaker

Clark, Elijah
Belleville, Richland, 1859-61
jeweler, clockmaker

Clark, A. J.
Chillicothe, Ross Co.
Columbus, Franklin Co., 1839-59
jeweler, watchmaker

Clark, (A. J.) & Co
Columbus, Franklin Co., 1852-56

Cleveland, Francis
Zanesville, Muskingum Co., 1815-18

Cleveland, (Francis) & Bliss (John)
Zanesville, Muskingum Co., 1815-18
goldsmith, silversmith
Employed Charles Hill who later joined A. C. Ross as Hill & Ross

Clymer, Charles
McConnellsville, Morgan Co., 1853-59

Cohen, Thomas
Chillicothe, Ross Co., 1815
silversmith, jeweler, clockmaker, watchmaker

Coleman, Joseph
Massilon, Stark Co., 1853 -80
jeweler
born in England; listed in the 1880 census as a dealer in watches and jewelry

Combs & Vautrot
Warren, Trumbull Co., 1853-56

Combs & Meiksch
1853

Conant, H. H.
Maumee City, Lucas Co., 1846
jeweler, watchmaker

Coppock, (G.F.) & Son
Columbus, Franklin Co., 1852-53

Conway, Newton S.
Catawba, Clark Co., 1853

Cook, H. T.
Toledo, Lucas Co., 1853-72
jeweler
listed, with son William, in the 1880 Toledo census as merchant jewelers

Cook, William H.
Toledo, Lucas Co., 1880
jeweler
son of H. T. Cook

Coon & Aaron
Medina, Medina Co., 1853

Coon, Jeremiah
Cleveland, Cuyahoga Co., 1846-56
b 1819 in NY; 1880 Cleveland census as a clerk in jewelry store

Coon, John W.
Cleveland, Cuyahoga Co.

Coonwell, M. A.
Copapa, Lorain Co., 1859
jeweler, clockmaker, watchmaker

Cooper, Henry
Wellsville, Columbiana Co., 1865-80
watchmaker
son of Wilson, listed in the 1880 census as a jeweler

Cooper, Wilson
Wellsville, Columbiana Co., 1853-80
watchmaker
listed in the 1880 census as a watchmaker

Coriell, A.
Portsmouth, Scioto Co., 1853-72

Cornwell, David Coleman
Athens, Athens Co., 1869-1900
silversmith, watchmaker, jeweler
son of John; listed in the 1880 census as a silversmith

Cornwell, John Goldsmith
Athens, Athens Co., 1832-1852, 1856-1869
jeweler
Wilkesville, Vinton Co., 1880
jeweler
Cornwell Jewelers (still in business) is the oldest in the country

Cornwell, Frank M.
Athens, Athens Co., 1880
silversmith
son of John; listed in the 1880 census as a silversmith

Covell, Lyman S.
Deleware, Deleware Co., 1853-72
jeweler, clockmaker, watchmaker
listed in the 1880 census as a farmer and jeweler

Cowles, Ralph
Cleveland, Cuyahoga Co., 1840-68
jeweler, watchmaker, silversmith

Cowles, (Royal) & Albertson (Joseph A)
Cleveland, Cuyahoga Co., 1849-53
jeweler, watchmaker, silversmith

Cowles, (Royal) & Co (Homer Micheal Goodwin)
Cleveland, Cuyahoga Co., 1857-89

Cracaw, E. A.
New Philadelphia, Tuscarawas Co., 1856
jeweler

Cram, Moses Bailey
Republic, Seneca Co., 1840-1860
b: 17 Oct 1804 in Weare NH; d: 18 Jun 1878 in Faribault MI

Crickmore, Peter
Lebanon. Warren Co., 1852-64

Crittenden, Newton E.
Cleveland, Cuyahoga Co., 1826-72
jeweler

Cross, R. A.
Maumee City, Lucas Co., 1856
jeweler

Custard, Joseph
New Lisbon, Columbiana Co., 1853-72
silversmith

Daller, H.
Ripley, Brown Co., 1853-68
jeweler

Davis, Pliny E.
Columbus, Franklin Co., 1850
jeweler

Deal or Dial, J.
Franklin, Warren Co., 1859-64
jeweler, clockmaker, watchmaker

Deardorf, P.
Lebanon, Warren Co., 1844-52
Dayton, Montgomery Co., 1853-68
clockmaker

Deardorf & Tucker
Dayton, Montgomery Co., 1849-51

Deardorf & Jenkins
Dayton, Montgomery Co., 1853

Defeu, C. F.
Chillicothe, Ross Co., 1866
Greenfield, Highland Co., 1868

Dehl, Charles
Wooster, Wayne Co., 1856
jeweler

Deitz, Bernard G.
Cleveland, Cuyahoga Co., 1859-68
watchmaker

Dietz (Bernard) & Bothers
Cleveland, Cuyahoga Co.

Demmet or Dammest or Dammert, Francis
Pomeroy, Meigs Co., 1853-56
Irontown, Lawrence Co., 1859
jeweler, watchmaker

Desnoyers, Pierre Jean
Gallipolis, Gallia Co., 1790

Deuble (George) & Brothers
Canton, Stark Co., 1856-72
jeweler, clockmaker, watchmaker, silversmith

DeVacht, Francois
Gallipolis, Gallia Co., 1792
watchmaker, silversmith

DeVacht, Joseph
Gallipolis, Gallia Co., 1792
watchmaker, silversmith

Dewey, Hiram Todd
Sandusky, Erie Co., 1853-64
jeweler

Dewey, R.
Sandusky, Erie Co., 1853-66

Dewing, John Lee
Athens, Athens Co., 1853

DeWitt, Frank C.
Oxford, Butler Co., 1870
jeweler
son of Zachariah

DeWitt, James
Wapakoneta, Auglaize Co., 1853-66

DeWitt, Zachariah T.
Oxford, Butler Co., 1856-68
silversmith, jeweler
birth: 24 February 1809 in Oxford, Butler, Ohio; death: 13 December 1870

DeYoung, R. J.
Leesburg, Highland Co., 1840
jeweler

Dickerson, T. H.
Marion, Marion Co., 1853-66
jeweler

Dickinson, Charles
Zanesville, Muskingum Co., 1815

Dickenson (Charles) & Safford (Harry)
Zanesville, Muskingum Co.

Deihl, E. H.
Wooster, Wayne Co., 1853-56
jeweler

Drayer, William E.
Hamilton, Butler Co., 1853-68
jeweler, watchmaker

Dreher, E.
Chillicothe, Ross Co., 1835-38
jeweler

Dresbach, C. F.
Columbus, Franklin Co., 1835-37

Droz, F. Humbert
Ohio City, Cuyahoga Co., 1853-68
jeweler, watchmaker

Dunbar, R. D.
Columbus, Franklin Co., 1852-68
jeweler, clockmaker, watchmaker, silversmith

Dungan, B. E.
Sunfish, Monroe Co., 1853

Dunkin & McLaughlin
Circleville, Pickaway Co., 1853

Dury, M.
Newark, Licking Co., 1853

Elliot, E. G.
Springfield, Clark Co., 1853-61

Elliot, Freeman
Lebanon, Warren Cp., 1828-31
jeweler, clockmaker, watchmaker, silversmith

Ells, Claflin & Co
Dayton, Montgomery Co., 1846
goldsmith

Embry, E.
East Liberty, Logan Co., 1853-66
jeweler, clockmaker, watchmaker

Emmons, S. F.
Youngstown, Mahoning Co., 1856
jeweler

Enyart, David
Lebanon, Warren Co., 1836-37
silversmith

Espich, Henry
Germantown, Montgomery Co., 1853-59
jeweler, clockmaker, watchmaker

Evans, J. S.
Franklin, Warren Co., 1859-61
jeweler, watchmaker, clockmaker

Ewatt, H.
Piqua, Miami Co., 1856-59
jeweler

Farver, J. K.
Gilboa, Putnam Co., 1853

Fee, Arthur
Felicity, Clermont Co.
birth: 18 Dec 1791 in Washington, Pa; death: 2 Jan 1879 in Clermont, Ohio; married: Sarah Miller, b 2 Mar 1798 in Kentucky

Fee, Arthur Jr.
Felicity, Clermont Co.
birth: 15 Jan 1821 Place: Clermont, Ohio ; death: 7 Apr 1879

Fee, M. D.
Felicity, Clermont Co.

Fee & Fee
Felicity, Clermont Co., 1856
watchmaker

Feighner, H. H.
Bucyrus, Crawford Co., 1853

Feller, George
Xenia, Greene Co., 1853

Ferguson
Dayton, Montgomery Co., 1845
clockmaker

Field, David E.
Cleveland, Cuyahoga Co., 1841-68
jeweler, silversmith, watchmaker

Field & Gray
Cleveland, Cuyahoga Co., 1853

Fletcher, J. F.
Ravenna, Portage Co., 1853

Folger, James Mott
Ravenna, Portage Co., 1849
clockmaker, watchmaker, silversmith

Ford, Daniel
Abbeyville, Medina Co., 1853

Foster, William
West Unity, Williams Co., 1853

Franklin, E. M.
Upper Sandusky, Wyandot Co., 1853

Fredericks, J. G.
Defiance, Defiance Co., 1859-61
jeweler, clockmaker, watchmaker

French, Thomas
Elyria, Lorain Co., 1859-72
jeweler, clockmaker, watchmaker

Frey, S. C.
Canton, Stark Co., 1853-56

Furtwangler, D.
Washington Court House, Fayette Co., 1853-68
silversmith

Gallup, William
Tiffin, Seneca Co., 1854-80
jeweler, watchmaker
working 1841-1845 in Licking OH; 1845-1853 in Covington KY; 1854-1880+ in Tiffin OH (listed there in the 1880 census as a jeweler).

Gantz or Zantz, David
Carrolton, Carroll Co., 1859-61
jeweler, clockmaker, watchmaker

Garden, Samuel, Jr.
Akron, Summit Co., 1846
jeweler, watchmaker

Garney, J. T.
Piqua, Miami Co., 1846
watchmaker

Gates, James
Lancaster, Fairfield Co., 1853-64
jeweler, watchmaker, silversmith
Also listed as an early silversmith in Chillicothe

Gates, Olmsted
Urbana, Champagne Co., 1859

Garrahty, James
Lancaster, Fairfield Co., 1853-56
watchmaker

Gelier, M.
Louisville, Stark Co., 1853-68

German, Michael
Lower Sandusky, Sandusky Co., 1841
watchmaker, clockmaker

Gillett, J.
Akron, Summit Co., 1853

Goodman, John
Cleveland, Cuyahoga Co., 1859-72
jeweler, clockmaker, watchmaker
born 1815 in England; listed 1880 census as a watchmaker

Goodspeed, Laban
Massillon, Stark Co., 1853

Goodwin, Homer Michael
Cleveland, Cuyahoga Co., 1857-1889
married Royal Cowles' sister Maryette in 1849; listed in the 1880 Sandusky census as an attorney

Gory, Volintine
Chillicothe, Ross Co., 1850
clockmaker

Gudgeon, D. L.
Bellefontaine, Logan Co., 1853

Green, H. N.
Mansfield, Richland Co., 1856
jeweler

Griffith, Humphrey
Lebanon, Warren Co., 1819-23
clockmaker, watchmaker
born 23 Dec 1796 in Wales; died 2 Jun 1870 in Indianapolis IN

Hall (A. B.) & Co
Ohio City, Van Wert Co., 1837
jeweler, watchmaker

Hall, J. C.
Urbana, Champaign Co., 1859

Hall, Ransom E.
Cleveland, Cuyahoga Co., 1833-36

Snow & Hall (Ransom)
1835

Haller (L. R.) & Son
Portsmouth, Scioto Co., 1853-36
jeweler

Handy, (J. J.) & Co
Morristown, Belmont Co., 1853

Hardman, J.
Lebanon, Warren Co., 1823
clockmaker, watchmaker

Harper, W. M.
Greenville, Darke Co., 1859-68
watchmaker

Harrison
Marrietta, Washington Co.,
jeweler, clockmaker

Hartman, Lewis
Tiffin, Seneca Co., 1863-80
watchmaker
son of John; listed in 1880 census

Hartman, John
Tiffin, Seneca Co., 1853-72
jeweler
born in Germany

Hasil or Hasic, Marcus
Cleveland, Cuyahoga Co., 1845-46
watchmaker

Hastings, B. B.
Cleveland, Cuyahoga Co., 1836-47
jeweler, watchmaker, silversmith

Hatch, John
Portsmouth, Scioto Co., 1828
clockmaker, watchmaker

Heath, Ralph
Chillicothe, Ross Co., 1815
jeweler, clockmaker, watchmaker, silversmith

Helfrick, A. B.
Dayton, Montgomery Co., 1853-64
jeweler, silversmith

Herancourt, Georg Micheal
Columbus, Franklin Co., 1835-42
jeweler, watchmaker, silversmith
Born in Bavaria; retail jeweler; proprietor of the Herancourt Brewery in Cincinnati

Herancourt, (G. M.) & Dresbach
Columbus, Franklin Co., 1835

Herancourt, (G. M.) & Hukill
Columbus, Franklin Co., 1834

Hewitt & Buck
Salem, Columbiana Co., 1853

Hill, Arundel
Steubenville, Jefferson Co.
born 5 Dec 1791 in Harrisburg PA, died 5 April 1848 in Steubenville; early spoon in private collection marked A. Hill Steubenv'e

Hill, (Charles) & Ross (A. C.)
Zanesville, Muskingum Co., 1833

Hill, Charles
Zanesville, Muskingum Co., 1815-33
Master to A. C. Ross, 1827-1831 and later his partner

Hinman, Stiles
Wilmington, Clinton Co., 1853-68
jeweler

Hoffman, George Washington
Plymouth, Richland Co., 1860-1880
silversmith
listed in the 1880 census as a silversmith; possibly the brother of Augustus Hoffman (Light & Hoffman)

Huffman, John
Bucyrus, Crawford Co., 1853-68
jeweler, watchmaker

Hunter, Merit A.
Jefferson, Ashtubula Co., 1856
jeweler

Hyde, Joshua
Mt. Vernon, Knox Co., 1853-72

Hyde, Zachariah D.
Roscoe, Coshocton Co., 1856-64
jeweler

Ingersol, William B.
Sandusky, Erie Co., 1840-45
Elyria, Lorain Co., 1846-50
jeweler

Ingersol, C. F.
Oberlin, Lorain Co.
Berea, Cuyahoga Co., 1853-59
jeweler, clockmaker

Irick, T. A.
Lebanon, Warren Co., 1837

Jacobs, John M.
Chillicothe, Ross Co., 1846
clockmaker, watchmaker

Jamison, Jacob
Dayton, Montgomery Co., 1853-66
clockmaker, watchmaker
In 1832 went from Springfield to Cincinnati then on to Dayton

Johnson, Joseph R.
Fairview, Guernsey Co., 1856
jeweler

Johnson, (E. D.) & Co E. D.
Urbana, Champaign Co., 1853-56
silversmith

Johnson, W.
Greenville, Licking co., 1859-64
jeweler, clockmaker, watchmaker

Johnson, W. J.
Somerset, Perry Co., 1853

Jones, G. A.
Akron, Summit Co., 1846
jeweler, watchmaker

Jones, George A.
Zanesville, Muskingum Co., 1856-68
jeweler

Julian, J. J.
Troy, Miami Co., 1856-68
jeweler

Karg, L.
Dayton, Montgomery Co., 1859
silversmith

Kelsey, Amos
Leatherwood, Guernsey Co., 1853

Kelvey, Thomas
West Union, Adams Co., 1820

Kesler, Frank
Columbus, Franklin Co., 1875-80
watchmaker
son of Herman; listed in the 1880 census as a watchmaker

Kesler, Herman
Columbus, Franklin Co., 1859-80
jeweler, watchmaker
born 1826 in Wurtemberg, Germany; listed in the 1880 census as a watchmaker

Kesselmeier, J.
Galion, Crawford Co., 1859-72
jeweler, clockmaker, watchmaker, silversmith

Kidd, (William) & Co William
Cleveland, Cuyahoga Co., 1853-72
jeweler

Kieffer, Lewis
Miamisburg, Montgomery Co., 1853-66
jeweler

King, Ashbel
Warren, Trumbull Co.
silversmith

King, Julius
Warren, Trumbull Co.
silversmith
He went on to graduate from the Cleveland Medical College and later founded the Julius King Optical Company in New York City

King, Walter
Warren, Trumbull Co., 1820-1853
silversmith, watchmaker
father of Ashbel, Julius and Walter Burnham

King, Walter Burnham
Warren, Trumbull Co.
silversmith

King & Brothers (Ashbel, Julius, and Walter Burnham)
Warren, Trumbull Co., 1856-64
silversmith

King, (Walter) & Son (Ashbel) W.
Warren, Trumbull Co., 1853-1855
silversmith, watchmaker

Kingsbury, R. R.
Ravenna, Portage Co., 1853

Kirkpatrick, Robert
Massilon, Stark Co., 1856-64
watchmaker

Kissell, John G.
Bryan, Williams Co. 1853

Kleeman Brothers, (Louis and Moses)
Columbus, Franklin Co., 1853-72
jeweler, watchmaker

Knight, C. M.
Hudson, Summit Co., 1853-64
jeweler

Knight, E. G.
Hudson, Summit Co., 1856
jeweler

Kramer, G. P.
Delphos, Allen Co., 1859
jeweler, watchmaker

Kranken or Krakran, E. A.
New Philadelphia, Tuscarawas Co., 1853-59
jeweler, clockmaker, watchmaker

Lafee, Paul A.

Laffere, A.
Dayton, Montgomery Co., 1856-72
clockmaker, watchmaker

Lebensberger & Lebolt
Dayton, Montgomery Co., 1856
jeweler, clockmaker

Lee, George
Pomeroy, Meigs Co., 1853-72
jeweler

Lee, John A.
Mansfield, Richland Co., 1853-72
silversmith

Lee, (John A.) & Wilkinson (Edward)
Mansfield, Richland Co., 1864-72
silversmith

Lehman, Christopher
Jerome, Union Co., 1853

Leppelman, Lewis
Fremont, Sandusky Co., 1853-72
jeweler, watchmaker

Leroy, Francis
Ohio City, Van Wert Co., 1836-37
goldsmith

Lesquereux, L.
Columbus, Franklin Co., 1853-68
jeweler, watchmaker

Lesquereux, F. A.

Licktennegger, F.
Columbus, Franklin Co., 1848-61
jeweler, watchmaker

Light (Joshua) & Hoffman (Augustus)
Plymouth, Richland Co. 1853-56, 1859-1872
jeweler

Likes, J. W.
Galena, Deleware Co., 1859-66
jeweler, clockmaker, watchmaker

Lindsley & Hatch (John)
1828

Lindsley, William
Portsmouth, Scioto Co., 1828
clockmaker, silversmith
Also a cooper and gunsmith. A partner of John Hatch

Liniger, John
Woodfield, Monroe Co., 1853

Lotland, John
Cadiz, Harrison Co., 1853

Love, James
Toledo, Lucas Co., 1846-68
jeweler, watchmaker, silversmith

Love (James) & Voight (Lucius N.)
1853-56

Madden, James
Tiffin, Seneca Co., 1853

Madison, Charles L.
Cambridge, Guernsey Co., 1853-80
jeweler, clockmaker, watchmaker
listed in the 1880 census as a watchmaker

Malcher, Francois Paul
Gallipolis, Gallia Co., 1790

Martin, A.
Dayton, Montgomery Co., 1859-61
jeweler

Martin, Joseph
Dayton, Montgomery Co., 1853-72
jeweler

Martin, J. M.
Cleveland, Cuyahoga Co., 1836-37

Masterson, P.
Chapel Hill, Perry Co., 1853

Matheny, F.
Athens, Athens Co., 1853

Matson, Newell
Painesville, Lake Co., 1853
jeweler

Matteson, Horace Elias E.
Seville, Medina Co., 1856
jeweler, watchmaker
listed in the 1880 census at Seville as a dry goods merchant

Mayer or Meier, Jacob
Cleveland, Cuyahoga Co., 1845-68
jeweler, watchmaker

Meads, Alfred
Cleveland, Cuyahoga Co., 1856-59
jeweler, watchmaker

Merrill, T.
Lebanon, Warren Co., 1837
With T. A. Irick, bought the stock of J. Probasco

Meyers, Frederick
West Union, Adams Co., 1853

Miers
Logan, Hocking Co., 1853

Miksch, R. P.
Franklin Mills, Portage Co., 1851-53
jeweler, watchmaker

Miller, Isaac W.
Newark, Licking Co., 1856-72

Miller, (John & William) John
Bellefontaine, Logan Co., 1859-72

Millner, Thomas
Ashtabula Ashtabula Co.

Miner, O. H.
Columbus, Franklin Co., 1848
watchmaker

Moeller, Peter
Cleveland, Cuyahoga Co.

Morison & Carey
Lexington, Richland Co., 1856
silversmith

Moyers, John
Hillsboro, Highland Co., 1853-72

Murphy, H.
Fairview, Guernsey Co., 1853

McClain, Robertson
Barnsville, Belmont Co., 1859-66
clockmaker, watchmaker

McCain, Benjamin
Ohio City, Summit Co., 1836-37
Akron, Summit Co., 1853
jeweler

McHenry, David
Circleville, Pickaway Co., 1856-72
jeweler. watchmaker
listed in the 1880 census as a grape grower

McHenry, Frank
Circleville, Pickaway Co., 1875-80
silversmith
son of David; listed in the 1880 census as a silversmith

McLaughlin, J.
Somerset, Perry Co., 1856
silversmith

McNeely, William
Paris, Stark Co., 1814
silversmith

McNeely (William) & Estep
Paris, Stark Co., 1814
St. Clairsville, Belmont co., 1827
silversmith, clockmaker, watchmaker

Nusley, V.
Sundusky, Erie Co., 1853-66

Oldein or Olden, David
Middletown, Butler Co., 1853-72
jeweler

Oldroyd, William
Mt. Vernon, Knox Co., 1856-59
jeweler

Olmsted, Philo Hopkins
Columbus, Franklin Co., 1835-46
Previously attributed, but not a silversmith; apprenticed as a printer in father's newspaper, which he later took over. Hotel owner, local politician, and prominent citizen

Parmele, John
Ravenna, Portage Co., 1853

Patterson & Wilkinson (James A.)
Mansfield, Richland Co., 1853-61
silversmith

Pauley, Milton R.
Lebanon, Warren Co., 1855-6
married Mary Benedict, 1857, in Mason OH; listed in the 1880 census there as a drygoods merchant

Shepherd & Pauley (Milton R.)
Lebanon, Warren Co., 1855-56

Paxton, Alexander
Steubenville, Jefferson Co., 1820
clockmaker, watchmaker

Paxton, Isaac
Hamilton, Butler Co., 1813
clockmaker, watchmaker, silversmith

Paxton (Isaac) & Wallace
Hamilton, Butler Co., 1813
clockmaker, watchmaker, silversmith

Peck, A. G.
Ashtabula, Ashtabula Co., 1823

Peugh, B. G.
Cleveland, Cuyahoga Co., 1845-46
jeweler

Phillippi, George A.
Portsmouth, Scioto Co., 1856-59
jeweler

Philpot, S.
Belleville, Richland Co., 1853

Picard, J. C.
Mowrytown, Highland Co., 1853
jeweler, watchmaker
Ad in Georgetown OH newspaper, 1834, states he is a French watch and clockmaker; listed in 1840 Cincinnati Directory

Pickett, Julius K.
Salem, Columbiana Co., 1853-72
silversmith
listed in the 1880 census as a hotel keeper

Pickett, Julius K.
Salem, Columbiana Co., 1870-80
watchmaker
son of Julius, Sr.

Pinkerton, D. C.
Chillicothe, Ross Co., 1838
McConnellsville, Morgan Co., 1838-59
jeweler, watchmaker

Platt, Benjamin
Delaware, Deleware Co., 1817-1833
silversmith
instrument maker working earlier in New Milford, CT

Platt, Cyrus
Delaware, Deleware Co., 1847-72
jeweler, clockmaker, watchmaker, silversmith
son of William; he was in Delaware by 1847, when he married; still working as a jeweler there in the 1880 census

Platt, William Augustus
Columbus, Franklin Co., 1830-50
jeweler, clockmaker, watchmaker
son of William; later president of Columbus Gas Light and Coke Co.

Platt, William
Columbus, Franklin Co., 1817-46
jeweler, clockmaker, watchmaker
son of Benjamin

Plowman, Thomas
Chillicothe, Ross Co., 1830-31
clockmaker, watchmaker

Powell, E. N.
Chillicothe, Ross Co., 1833-36
jeweler

Pratt, Ephraim P.
Chillicothe, Ross Co., 1839
silversmith

Pratt (Ephraim P.) & Bangs (John)
Chillicothe, Ross Co., 1839-41

Preston, H. W.
Norwalk, Huron Co., 1856
jeweler

Probasco, John
Lebanon, Warren Co., 1823-52
jeweler, clockmaker, watchmaker, silversmith

Punghes, (Punches) W.
Bryan, Williams Co., 1859-64
Ashtabula, Ashtabula Co., 1868
jeweler, clockmaker, watchmaker, silversmith
b. 1811 in PA; recorded as a jeweler in Bryan in the 1880 census

Pugh, Richard
Cleveland, Cuyahoga Co., 1861-72

Quest, Benjamin K.
Cadiz, Harrison Co., 1856-80
jeweler, clockmaker, watchmaker
listed in the 1880 census as a clock repairer

Ralston, William
Ashland, Ashland Co., 1853-72
jeweler, clockmaker, watchmaker, silversmith
apparently working for several years in the 1870s in Fayetteville TN

Ramsay, George
Clyde, Sandusky Co., 1859-64
jeweler, watchmaker

Reeks, H.
Dayton, Montgomery Co., 1853-61
jeweler

Reeves (E.) & Son (John)
Dayton, Montgomery Co., 1844-72
watchmaker, silversmith

Reeves, E.
Dayton, Montgomery Co.

Reeves, John
Dayton, Montgomery Co.

Reeve (George) & Richard
Zanesville, Muskingum Co., 1809

Reeve, George
Zanesville, Muskingum Co., 1809-14
jeweler, silversmith

Reniff, T. W.
Toledo, Lucas Co., 1853-66

Ricaby, William
Cleveland, Cuyahoga Co., 1953

Richard, C. A.
Columbus, Franklin Co., 1836-37
clockmaker, watchmaker

Richards, Joseph
Gallipolis, Gallia Co., 1853

Ricksecker, Israel Canal
Dover, Tuscarawas Co., 1853

Reiter, Alexander
Alliance, Stark Co., 1859-68
jeweler, clockmaker, watchmaker

Robert, Jules
Gallipolis, Gallia Co., 1859-61
watchmaker
listed in the 1880 Gallipolis census as a jeweler, b. 1830 in Switzerland

Robinson, John R.
Mansfield, Richland Co., 1856
jeweler

Ruff, Christian
Upper Sandusky, Wyandott Co., 1859
jeweler, clockmaker, watchmaker
in the 1880 census at Upper Sandusky, Christian Ruff, b. 1806 in Wurtemberg, Germany, is listed as a carpenter

Robinson, William
Chillicothe, Ross Co., 1810-15
silversmith

Roff, Conrad
Dayton, Montgomery Co., 1856-59
silversmith, watchmaker

Rogers, Soloman
Elmira, Fulton Co., 1859
jeweler, clockmaker, watchmaker

Rohman, B.
Rossville, Butler Co., 1853
Hamilton, Butler Co., 1859-72
jeweler

Rose, M.
Canton, Stark Co., 1853

Rosenfield, S.
St. Marys, Auglaize Co., 1856

Ross, Alexander Coffin
Zanesville, Muskingum Co., 1829-64
jeweler, clockmaker, watchmaker
Apprenticed to Charles Hill, 1829-1831 and his partner in 1833. A man of many talents and an ingenious turn of mind. He is credited with being the inventor of sulphur matches and with producing the first daguerreotypes west of the Allegheny mountains after reading an account of the discovery of the process in a London journal. He operated the first telegraph line in Zaneville and is credited with writing the famous song Tippecanoe and Tyler Too, in the Harrison presidental campaign

Ross, James J.
Zanesville, Muskingum Co., 1853-61
jeweler, watchmaker
brother of Alexander, for whom he probably worked

Russell, Daniel N.
Lebanon, Warren Co., 1836
clockmaker, watchmaker, silversmith

Safford, Harry
Zanesville, Muskingum Co., 1816
jeweler, clockmaker, watchmaker, silversmith, goldsmith
Probably came from Gallipolis; worked in Marrietta, 1810. Later a merchant and postmaster of Springfield

Saffer & Allen
Dayton, Montgomery Co., 1853

Sage, Henry
Circleville, Pickaway Co., 1856-64
jeweler, watchmaker

St. John, R. H.
Bellefontaine, Logan Co., 1853-56
watchmaker

Sanderson, Robert
Athens, Athens Co., 1839-64
watchmaker, silversmith

Sargent, A. G.
Lower Sandusky, Sandusky Co., 1836
watchmaker, silversmith

Sargent, J. C.
Bellefontaine, Logan Co., 1859
jeweler, watchmaker

Sarratt, J. H.
Steubenville, Jefferson Co., 1853-72
jeweler

Satterthwaite, Isaac
Lima, Allen Co., 1853-72
silversmith
also a gunsmith

Savage, John T.
Columbus, Franklin Co., 1853-56
jeweler

Savage, James Y.

Savage, William
Columbus, Franklin Co., ca. 1840-1880
jeweler
b 1815 in VA

Savage, James
Columbus, Franklin Co., ca. 1860-1880
jeweler
son of William

Sayler, Jacob
Hillsboro, Highland Co., 1853-72
silversmith

Saylor, Samuel
Jackson, Jackson Co., 1853-68
jeweler

Schreckengaust (S. & J.)
Chillicothe, Ross Co., 1850-72
jeweler, silversmith

Schneider, George
Cleveland, Cuyahoga Co., 1859-72
jeweler, watchmaker

Schroeder, A.
Cleveland, Cuyahoga Co., 1844-46
jeweler, watchmaker

Schroeder (A.) & Wangelin
Cleveland, Cuyahoga Co.

Schwabe, Theodore
Zanesville, Muskingum Co., 1846-56
silversmith

Schwarz, John
Hamilton, Butler Co., 1859
jeweler

Shober, Wiliam
Gallipolis, Gallia Co., 1859-72
jeweler, clockmaker, watchmaker

Seewald, Philip
Tiffin, Seneca Co., 1853-66
jeweler

Selenberger, E. C.
Feesburg, Brown Co., 1853

Shaw, (P. & R.)
Sarahsville, Noble Co., 1853

Shaw, T. M.
Feed Spring, Harrison Co., 1853

Sheldon & Ewalt
Wooster, Wayne Co., 1853

Sheldon, Philo S.
Bellefontaine, Logan Co., 1856
jeweler

Sheldon, P. S.
Wooster, Wayne Co., 1856
jeweler

Shepherd
Wilmington, Clinton Co., 1853

Shepherd, Amaziah
Lebanon, Warren Co., 1853-56

Shepherd (Amaziah) & Pauley (Milton)
Lebanon, Warren Co., 1855-56

Shepherd, J. B.
Ashtabula, Ashtabula Co., 1853-56
jeweler

Sherwood, John
Dayton, Montgomery Co., 1859
clockmaker, watchmaker

Sherwood, N. D.
Jefferson, Ashtabula Co., 1853

Shrock, Jacob M.
Newark, Licking Co., 1853-72
jeweler
1880 census as a watchmaker

Shrock & Cook
Millersburg, Holmes Co., 1853

Sill (E. J. & C. S.)
Cuyahoga Falls, Summit Co., 1853-56
watchmaker
also a druggist

Simpson, Walter
Sandusky, Erie Co., 1853-56
jeweler

Smith, F.
Winesburg, Holmes Co., 1853

Smith, J.
1803
watchmaker, silversmith, goldsmith
Advertised in Scioto Gazette, 21 May 1803

Smith, J.
Appleton, Licking Co., 1859
jeweler, clockmaker, watchmaker

Smith, M.
Franklin, Warren Co., 1817
clockmaker, watchmaker, silversmith

Smith, William B.
Coshocton, Coshocton Co., 1859-72
jeweler, clockmaker, watchmaker

Snow, William H.
Cleveland, Cuyahoga Co., 1835-37

Snyder, C.
Georgetown, Brown Co., 1853

Southwell, George
Columbus, Franklin Co., 1848
watchmaker

Spear or Speer, Robert
Steubenville, Jefferson Co., 1853-61
jeweler

Sprague
Newark, Licking Co., 1853-72
jeweler
Hezekial S., Henry Day, and Henry S. Sprague all worked as jewelers in Newark. The first two were the brothers of Lindel Sprague and the third his son

Sprague, Lindel
Wooster, Wayne Co., 1853-72
silversmith

Spurk, Peter
Chillicothe, Ross Co., 1810
silversmith

Staford, Thomas
Auburn, Geauga Co., 1859
jeweler

Stanley, Joseph E.
Cleveland, Cuyahoga Co.
Zanesville, Muskingum Co.
silversmith

Stanley, Jos. M.
Zanesville, Muskingum Co.
goldsmith, silversmith

Starbuck, Robert P.
Bealsbille, Monroe Co., 1856
watchmaker

Stark, William Trammell
Xenia, Greene Co., 1853-58
jeweler
born: 1790 in Loudoun VA; died: 11 Sep 1858 in Xenia

Starr, L.
Bedford, Cuyahoga Co., 1853

Starry, James H.
Hillsboro, Highland Co., 1842
Clarksville, Clinton Co., 1843-50
silversmith
first silversmith to work in the city

Stedman, Oscar
Nelson, Portage Co. 1853

Steele, A. W.
Ashtabula, Ashtabula Co., 1853-64
jeweler, clockmaker, watchmaker, silversmith

Stein, D. O.
Circleville, Pickaway Co., 1859
jeweler, clockmaker, watchmaker

Stevens & Heath (Ralph)
1815

Stevens
Chillicothe, Ross Co., 1815
jeweler, clockmaker, watchmaker, silversmith

Stone, Levi
Mt. Vernon, Knox Co., 1856-72
jeweler
probably apprenticed to Joshua Hyde. Member of Young, Stone & Hyde

Stow, Dwight Foster
Toledo, Lucas Co., 1846-53
jeweler, clockmaker, watchmaker, silversmith
working 1832-1845 in NYC

Strieby, C. H.
Mt. Vernon, Knox Co., 1853
clockmaker

Sturdivant & Brothers
Deleware, Deleware Co., 1853

Sumner, Edward
Bellevue, Huron Co., 1859-64
jeweler

Sumner (Edward) & Weiker
Bellevue, Huron Co., 1853

Sweny, J. R.
Harveysburg, Warren Co., 1859
jeweler, clockmaker, watchmaker

Swope, James Willard
Dayton, Montgomery Co., 1859-72
jeweler, clockmaker
born: 1835 in La Porte IN; died 15 JUL 1909 in Dayton

Talcott & Co
Cleveland, Cuyahoga Co., 1853-59
jeweler, watchmaker

Tallman, William
Akron, Summit Co., 1856-61
jeweler, clockmaker, watchmaker

Thiele & Hofer
Cleveland, Cuyahoga Co., 1853
jeweler

Thiele & Co
Cleveland, Cuyahoga Co., 1856
jeweler

Thoma, August
Piqua, Miami Co., 1846-72
jeweler, silversmith

Thomas, William
Urbana, Champaign Co., 1853-56
jeweler

Thompson, Seth
Chillicothe, Ross Co., 1804-06
jeweler, watchmaker, silversmith, goldsmith

Thrift, John
Kalida, Putnam Co., 1859
jeweler, clockmaker, watchmaker

Tight or Zight, G.
Granville, Licking Co., 1859-64
jeweler, clockmaker, watchmaker

Truman, Jeffery
Maineville, Warren Co., 1822-23
Franklin, Warren Co., 1822-23
watchmaker, clockmaker

Van Deren & Gadner
Chillicothe, Ross Co., 1836

Vandyke, D. W.
Mason, Warren Co., 1853-68
listed as a gunsmith in 1880 census

Vantrot, Jules
Warren, Trumbull Co., 1856-72
jeweler
born in France; listed in 1880 census as a jeweler, as was his son, Jules Jr.

Vantrot (Jules) & Mieksch
Warren, Trumbull Co., 1853

Vantrot (Jules) & Ackley
Warren, Trumbull Co., 1868

Varner & River
Covington, Miami Co., 1859
clockmaker, watchmaker

Vellage, B. C.
Athens, Athens Co., 1856
watchmaker

Venen (Joseph Albert & Darwin Plummer)
Conneaut, Ashtabula Co., 1853-72
jeweler, clockmaker, watchmaker

Venen, John D.
Conneaut, Ashtabula Co., 1853-56
jeweler

Vincent, Antoine Claude
Gallipolis, Gallia Co. 1790

Vincent (Benjamin) & Green (Jesse)
McConnellsville, Morgan Co., 1856
jeweler, watchmaker

Wadell, Robert R.
Georgetown or Hillsboro, 1857
jeweler

Wangelin (Louis & Edward)
Cleveland, Cuyahoga Co., 1844-46
goldsmith

Warner, John
Columbus, Franklin Co., 1816-31
jeweler, silversmith

Washburn, Wellington
Cuyahoga Falls, Summit Co., 1859
jeweler, clockmaker, watchmaker
apprenticed in Akron, 1852-1859; working 1859-1875 in Galesburg IL

Wassignsra, P.
East Liverpool, Columbiana Co., 1853-59
jeweler, clockmaker, watchmaker

Weber, C. B.
Ironton, Lawrence Co., 1853

Webb, N.
Greenville, Darke Co., 1853-72
jeweler
also sold books

White, Alex
Galigher, Guernsy Co., 1859
jeweler, clockmaker, watchmaker

White, D. C.
Elyria, Lorain Co., 1853-68
jeweler, clockmaker, watchmaker, silversmith

White, Edward
Cleveland, Cuyahoga Co., 1859
jeweler, watchmaker

Whitemore, Levi
Cleveland, Cuyahoga Co., 1845-46
jeweler

Whitemore, J.
Medina, Medina Co., 1853

Whitesides, R.
Chillicothe, Ross Co., 1806-08
jeweler, silversmith

Wight (J. W. & H. W.)
Garrittsville, Portage Co., 1859-64
jeweler, clockmaker, watchmaker

Wilcox, John
Cardington, Morrow Co., 1853
Belleville, Richland Co., 1859-64
jeweler, watchmaker

Wiler, J. V.
Mansfield, Richland Co., 1853

Wilkinson, Edward
Mansfield, Richland Co., 1853-72
silversmith, jeweler
listed in the 1880 census as a retired jeweler

Wilkinson, Milton G.
Mansfield, Richland CO., 1857-80
jeweler
son of Edward; listed in 1880 census as a jeweler

Wilkinson (James A.) & Co
Norwalk, Huron Co., 1856-80
jeweler
son of Samuel; listed in the 1880 census as a jeweler

Wilkinson, Samuel
Norwalk, Huron Co., 1830-60
jeweler
listed in the 1880 census as a retired jeweler, living with his son

Wilkinson, Thomas
Gallipolis, Gallia Co., 1853-64
jeweler

Williams, John H.
St. Clairsville, Belmont Co., 1851-53

Wilson, C. B.
Findlay, Hancock Co., 1853-56
jeweler

Withington, Martin A.
Massillon, Stark Co., 1845-66

Wolcott, S. B.
Elyria, Lorain Co., 1859-72
jeweler, silversmith

Wofram, C.
Dodsonville, Highland Co., 1853

Woltze, W. E.
Dayton, Montgomery Co., 1859-61
watchmaker

Woods, S.
Rossville, Butler Co., 1832
clockmaker, watchmaker

Woolnough, J. H.
Cleveland, Cuyahoga Co., 1853

Young, William Mitchell
Mt. Vernon, Knox Co., 1854-1880
jeweler
apprenticed to Joshua Hyde in 1849. He joined him as a partner in 1854

Young (William Mitchell), Stone (Levi) & Hyde (Joshua)
Mt. Vernon, Knox Co., 1854-72
jeweler
Levi Stone became a partner in 1856; Joshua Hyde retired in 1872

Zoellner, Albert
Portsmouth, Scioto Co., 1858
jeweler
son of Phillip; born: 27 APR 1859 in Portsmouth

Zoellner, Phillip
Portsmouth, Scioto Co., 1858
jeweler, watchmaker
born: 22 NOV 1832 in Bavaria; died: 28 DEC 1906 in Portsmouth

www.ingramcontent.com/pod-product-compliance
Lightning Source LLC
Chambersburg PA
CBHW060459010526
44118CB00018B/2465